THE MOHAWK

RIVERS OF AMERICA BOOKS
already published are:

★ ★ ★ ★

Rivers of America

EDITED BY

Hervey Allen AND *Carl Carmer*

AS PLANNED AND STARTED BY

Constance Lindsay Skinner

ASSOCIATE EDITOR · JEAN CRAWFORD

ART EDITOR · FAITH BALL

The Mohawk

BY

Codman Hislop

ILLUSTRATED BY

Letterio Calapai

RINEHART & COMPANY, INC.

NEW YORK • TORONTO

917.47
H62m

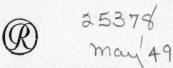

25378
may '49

FOR GERTRUDE

AND "C. N. W."

Contents

PART TWO

THE NEW BREED

Lines Written at the Cohos, or Falls of the Mohawk River

From rise of morn till set of sun
I've seen the mighty Mohawk run;
And as I mark'd the woods of pine
Along his mirror darkly shine,
Like tall and gloomy forms that pass
Before the wizard's midnight glass;
And as I view'd the hurrying pace
With which he ran his turbid race,
Rushing, alike untir'd and wild,
Through shades that frown'd and flowers that smil'd,
Flying by every green recess
That woo'd him to its calm caress,
Yet, sometimes turning with the wind,
As if to leave one look behind,—
Oft have I thought, and thinking sigh'd
How like to thee, thou restless tide,
May be the lot, the life of him
Who roams along thy water's brim;
Through what alternate wastes of woe
And flowers of joy my path may go;
How many a shelter'd, calm retreat
May woo the while my weary feet,
While still pursuing, still unblest,
I wander on, nor dare to rest;
But, urgent as the doom that calls
Thy water to its destin'd falls,

I feel the world's bewildering force
Hurry my heart's devoted course
From lapse to lapse, till life be done,
And the spent current cease to run.
One only prayer I dare to make,
As onward thus my course I take;—
Oh, be my falls as bright as thine!
May heaven's unrelenting rainbow shine
Upon the mist that circles me,
As soft as now it hangs o'er thee!

THOMAS MOORE, 1804.[1]

[1] Author's footnote: "There is a dreary and savage character in the country immediately about these falls, which is much more in harmony with the wilderness of such a scene than the cultivated lands in the neighborhood of Niagra. . . .

"The fine rainbow, which is continually forming and dissolving, as the spray rises into the light of the sun, is perhaps the most interesting beauty which these wonderful cataracts exhibit."

Preface

ONE becomes aware, at times, of tides, onrushing and receding, mountainous and terrible, and all the water motions in between, down to the shallows' ripple, moving not only through oceans but through nations. There was the tidal drift of tribes and races across Asia and Europe, and then the veering of great human currents, east out of Asia and west out of Europe, into the New World. Egypt and Greece and Rome ran like strong rivers into the reservoir of medieval Europe, mingling with its waters, and then spilling west into the Americas.

We mark out the great tidal lines, onrush and recession, as men, brown, red, black and white, moved like the projecting arms of a rising sea into America. Who sent them? What did they carry as they traveled? What did they leave by the way as they moved into the new river valleys, onto the new plateaus and highlands? What did they exchange when they met? The answers to these questions, too, are tidemarks.

White men moved against the Amarind civilizations they found in the Americas at different speeds, driven forward by kings and empire builders, trading companies, by popes, by all the special pleaders of religion. Men from Spain, gold-hungry and heaven-hungry, gentlemen-adventurers and prison-pale bondmen, and all the in-betweens a seething England could throw into the west-moving flood; Dutchmen, Frenchmen, Pala-

tines singly and by the hundreds and thousands they came in
the clothes of their trades, in uniforms and cassocks, in court
silk and Puritan homespun, smug company clerks, sailors, trappers, priests, farmers—the motley that are the life of cabin
clearings, of towns and nations.

We can follow out some of the tidal lines here in the
Mohawk Valley. The explorers and the hunters and the traders,
the cabin builders and the town makers followed each other
up this "river that flows between mountains," each loaded with
different gear, each leaving his special mark upon the land.

And each of them, in turn, for instance, who crowded into
the Mohawk country, infecting the Five Nations of the Iroquois
with a mortal fever that could be satisfied only with rum, muskets and trade goods, found themselves in turn struggling
against countertides. The Indian watched the white man, Englishman and Frenchman, burn with ugly schemes to possess
his land and his allegiance. Ideas changed. Ideas, for instance,
about a man's freedom and his relations to his king and state
changed in the harsh countertides of frontier life until they
broke in waves of revolution.

There are hundreds of subtle wave lines to be read if we
are to follow the flood, always rising, merging here, and here,
forest trail becoming wheel rut, wheel rut becoming turnpike,
turnpike linking valley to valley. Each time a new book moved
west in the pack of a traveler, each time a printing press was
moved into a new town, just so much did the tide of civilization
rise.

Who brought the first school into your valley? The first
college? Who were the adventurers who brought in the first
railroad? When did the courthouses rise? When did the stove
take the place of the open fireplace, and oil the place of the
guttering candle?

Who told the stories of your local heroes, and made music

about them? When did your myths begin to grow, turning your forebears into bewigged deities with a smell of sanctity about them?

And who were your arbiters of taste? Who dictated the shape of your buildings? Never mind that we find your first Roman arch in a rude bridge between a stagecoach tavern and the frontier road beyond it. The arch will move now, from church to church, courthouse to courthouse, to banking building and private house, the mark of Rome, two thousand years away.

What do we read in the records of our storekeepers? What was on their shelves? How much did things cost? If we know these things we will know what moved people.

Line by line, your story and our story here along the Mohawk River can be told as we read and evaluate the wave lines about us. At this point, and at this, the lines merge, and our two stories become one. Then we know that the isolation of our valleys at those points is over. The lines continue to merge, and we begin to see the pattern that is, finally, America.

The wave lines are forever joining. Our techniques for perceiving them are improving. The sociologist-historian may, in time, become a forecaster, able to predict enough of the mortal storm to save much that now goes down in ruin. Perhaps he may one day record the first joining of the wave lines that mean the emergence of a world community.

PART ONE

Gateway to the West

"Who looks upon a river in a meditative hour and is not reminded of the flux of all things?"

RALPH WALDO EMERSON

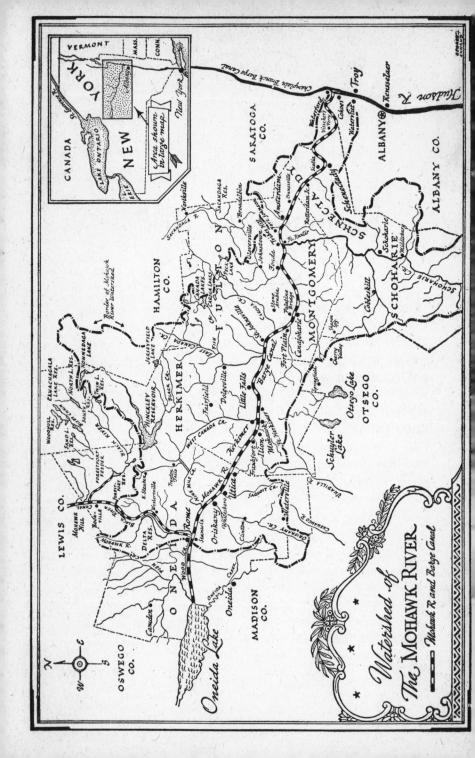

Watershed of
The MOHAWK RIVER
━━ Mohawk R. and Barge Canal

1

Upstream

This is Te-non-an-at-che, "the river flowing through mountains," the Mohawk, along whose banks France failed to win great allies in the fight to dominate America, and England lost her key battle to hold the Thirteen Colonies. This river and its valley are worth knowing.

This is the river that cut a gate through the rock wall of the Appalachian Plateau, the only entrance into the Western Plains between Georgia and the St. Lawrence Valley. Let your imagination dwell on that one fact for a moment. As tides flow over the land, so, too, did streams of men flow north from the Atlantic seaboard up the forested basin of the Hudson to the Mohawk Valley, and then west into the Genesee country, the Great Lakes country, and the seemingly limitless America beyond.

Struggle and battle on a hundred levels took place to possess this river valley. To possess it meant to possess America. No? Look at your map. Follow the Mohawk west. From Cohoes, where it joins the Hudson, to Rome one hundred miles inland, where the New York State Barge Canal continues on to Lake Ontario and Lake Erie, you climb, step

by step, up the twenty locks of the canal until you stand 420
feet above the Mohawk's level at the Hudson. At Rome the
river makes an abrupt right turn to the highlands country of
the Delta Reservoir, one of the huge canal control basins.
Up and north it goes to a junction with the Lansing Kill. Not
"Lansing Creek," mind you. The Dutch word "kill" has hung
on in the Mohawk country. Here in a narrow valley you find
the river and the kill different only in name. The Mohawk now
dwindles west and north again until it recedes at last to its
source on the lonely reaches of Mohawk Hill, 1,800 feet above
sea level.

But there's none of the river's poetry in altitudes and
mileages. Listen rather to the music in the names of the
streams that drain into the river from the western Catskills,
and the lowlands of the Adirondacks. Say them out loud.

> The Maquas, the Mohaugs, the Mohawk, many and one,
> Depending on your angle and when you were born.
> Our creeks and kills belong to us and to none else;
> The Chuctanunda, Potash Creek, Burch,
> Briggs Run, Kayaderosseras, the Sandsea Kill,
> Schoharie, Otsquago, Alplaus and the Stony;
> Garoga, Canajoharie, the Sauquoit and the Flat;
> They all make one river, friend,
> The Maquas, the Mohaugs, the Mohawk, many and one,
> Many yet one, compounding a thousand streams
> That drain these hills. . . .

New York's two greatest rivers, the Hudson and the
Mohawk, join about a mile below the falls of the latter, at
Cohoes. Green Island, Van Schaick Island, and Peebles Island
break the Mohawk here into four arms. North of the upper
arm is the town of Waterford. From here, like a great vein,
runs the New York State Barge Canal, outgrowth of the
empire-building Erie Canal. Here are the first locks of that

tremendous inland waterway that connects the Atlantic Ocean with the Great Lakes. Opposite Cohoes and Van Schaick Island is the north end of the city of Troy, and south of Green Island is an ugly huddle of houses and tenements, on the site of the ancient Dutch community of Watervliet.

Rather than river's end, let this be, for us, river's beginning. Men have always looked upstream when they came to the Mohawk, for upstream was west. Let us head west, then, with that low-lying barge, the *Seneca*, heavy with gasoline, as it climbs the first water-stairs on its way to ports on the Great Lakes.

The once-renowned falls at Cohoes, which the canal by-passes, are now for most of the year a poor trickle of water, for the river here is drained into power flumes for the benefit of the factories that crowd around the last few miles of the Mohawk's course. The river winds northwest from the falls between shadowing low palisades until it enters a gentle country, farmers' country, with cedar groves along the banks and fields flowing south and north in soft curves. Now the *Seneca* passes the south shore town of Niskayuna and the north shore towns of Half Moon and Crescent. Soon it twists into a deep gorge east of Rexford, or Aqueduct, as the village is sometimes known, for here the old Erie Canal was carried from the south to the north shore of the Mohawk on a great stone bridge that gave Rexford its nickname. From the high palisades here, just east of the river's great bend at Schenectady, you can see a reach of water as lovely as any in America. West is the Dutchman's "Groote Vlachte," the Great Flat, and on beyond is the high, bold line of the Helderbergs and the Princetown Hills, walling in what Schenectady's first settler, Arendt Van Curler, called "the most beautiful land."

It takes seven canal locks to raise the *Seneca* upstream

beyond the Mohawk rapids, and on into the Rexford gorge. There's quiet river sailing for quite a way, now.

That wide, water-filled ditch bordering the north bank of the Mohawk at the "Aqueduct" is all that is left here of the old Erie Canal. The wonderful, unmortared stonework of the Scotch stonecutters is still there, but the bawling "canawlers," shouting at their mules, untangling towlines, drinking, and yarn-swapping in the town's barnlike hotels, they are all gone.

Our barge soon passes Schenectady, "the place-beyond-the-pine-plains," today quieting down from the rush of war. Here are the sprawling plants of the General Electric Company and the American Locomotive Works, and, far older than either of them, the gray, ordered buildings of Union College. Schenectady is still full of Dutch names and there are Dutch houses here, rare now in America, crowded together in the lower part of the city, on streets that were once laced tight by a high, wooden stockade. Here one segment of the frontier of America ended, really, until the Revolution cleared the way for large-scale settlement of the Indian country.

South of Schenectady the river swings in a great bend again west, through meadowlands that have been farmed since they were made available to settlers by Holland's Dutch West India Company, and the Mohawk Indians, into whose old hunting grounds our barge now moves against the stream and the prevailing west winds.

The *Seneca* passes Scotia, whose name implies that its first settler could not forget his native Scotland; it passes the vast navy storage depot, as the hills north and south begin to crowd the fields of the Groote Vlachte. Eight miles beyond Schenectady, on the south shore of the river, is Rotterdam Junction, a railroad center, elbowed close to the riverbank by the Pattersonville Hills.

By the time our barge has reached Amsterdam it has climbed ten of its lock-stairs on its way to the Great Lakes; it is now about thirty-six river miles from the Hudson and 254 feet above it. Slowly this town, famous for its rug factories, is trying to take some of the beauty that goes into its looms and weave it into its pattern of crowded, factory-colored streets.

Just beyond Lock No. 12 the *Seneca* pushes through waters that flow out of the mouth of the Schoharie Creek. You're in Mohawk country now. Down the wind, out of the night, above the pulse of the *Seneca*'s diesels, the ear in tune can hear the far sounds of the frontier, of Johnson's "Blue Eyed Indians" on their ugly business of murder in the cabin clearings, shouts of the rivermen, poling their bateaux west, the sounds of musket drill in the shadow of Fort Hunter, and, faintly, the bell of Queen Anne's chapel. Schoharie Creek drains historic country.

Strong engines pushing gasoline west in a slow, easy trip stop only long enough to let the waters from upstream gather in the locks. Gently, up the gray stone walls of the lock our barge rises and then moves west again. Stair by stair, it climbs these colossal steps until it comes to the highest of them all, on the threshold of the gateway the river has opened through the plateau to the Great Lakes beyond.

First, though, as it rises to the higher levels, it passes Canajoharie, "the pot that washes itself." Here is a clean-scrubbed village on the river's south shore, where the Beech-nut Company adds to the foodstocks of the nation. Palatine Bridge, on the north shore, is a part of the German Flats country into which the eighteenth-century Palatines moved, and where they put down roots the frontier raids of the Indian wars and the Revolution were never to unearth. Fort Plain and St. Johnsville slip by as the *Seneca* heads for Lock No. 17, at Little Falls, the giant step up which the waters of the

Mohawk lift our barge more than forty feet. Here, in strange contrast to the town's name, once roared the vast falls of the prehistoric Mohawk, grinding out a channel whose high palisades now close in on both shores of the river.

River, highways, and railroads bottleneck here. Here, somehow, the eastern slope of the nation seems to have tapered gently up to a thin pass beyond which lie the ever-widening plains. Look at your map again. Now it should be clear to you how much the Mohawk has meant to America. The colonial power that controlled this river controlled America. The names of some of its towns still begin with "Fort." Buried under the streets of other towns, west to the Great Lakes are the kitchen-middens of ghost forts. Here once was a line of armed camps whose function was to act as a dike to hold back the French tide, poised for more than a hundred years to sweep through the Mohawk Valley, down the Hudson to New York, drowning Englishmen wherever it found them.

West of Little Falls at Rome was Fort Stanwix, later Fort Schuyler. If, during the American Revolution, the English force under Barry St. Leger had been able to push east down the valley, burning and pillaging, as they had planned, and then to have joined forces with Burgoyne, it is possible that all our heroes of those days would have been hanged, and remembered only as the leaders of a rabble in arms.

Slowly, low in the water, the *Seneca* moves to the heavy rhythm of its engines, past Little Falls, through the gateway to the west.

The mountains move south and north and our barge follows the canal channel through farmlands that were once vital to the larder of the Northern Revolutionary army. Herkimer, Mohawk, Ilion, Frankfort, which we now pass on the way to Utica, revolve today about the Remington Arms

and Remington-Rand factories. In them, and in many of the great plants that now bid for the valley's workers, new loyalties and alignments of men have been taking shape for many years. The right to farm Mohawk land is no longer the issue. Arguments and battles over property rights have turned into contests over the right to work and the conditions of work.

At Utica the *Seneca* has moved more than a hundred miles west from the Hudson and has climbed a little over four hundred feet. The river east to Frankfort and west to Rome is now really a canal, and the Mohawk is a captured stream in a huge man-made channel. Utica, almost at the geographical center of New York State, spreads out on a wide plain bordering the old south shore of the Mohawk. Here once met the Iroquois trails that ran north up the Black River valley toward Canada, south into the rich Susquehanna Valley of Pennsylvania, and east and west between the Hudson and the Great Lakes. The highways out of Utica still follow these old forest paths.

Utica, if one thinks of the valley towns and cities to the east, is a new city. Its first merchant arrived as late as 1790, to capitalize on the growing throngs of settlers moving into the "western lands." Today its wide streets prove that its growth began well after the stockade period. Great fountain elms, which are the glory of the Mohawk Valley, line Utica's streets. Overhead there is often a veil of smoke to mark the city as the home of dozens of industries making everything from textiles to machine guns.

Fourteen miles west of Utica you could see, if you were standing on the south side of our barge, a tall gray stone shaft not far above the old shore line of the river. Someone among the crew might tell you it was the Oriskany Battle Monument, though, more likely, he would shrug his shoulders and go off on some important business. There, Nicholas Herkimer and his undisciplined Palatine neighbors stopped England. There, the Continentals' success at Saratoga was made possible and a free United States became something more tangible than the paper domain decreed by the Declaration of Independence.

West of this historic ground lies the great Oriskany Swamp, today a rich bottom land crowded with truck gardens; it, too, fades east as the *Seneca* glides into Rome.

Now look at your map again. Through this peaceful, elm-walled city walk and ride the ghosts of empire builders. Here the great highway of the Mohawk ends. Here was the Wood Creek "carry" and then Wood Creek, down which colonials ferried their trade goods to the "far Indians" of the Lakes country. For our barge carrying gasoline to the cities of the Great Lakes the fact is marked only by the disappearance of the river's winding, almost empty channel, which here bends north to the Adirondack highlands country.

The *Seneca*, however, pushes on west in its man-made channel, still carried on the canalized waters of the river that has brought it to Rome, 128 miles inland from the Hudson, 420 feet above the entrance to its first lock at Waterford.

It all seems so easy now. There is the nasal honk of the Twentieth Century Limited as it pounds west out of the valley on the New York Central tracks. Train after train, they pile past Rome, east and west, night and day, on one of the world's tightest schedules. West and east on the valley's arterial highways roar the cars and trucks whose life depends on the cargo of such barges as the *Seneca*. It all seems so easy. Up from the Atlantic as you like, by road or rail or by river, north with the Hudson to the Mohawk. And then west. There are no seams in this travel pattern. Through the Mohawk Valley you can go now, at whatever speeds suit your convenience: ten miles an hour through the canal's river and lake channels, six miles an hour through the canal's man-made links, up to fifty miles an hour on the river's north- and south-shore highways, seventy and more if you ride the Century.

And so through Rome, and out of the valley, into the west.

So easy? Look at your map. What did we have to begin with before "Clinton's Ditch," the old Erie Canal, began to make things easier? Before the Iron Horse began to scare his flesh and blood predecessor out of the traces; before we became Americans? We had only the river. But what this Mohawk has meant to America! It was Te-non-an-at-che, the "river flowing through mountains," the river that cut the only gate through a rock wall rearing from Georgia to the St. Lawrence. Possessing it was not easy. Developing it to please the ambitions of each new generation has not been easy. In this struggle to possess and to build, however, is our MOHAWK RIVER story.

2

The Skeleton in the Pothole

WORKMEN found the skeleton on Thursday, the last week in September, 1866. Probably there was autumn haze west of the Cohoes Falls, west of the harvested flats between the falls and the Aqueduct, deeper haze west of the great bend in the Mohawk at Schenectady, blue shadowing haze beyond the Princetown Hills, west, up the broad reaches of the valley. It would have spread beyond the narrowing walls of rock that cut the sheet of river to a silver ribbon at Little Falls, a haze of autumn like a curtain drawn across the Valley of the Mohawk, across the Western Gateway.

Professor Hall's report, made shortly after the discovery, has a clean, accurate, sterile quality:

> In the month of September, 1866 the workmen engaged in excavations for the foundation of a new mill to be erected by the Harmony Mills Company, of Cohoes, N.Y., discovered the lower jaw of a mastodon with a single foot bone, resting upon a projection of the rock between two depressions or concave walls of small pot-holes, in the margin of what afterward proved to be a larger pot-hole.

Ten thousand years before that autumn the mastodon moved through the cold marshes of the valley, his coarse long hair wet by the mists that drifted south from the shrinking ice sheet. Sound of falling water, huge, hoarse, and endless, rolled back on the wind as the vast river near which he grazed fell to its last level before it ran, yellow with backcountry clays, into the geologists' "Lake Albany."

The Hall report continued:

> Several thousands of loads of muck or peaty soil with trunks and branches of decayed trees had been removed previous to coming to the level where the jaw was found. . . . The discovery of the jaw with a single bone in such a position led to the inference that other parts of the skeleton would be found at the bottom of the pot-hole, could it ever be reached, and the progress of the excavation was watched with great interest. After considerable delay, the excavation was resumed and the peaty earth was removed from the eastern and central part of the pot-hole, which later proved to be the deepest portion. In the bottom of this cavity, lying upon a bed of clay, broken slate, gravel and water-worn pebbles, and covered with river ooze and vegetable soil, lay the principal parts of the mastodon skeleton . . . the head, with tusks unbroken and undisturbed, was directed to the eastward. . . .

"The head with tusks unbroken and undisturbed . . ." There was Professor Hall's watch, to tell the time of day, and the almanac of the patent medicine company on the desk of the Harmony Mills superintendent to tell the day of the month and bemuse that gentleman with dark prophecy of the year's weather, and then there was this other measure to which, in his academic way, Professor Hall was sensitive. This was a clock to time the centuries, this Mohawk River pothole on the 50-foot level of which lay the "head with tusks unbroken" of a mastodon, cousin to the elephant, ten thousand years dead.

This pothole, near the site for building No. 3 of Cohoes'

Harmony Mills Company, marks the passage of bleak and numberless years. The Mohawk of today idles gently east one hundred feet below the surface of the rock in which the giant hole was worn by the Iromohawk. The waters that spun the grinding stones around and around its smooth walls began, not in the Catskill and Adirondack rills and streams of New York that give rise to our Mohawk, but in the drainage of the glaciers that fed the great inland seas of the Pleistocene period. The Iromohawk drained Lake Iroquois, huge predecessor of Lake Ontario, drained that whole body of inland water that now, as the Great Lakes, flows north and east to the sea through its "new" channel, the valley of the St. Lawrence.

The Mohawk gateway to the west was thrown open when the last ice sheet retreated far enough to the north to allow the impounded waters of Lake Iroquois to spill east across the great plateau at what is now Little Falls, New York. What geologists call the Rome River, a preglacial stream, had once flowed west from this high land before it disappeared. With the rush of water to the east across this spillway the preglacial valley of the Mohawk was filled with roar and rush and the grinding of ice. The flood poured east, cutting out the farmed, green reaches of today, tearing down not only the rock gate at Little Falls, but another stone barrier at what is called "The Noses," huge projections which the quiet river now divides a few miles west of the village of Fonda.

These "gateways" were thrown open centuries before the last stumbling mastodon died in the valley marshes, victim of an environment changing too fast for him to pace. For centuries the Iromohawk ground down the vaults of rock in a storm of water that would have drowned Niagara, pouring for generations into ice-filled Lake Albany, which spread west to what is now Rotterdam Junction, a few miles beyond Schenectady, north into the Saratoga country, and south to the Highlands of the Hudson. Three hundred or more feet below the surface of Lake Albany was the land that would in our time become farm and town, but which had to wait for the final retreat of the ice sheet into the north and the slow collapse of the rubble and ice barrier the glacier had left across the Hudson Valley to the south.

Into this slowly shrinking lake the Iromohawk poured the clay and sands and gravel of the valley it was cutting on its sweep east. Schenectady, "the place beyond the pine plains," carries in its Indian name a reminder of the sand plain that stretches east of it to the Hudson Valley, a barren level of dunes and scrub pine, out of keeping somehow with the lush country the railroad traveler sees south of it along the Hudson, and west through the Mohawk Valley that was once one of the granaries of the American Revolution.

Before there were men in the valley the Iromohawk began to build for itself its final channels. With the retreat of the ice sheet toward the St. Lawrence Valley and the lowering of Lake Albany, land began to rise, land which had been the floor of the lake. When the kind of time passed that has nothing to do with watches and almanacs the Iromohawk was forced to find a new outlet, for the delta bottom it had spread across Lake Albany, free at last of the vast pressure of the ice sheet, rose to become a barrier to the river's straight course east.

Rivers, like men, will "borrow" the work of others when it suits their purpose. Running north from Schenectady was an ancient preglacial valley once occupied by what geologists have called the Ballston River. With drying swamps to the east of it the Iromohawk slowly accepted the discipline of the older channel and swung north in a great curve, beginning south of Schenectady, cutting out a huge basin, cutting deeper and deeper below the floor it had once laid on the bottom of

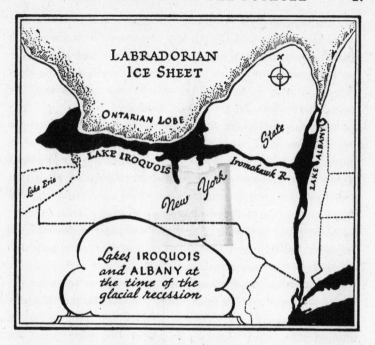

a vanishing lake. How long the cold and swollen river flowed north no one knows. Ballston Lake and deep Round Lake belong to the history of the Iromohawk, for it was through channels across which they now lie that the river found three new outlets to the Hudson Valley and the sea. And still the land rose and the once-wide lake drained away into pockets. And then the last of the river's valley making took place, for the rush of waters from Lake Iroquois had still to find a new outlet down the St. Lawrence before the Iromohawk would become the Mohawk and one valley would be enough to carry a quieter stream.

One can imagine the river's playing a giant's game with the ice-scarred land. Which of the three channels it had forced into the Hudson Valley would it make its own? Would it leave them to cake in the drying sun, and carve out a new bed to carry off the waters of the dying glacier and the Great Lakes? Rivers practice the economy men practice when they carve out their roads through a rough terrain; they follow the lines of least resistance, the easy slope, the shortest distance. As Lake Albany withered and dried into marshland, the river that spilled north of today's Schenectady cut deeper and deeper into the new land, channeling its way first through the sediments the ancient lake was deserting and then, as the land tipped slightly from north to south, cutting east through the rock that now stands up in massive palisades near the old Erie Canal town of Rexford.

The northern channel the Iromohawk had borrowed from the older Ballston River could not compete with the new valley that was being carved east of it. By the time Professor Hall's mastodon was grazing in the river swamps there was no longer any need for the river's northern outlets, the valley of the Mourning Kill, the Drummond channel, and the gorge running into Round Lake. The new valley was then deep enough to carry all the water that still swept through this western gateway to the Hudson Valley, would continue to rush east in enormous volume until the Great Lakes appropriated the St. Lawrence Valley, their final outlet to the sea.

Head and tusks, spinal column, scapula and pelvis, bone by bone the "Cohoes mastodon" emerged for the edification and the wonder of the thousands who saw it in the offices of the Harmony Mills Company. The excitement it aroused justified its exhibition at the Troy County Fair. Two thousand dollars was voted by the state of New York to assemble the almost complete skeleton; in 1867 it was placed on view in what was elegantly known as the "State Cabinet of Natural History" in the Capitol at Albany.

To the Cohoes *Sentinel* for September 29, 1866, one

would like to give the last word of comment; the editor wrote, under the spell laid upon him by the discovery of the skeleton:

> . . . be assured there are more things in heaven and earth than are dreamed of in our philosophy! Those who, during the past generations, have trod the earth of Cohoes have never taken into their wildest imaginings what were concealed beneath the surface.

Nor could they have heard the thunder of a forgotten river vast enough to drain the Great Lakes, to carve a gateway through the Appalachian Plateau, to spin rock drills deep enough into the heart of the land to make a trap for mastodons.

3

"Adodarhoh Did Not Make
The World"

". . . and the corn, the beans and the squash were once sisters, but Adodarhoh, eater of men, drove them apart."

The old man worked his rubbing stone against the strip of wolf's bone, slowly rounding the end of it. He looked for a moment at the small boy who was trying to untangle the weight-lines of a fish net.

"Tonight Soi-ka-Gakwa, our Grandmother, the Moon, will come again and Adodarhoh, eater of men, will climb the pine tree, and fill his mouth with clay, and imitate the screech owl. And then Hayonwatha will lose another of his seven daughters."

The stone net-sinker fell out of its knot at the end of one of the weight-lines, fell hard on the small boy's right foot, and rolled into the river. There was an anguished cry as the boy dropped the weight-lines, grabbed his foot, and tried to rub out the pain.

"I have heard a woman cry like that, and Hagoks, the Heaven Bird, cried that way when Adodarhoh shook him to make his feathers fall to the ground." The old man didn't look up as he pressed his rubbing stone against the flat spoon end of the bone he was slowly shaping to make into a pair of fish hooks. Soon there would be a hole in the flat end of the bone, which he would then split into two rough hooks that would only need sharpening.

"You have spoiled Ohsinoh's net. Be quiet now, and get my pipe, and sit by me. Then I shall tell you how the world began." The hole was coming now in the bone. The boy threw down the net, poked his wet hand into the old man's deerskin bag, and brought out the tobacco pouch and the clay pipe whose bowl was shaped like a bird.

At their feet was the river-which-flows-like-a-small-sky, which flows-through-mountains, flowing east through the Nation of the Flint.

While the old man filled his pipe, the boy limped over to the burning pile of corn shocks the women had left on the cleared bottom land; he drew out a smoldering stalk and hurried back. Squatting on the tangled net, he waited for the lazy curl of smoke to rise from the pipe and the story of how the world began.

The old man put the wolf's bone and his rubbing stone down on the dried grass by his side. He stared west up the long reach of river, its water white under the noon clouds like the down of the globe thistle. The quiet line of the long hills rounded into the marshes on either side of the river; there was the same grace in these curving flanks of hills that there was in the autumn flank of Senoto wanne, the Elk.

Senadondo, the boy, and Canonou, the old man, and the still, full waters of Te-non-an-at-che at the foot of the hill, all seemed bound, for a breathless moment, in a great circle drawn against the sky by the wheeling geese. Canonou watched them as they closed the circle and then dropped in a wind-bent line to the cool marshes by the side of The-Sleep-ing-Woman hill.

"Adodarhoh did not make the world. He could destroy men, and his body was bent with seven crooks, and his hair was a clot of snakes, but his strong magic did not make the world.

"Nor do I believe the story told by the People of the Great Hill that the Holder of Heaven raised the land of Kono-shioni above the Endless Waters and that he sowed there five handfuls of seeds from which we and our brothers of the Long House have come."

The old man turned his head ever so slightly, as though he were listening to the voices of Kahanckt, the Geese, as they wound their way through the marsh alleys, talking of the Land of the Crooked Tongues.

"No, Senadondo, I do not believe these stories. I had the true story from my father, who heard it in council beneath the Tree of the Great Peace."

Senadondo watched the blue smoke float above the bird pipe. Dare, the Crane, walked with dignity into the shallow water that lapped the far bank of the river. Sitting here, by the weir shallows, with the last of summer shimmering above the river, it was hard to think of the beginning of the world.

"The world, Senadondo, is the back of the Great Turtle. I know this to be true, from my father. This, of course, was true before our Nation, the Ga-ne-ga-o-no, and our Brothers, the O-na-yo-te-ga-no, and our Brother Nation beyond them, the O-nun-dah-ga-o-no, and the fourth Nation, the Gue-u-ghew-O-no, and the Nun-da-wah-o-no, who keep the west door of the Long House, before all the Five Nations sat down beneath the Tree of Great Long Leaves. This was the time when the Turtle moved in a land of darkness which was not the world, among strange animals."

The old man looked at the small boy. "Our hunters would drop their bows and run like women, should they see such animals." Senadondo thought this hard to believe, for even Ochquari, the bear, frightened only the youngest hunters.

"Above the Turtle," Canonou continued, "was a land as bright as Endeka-Gakwa, the Sun, could make it. There lived the virtuous people, the people of dreams. Among them was a woman large with child who cried out in her pain that she must go to the land of darkness, for, of her two children about to be born, one she knew was evil and would find no home in the upper land of light.

"The monsters in the land of darkness heard the woman's cry of pain, and prepared a place on which she should fall, when her time had come. They placed the Turtle in the center of the darkness, and varnished his back with earth.

"Out of the light and into the blackness fell the woman large with child, fell through the emptiness until she rested at last on the back of the Great Turtle. Out of her pain and her dying two children were born, each hating the other, each possessed of strong magic. There, in the underworld, they fought to possess the Great Turtle who had become the world. The bad child created snakes and mountains to halt the work of his good brother. The child of light, however, then formed our river Te-non-an-at-che, which finally cut through the mountains, into the land of the Long House."

Canonou picked up his wolf's bone and the rubbing stone. They could still hear the voices of the geese in the marsh alleys. "That is truly the way the world began, for that is the way I had it from my father."

Senadondo and Canonou were People of the Flint, the Elder Brothers of the Brotherhood of the Five Nations, the Iroquois. What was their world? First, for them, it was the river Te-non-an-at-che. Their river was not just a valley maker, a water highway. Their river was a way of life; it was life. Dare, the Crane, and Kahanckt, the Geese, and Sateeni, the Dog, and Tawyne, the Otter, and all the living things that drank from the river and lived by the river were citizens of its simple and reasonable world.

This Iroquois world was a reasonable world, for it was a world of primitive men. In it you name things. You follow the river-flowing-through-mountains, and in time the name comes, for the name is simply a shorthand way of telling something about the thing you have watched.

Senadondo and Canonou lived, too, in a world of river- and forest-gods. These were as real as the otter and the dog, and they were as necessary. A storm is a great and super-human work. The sun is a stupendous performer. Lightning splits the tallest tree. Men cannot do these awesome things that crowd night and day, wonder piled on wonder. But then the name comes, and it is the link between the namers and the Wonder-Worker. It is this process and this act of naming that are so reasonable; the naming talent was the only unique talent these Indians had, really, as citizens of the world that is the Turtle.

Senadondo and Canonou, as People of the Flint, had been given the name "Mohawks," "the eaters of living creatures," by their enemies. It is as Mohawks that we commonly know them, though these Keepers of the Eastern Door of the Long House called themselves "Ga-ne-ga-o-no," the Flint Owners.

These Mohawks were not modest, nor were their "brothers" west of them along the Iroquois trail, the Oneidas, the Onondagas, the Cayugas, and the Senecas. Collectively, as the Iroquois, they called themselves the Onk-we-on-we-ke, the "only real men."

The name "Iroquois" itself is probably a French nick-name, a translation of two Indian words with which the speakers of the Five Nations usually ended every pronouncement: "Hiro" ("I have spoken") and "Cooer," which seems to have indicated approval or disapproval according to the inflection given it by the speaker. Certainly the French had every reason to think of the Iroquois as a boastful people, more disapproving than approving. Others have said Iroquois was an Algonquian epithet meaning "real snakes."

We, of course, know how the world began. We are confident that our information comes from more reliable sources than from the legendkeepers of the Long House. We can never know Senadondo and Canonou, however, nor any of these mercurial, passionate, brutal, and sometimes brilliant dwellers beneath the Tree of the Great Long Leaves, unless we can, for a moment, forget Jeans and his Expanding Uniserve, Einstein, and the sweet reasonableness of nuclear fission. Hear for a moment, if you can, these faint, far-off, thousand voices this Mohawk boy really heard by Te-non-an-at-che: the "river-that-flows-through-mountains."

How did these Iroquois get possession of the Mohawk Valley, their "land of Konoshioni"? Of all the tribes that pushed east out of the shadows of history, east across the ranges of the Appalachians or down the great corridor of the St. Lawrence to the Atlantic, none became so potent as the Iroquois of the Long House. At the height of their power, their name struck terror to their tribute-paying neighbors from Hudson Bay on the north to the forests of the Cherokees, the Creeks, and the Choctaws at the southern end of the Piedmont. The tribute gatherers of the Iroquois were seen in the villages of the New England Indians, padding down the trails into the Ohio country, disciplining their erring "children" along the banks of the Illinois.

There's necessary groundwork to be done, however, before you can understand the size and the strength of the Long

House culture these people built here in the Mohawk River country.

First, a date: 1609. In September of that year Henry Hudson sailed *De Haelve Moen* up a new river, looking for China. He didn't find China, but he met the "loving people" of a new country. He anchored the *Half Moon* probably off the shore of the land that is now occupied by Albany. His long-boats were rowed upstream some "eight or nine leagues, and found but seven foot of water and unconstant soundings." His sailors must have dropped their anchor lines about opposite the site of the present city of Cohoes; they may have cursed as the currents set up by the Mohawk's confluence with the Hudson shifted their boats toward the opposite shore. China wasn't that way, either north up the new river or through the channels that seemed to open to the west.

During that September, however, the "loving people" as Mate Robert Juet of the *Half Moon* called them, met the men of Europe for the first time. West from the Hudson Valley, west up the Mohawk Valley, west across the plains country to the mountains and the Pacific beyond, stretched the culture of the Stone Age. East was civilized Europe. The Christian culture of the white man had already established contact points with the Stone Age culture of the Indian at other places in America, but not here.

It was a great meeting. Hudson's men had got the Manhattan Indians drunk immediately. Robert Juet noted in his diary that the best the Indians had "could be bought for trifles." On the journey up the river, Sailor John Coleman was killed by "hostile Indians" for unnamed reasons. A few days later the crew grabbed two visiting natives and held them captive in the ship's cabin. Mate Juet noted a day or so later: "This morning our two savages got out of a port and swam

away. After we were under sail they called up to us in
scorn."

It was in September, 1609, then, that the great human
tides flowing east out of Asia and west out of Europe met
for the first time in this most vital area of the New World. It
is too bad, in a way, that the agents of great events are not
prepared to play their roles in the grand manner. The "lovinge
people" did the best they could with their offerings of tobacco and maize and the great "Platter full of Venison." Hudson's men gave the natives a private showing of what Europe
was to deliver soon in great quantities: rum, guns, trade
goods.

There were probably no Iroquois representatives at the
meeting. In 1609 Hudson would have met Algonquin tribes
along the shores of the river that was finally to bear his name:
they were Lenapes ("the first come") Minsis, Wappangers,
Mahicans. If it had been sixty or seventy years later, the "lovinge people" would have sent out runners hotfooting for the
nearest Mohawk castle; the council fires of these less trustful
Brothers would then have indicated that the proper ceremonials were under consideration. The royaneh, the tribal
nobles, would have examined this man Hudson and his boat
and his crew with dignity and reserve and caution. Robert
Juet would have had to find a more apt term than "lovinge
people."

In 1609, however, the Mohawks were still newcomers
along the banks of Te-non-a-nat-che. By 1614 they seem to
have pre-empted the west-shore Albany area of Hudson's new
river. They may have thought of themselves as the "Only
Real Men," but they had yet to persuade the Algonquin
neighbors that there was anything to the idea. West, up the
Mohawk valley and beyond, were the Oneidas, the Onondagas, the Cayugas, and the Senecas, Iroquois, all of them,

but still restless, comparatively new to the lands they were hunting, fishing, and beginning to cultivate. Their great and dreaded league was still an incipient affair, good to draw their five nations together in the face of total war, but not yet strong enough to prevent the dignified and exciting business of scalp taking and village burning among themselves.

The month of March fools you so often, slipping in, lamb-like, on the heels of February. The Algonquin Indians of the Hudson Valley and New England must have felt the Iroquois had put over a March trick on them, slipping so modestly into the forests and the clearings of the Mohawk country. The Mohawks and the Oneidas probably arrived no more than thirty or forty years before Henry Hudson began note taking off Manhattan, that "island-where-we-all-got-drunk."

It's not hard to tell where they came from. If you dig, for instance, into the soil of Garoga, one of the four earliest Mohawk village sites, about ten miles north of the outlet of Garoga Creek into the Mohawk River, you'll find the answer. You'll dirty your hands in the ashes of Long House fires, and out of the ashes you'll sift, one by one, broken bits of children's toys, heavy chunks of water carriers, fragments of clay pipes shaped to resemble birds and animals, arrowheads, axheads, all of them mixed in with the refuse of numberless Indian meals. The important thing is that here at Garoga is pottery identical in manufacture and decoration with pottery found in the once-great Iroquois-Mohawk settlement of Hochelaga, near today's Montreal. Jacques Cartier found a warm and exciting welcome at Hochelaga in October, 1535. When Champlain returned to the St. Lawrence in 1603, the Iroquois were gone and Algonquins were living in their cleared lands.

What happened? The Algonquins gave Champlain a romantic sort of story about how their good neighbors, the Mohawks, who were farmers, wanted to prove that they, too,

could hunt as well as could the Algonquins. The story goes
that the Algonquins took out a party of Mohawks, who soon
killed so much more than the Algonquins killed that the latter
couldn't take it. There was murder in the night. Outrage swept
the Mohawk nation, which withdrew from the St. Lawrence
country into the Vermont valleys to plot revenge. Whatever
the cause of the Mohawk and Oneida break with their Algonquin neighbors, the evidence of the transfer is clear in these
unfired pottery fragments and weapons of Garoga. By 1580
the Mohawks and the Oneidas had found new homes. The
Mohawk Valley had been occupied at last by a people who
would grow strong enough to hold it and to exploit it.

Our Iroquois of the Five Nations came by accident and
without plan into this most strategic valley along the Atlantic
seaboard. They were, however, by no means the only "Iroquois" group. Ethnologists lump them into a huge catchall
called the Huron-Iroquois-Cherokee linguistic stock. Somewhere they had their family origin. Evidences of them are
found in the Mississippi Valley long before their migrations
into the east and their breakup into the separate nations and
tribes of historic times.

What made them leave such a comfortable, mothering
land? By the thirteenth century these Iroquois people seem to
have built up an agricultural-traders' civilization capable of
providing a rich life in terms of what forest and stream and
corn lands can give.

But by the beginning of the fourteenth century they seem
to have begun their search for new land. One can only guess
at the reasons for the breakup. Perhaps drought or flood. Perhaps jealous, less well-fed neighbors who had not lost the skill
of war began to move in on them. Whatever it was, these people began to push east through the forests. Hurons and Neutrals, Eries and Susquehannocks, and our Five Nations moved

slowly up the Ohio Valley, stopping, moving on again, pushing ahead of them or absorbing those Algonquins who had arrived, wave on wave, generations ahead of the Iroquois migration.

East, too, out of the Mississippi Valley moved the Tuscaroras and the Meherrin and the Nottoways, part of the original family grouping, to settle, finally, in the eastern Carolinas. The Iroquois-Cherokees drifted into the western Carolinas and Tennessee, Kentucky, Alabama, and Georgia.

Don't think, for a moment, that common language roots meant that these people shared a common affection. Kinship was claimed only when it meant more beaver skins for the claimants, better defense against common enemies. The Hurons, the huge Iroquois group from which our Mohawk-Oneida-Onondaga nations apparently broke off, stirred always with harsh, intertribal wars. The Hurons, or Wyandots, and the Neutrals, and Eries of the Great Lakes region were practically wiped out by their cousins of the Long House in the bitter seventeenth-eighteenth century struggle to compete successfully for the rum and trade goods of the French and English.

But that was the way the pattern took shape. For three hundred years there was a continual jockeying for position, a search for security and advantage, until, by the time Henry Hudson was eating the "Platter full of Venison" not far below the mouth of the Mohawk River the pattern had taken significant form. The Stone Age was aligned, by 1609, for better or for worse, to deal with guns and rum and bright cloth, with priests and the white man's diplomacy of broken promises.

The Hurons were in position. They spread west, north and east of Lakes Erie, Huron and Ontario, and on east down the St. Lawrence.

The Neutrals were in position south of Lake Ontario, between the western end of the Seneca country and the northern reaches of the Erie's lands, which stretched along the south shore of Lake Erie.

The Five Nations were in position. How good that position was they probably didn't know at the time, but the Mohawk Valley was theirs. Their Confederacy was weak, but it would be forced to grow strong as it fought for life.

The Susquehannocks were ready to deal with the Quaker Penns, and with the Swedes, Dutch, and Marylanders, in the hunting grounds and along the trading paths of the Susquehanna and Delaware valleys.

This is, briefly, the Indian pattern of distribution in 1609. The Algonquins played a part in the crises that followed; but their role was of more concern to New Englanders, and the Manhattan-Hudson Valley Dutch, and the English of the tidewater regions. In the great showdown for the possession of North America it was the Iroquois stock that counted. And of the Iroquois it was, finally, the Long House Nations, the Senecas, the Cayugas, the Onondagas, the Oneidas, the Mohawks, and later the Tuscaroras, who counted most. It was they who possessed the Land of Konoshioni, who possessed the valley of the Mohawk, and Te-non-an-at-che, the "river-flowing-through-mountains."

4

"The Tree of the Great Long Leaves"

The speech that Ondaaindiont [the Huron] made at his arrival was not long. He told them that he came from the land of Souls, where war and the terrors of the enemy had laid everything waste, where the fields were covered only with blood, where the cabins were filled only with corpses, and that there remained to them no life except that which was needed to come and tell their friends, that they might have pity on a land that was drawing to its end.

". . . have pity on a land that was drawing to its end." The Susquehannocks, to whom the Huron ambassador delivered these words, must have felt the cold shadow of Hagoks, the Heaven Bird, fall upon them. In the Huron's mouth the words must have been ashes.

This report of the death of a great Indian nation was made only thirty-eight years after Hudson's *Half Moon* had turned back to Europe. The events that lie between those dates are pure Greek tragedy for the Hurons, the last act of which was to find them reduced from a nation of twenty thousand to a beggar group of three hundred. And, as in a

Greek tragedy, there were terrible sequels to this first play in the cycle. The Iroquois of the Long House, like the pursuing Furies, wreaked an awful vengeance not only on Hurons but, in the twenty years following the death of that nation, on the Tobacco Nation, the Neutrals, and the Eries. By 1680 the Confederacy of the Five Nations had defeated the Susquehannocks and were sending out their war parties to attack the Illinois.

The final curtain falls on the whole ugly, brutal drama with a chorus of white men, trappers, priests, politicians, chanting the lines of the denouement, telling of the end of the Long House itself. If one looks carefully at the chorus one will see, hanging from its belts, beaver skins and the captured totems of Iroquois and Algonquin alike; one notices, too, that the clothing of the chorus is covered with the dried blood of a hundred tribes.

If Hudson had gone inland, west, up the Mohawk Valley in 1609, he would have found only the stage ready for the tragedy that was yet to be played. But he would have found the main prop in place, the Tree of the Great Long Leaves. The Indians, not yet insulated from the invigorating currents that flow directly from the soil and the air, were, by nature, poets. The Long House legendkeepers might have told Hudson about Gayanashagowa, their Great Binding Law, and perhaps, if that China-bound navigator had concealed his confusion, of Dekanawida and Hayonwatha, or Hiawatha, whose strong magic had planted the Tree of the Great Peace around which sat the Five Nations.

Hudson, being a practical man, agent for a tough-minded group of Dutch merchants out for huge profits, might, if he had been astute, have predicted the fate of this poets' league. If he had thought in dramatists' terms he would have seen himself as Prologue to the tragedy.

In 1609, however, the Long House Confederacy was a pattern of poetry and political expediency. For savages, the two were not incompatible. Then the Tree of the Great Long Leaves was a fitting symbol for the campfire councils that had to determine the simple matters of war and peace for men of the Stone Age.

Seth Newhouse, a Mohawk Indian, found the story among Iroquois records, in the years before World War I; he pieced together the poetry of its beginning, and the basic facts of its realistic provisions. Somewhere in the misty regions of prehistory the story begins. Virgin birth, the perils of black magic, a Moseslike parting of the waters for the passage of the prophet—the legend is rich with elements and symbols which show that it probably goes back to a time long before the Iroquois moved out of the west.

Dekanawida, son of a virgin, the planner of the Law, and Hayonwatha, the orator who explained its provisions around innumerable campfires, are the chief figures of the drama. Hayonwatha and Longfellow's Hiawatha are the same man, though Longfellow chose to rob the old Onondaga chief of his birthright, make an Algonquin of him, place him in what is now Michigan, and tell his tale to the rhythms of a Finnish folk story.

Dekanawida was born in the Land of the Crooked Tongues, the village of Ka-ha-nah-yenh. Here lived an old woman whose daughter, to the amazement of her tribe, gave birth to a son without first having conceived. The grandmother listened to her daughter's prophecies of what marvels the boy was to accomplish, how he was to go to the Land of the Flints and the Many Hills people and there raise up the Tree of the Great Peace.

Seeing only evil in this virgin birth, the grandmother demanded that Dekanawida be dropped through a hole in the ice that covered their lake. Twice did the obedient daughter do as her mother ordered and twice was the child found the next morning back at its mother's breast. Once more the boy was thrust into the cold waters, this time by his grandmother. And once again there was the miracle. When the old woman found Dekanawida again at his mother's side, she too believed all that her daughter had said would come true.

Dekanawida, in the eyes of his tribe, grew into a strange and unwelcome man. He hated war. His voice intoned against war around the very campfires where war was being planned. "Their hearts," say the legendkeepers, "grew bitter against a man who loved not war better than all things."

There was no room for this man in the Land of the Crooked Tongues. Driven out by his puzzled tribesmen, he made his way slowly south through the towering forests until he came to a great falls, in the country of the People of the Flint. Here where their river broke into mists and rainbows he told the Mohawks he had come to establish the Great Peace. "Peace and comfort," he said, "are better than war and misery for a nation's welfare."

To quiet the scoffers and the doubters Dekanawida agreed to prove that he was, indeed, possessed of strong magic, strong enough to make the Great Tree of Peace grow where no such tree had ever grown before. He climbed a tall pine that leaned over the chasm of mists and shifting rainbows. "Cut down the tree!" he called to the scoffers and the doubters. "Cut down the tree!"

The Mohawks toppled the tree. The sound of its breaking was lost in the thunder of the water. Tree and the man who would end war fell through the swirling shadows and vanished. The Mohawks, after searching in vain for Dekanawida among the rocks below the falls, returned to their castle convinced that they had seen the last of this madman.

Next morning runners reported smoke rising above a long-empty cabin, and in it, they said, they had seen the man who would end war and misery. Chiefs and tribesmen pushed their way through the cedar groves to the cabin.

"Netho, netho, netho!" rang through the clearing as Dekanawida stood before the crowding Mohawks. "Netho, netho, netho! . . . It is well!" "Then," say the legendkeepers, "were the chiefs and the people convinced that indeed Dekanawida might establish the Great Peace."

How long Dekanawida had to wait among the People of the Flint for the coming of Hayonwatha the legend does not say. His strong magic, however, told him that the Onondaga orator would finally join him so that together they might go among the nations, planting the Great Tree of Peace, ending war under the rule of the Binding Law.

Hayonwatha's journey from the land of the Many Hills to meet Dekanawida is a magic-filled pilgrimage. Bitter at the death of his seven daughters, saddened because Adodarhoh, the Magician, destroyer of men, held the Onondagas in terror of their lives, he finally "split the heavens" and departed, despairing of all human goodness.

In his journey through the Rush-lands, he performed the first of his miracles. Below the waters of a lake Hayonwatha saw, winking in the sands, purple and white snail shells, as beautiful as any he had ever seen. It would quiet his grief to gather them.

Everywhere on the surface of the lake, hundreds of ducks and geese were resting, waiting for the winds that would tell them it was time to fly south. Hayonwatha spoke to them, then stooped, cupped his hands, and lifted them, filled with lake water. Immediately, over the whole surface of the lake, there was a wild beating of wings. A huge shadow seemed to rise, then, caught in the wind, it rushed south. The honking

of the geese drifted back fainter and fainter as Hayonwatha walked across the marshy bottom of the empty lake, gathering the white and purple snail shells. When he had gathered enough for a dozen strings he stood on the far shore and clapped his hands. Before he had gone a dozen paces along the trail to the east he heard the beating of wings again; he turned just as the sun vanished beneath the north-rushing cloud of returning birds. As they circled the dry lake it was as though a spring rain fell from their wings and breast feathers. As Hayonwatha turned back he could see, everywhere, on the surface of the newly filled lake, his ducks and geese, resting, waiting for the south-riding wind.

When the still-despairing Onondaga was a day's journey nearer the Land of the Flint People he came on a group of old chiefs in council. He joined them, thinking that perhaps out of his own bitterness he might find words which would be of help. Never once was he asked for advice. The old chiefs talked and talked and talked through the end of a night and a whole day, and nothing was accomplished.

Hayonwatha, deeper in sorrow than before, left the council and made a lonely camp in an alder clearing. In front of his fire, as had become his custom, he put up two poles, pronged at the top to carry a horizontal pole on which he hung three strings of wampum. As his fire burned down into the coals he repeated to himself the lament he repeated each night before the coals became ash: "Men boast what they would do in time of trial but they do not do what they promise. If I should see anyone in grief I would remove these shells from this pole and console him. The shells would become words and lift away the darkness with which he is covered. Moreover, I would truly do as I say."

On the eleventh day of his journey Hayonwatha joined a second council, a great gathering of chiefs and villagers who talked for seven days, but never arrived at a decision. No word was asked of Hayonwatha, nor was he ever consulted. Suddenly, in the midst of the endless talk, on the seventh day, a messenger arrived from the east and called out, "The man from the north and the man from the land of the Many Hills are to meet near the great falls of the Flint People."

With five chiefs of the council at which he had been a worthless guest Hayonwatha hurried east for five days, arriving, on the twenty-third day of his journey, in the appointed village of the Mohawks.

Dekanawida's first words, on meeting Hayonwatha for whom he had been so long waiting, were words of sympathy: "This, then, is my younger brother who has suffered deep grief." It was not until Dekanawida overheard Hayonwatha's fireside lament, however, that he discovered how he could best quiet his friend's sorrow. Hayonwatha's voice, as it intoned the lament, had in it the grief of winter wind: "Man's work," he whispered, "is useless, for the people only boast what they will do, saying, 'I would do it this way,' but they do nothing at all. If what has befallen me should happen to them I would take down the three shell strings from this upright pole, and I would address them and I would console them, because they would be covered with darkness."

Dekanawida, hearing these words, stepped out of the shadows, laid fresh wood on the darkening coals, and then spoke to Hayonwatha: "Your griefs and rages have been great; but now they must be removed. Have you no more shell strings on your pole?"

Hayonwatha looked up at the firelit giant above him. "I have no more strings," he said, "but I have many shells in a tanned deerskin."

Dekanawida said, "My younger brother, I shall string

eight more strands, because there must be eight parts of my address to you."

As soon as he had strung the wampum so that there were thirteen strings, bound in four bunches for the thirteen condolences, he began the first of his ceremonial addresses. When he had finished the eighth he knew that the mind of Hayonwatha was again clear, that he could once more judge things rightly. There, as the fire burned down, the two men talked of the Great Peace. The peace Hayonwatha now felt in his own heart he grew impatient to extend to all men.

Peace, they found, took many wonders to establish, for men would not believe in it. The Mohawks, who had seen Dekanawida's miracle at the falls, accepted the plan of the Great Binding Law first. But the Oneidas kept saying, "Tomorrow, tomorrow, tomorrow." After a year of councils and the giving and taking of many belts of wampum, Hayonwatha won a reluctant consent from them. They would abide by the Great Binding Law.

But "tomorrow, tomorrow, tomorrow" became a doleful chorus in the ears of Dekanawida and Hayonwatha, for it was taken up next by the Onondagas, who clung to the dignities of war for still another year before they accepted the Law. And so it went. The Cayugas took a third year to make up their minds to embrace peace. The Senecas, the People of the Great Hill, at the very western door of the Long House, were the last to sit down under the Tree of the Great Long Leaves, for their war chiefs were the least willing to bury the war hatchets.

Then came the composing of the Peace Song, for it must be sung on the journey to pacify the magician of the Onondagas. Hayonwatha knew it was Adodarhoh's magic that was the last barrier to peace. "Seek out his fire and look for his smoke. His mind shall be made straight like the minds of other men if the singer remembers and makes no error in his singing of the peace song from beginning to the end."

Spies were finally chosen who "were strong by the magic of the deer and the bear." Days later they returned and reported that they had found the swale where Adodarhoh lived, and that he was terrible to behold. "We tell you," they said, "that the body of Adodarhoh has seven crooked parts. His hair is infested with snakes, and he eats men."

The evil magician of the Onondagas must be made straight as other men, or they could never plant the Great Tree of Peace. Dekanawida and the council of the Mohawks decided then to march to the Land of the Many Hills. For a long time Dekanawida "stood before the door of the Long House singing the new songs." Many came and learned them so that they might be made strong for the journey west.

As they marched toward the swale of Adodarhoh, in the land of the Onondagas, singing the song of peace, they were joined by other tribes. They passed many abandoned village sites whose names were like echoes in the memories of the old men. Families and clans adopted them, for they wanted names by which they could be known around the council fire of the Tree of Peace they were soon to plant.

When they came to the edge of the Onondaga country they built the customary signal fires, and waited until the Onondaga chiefs invited them in. Then, accompanied by the whole nation of the Many Hills people, they all "marched to the fireside of Adodarhoh, the singer of the peace hymn leading the multitude."

Mohawks, Oneidas, Onondagas, sworn to plant the Tree of the Great Long Leaves with their brothers to the west, surrounded the swamp where Adodarhoh had made his fire. The first singer to approach the raging, twisted magician was so frightened that he made an error in his singing of the peace song. A second singer was appointed, but he, too, failed.

At last Dekanawida "sang and walked before Adodarhoh's house. When he finished his song he walked toward Adodarhoh and held out his hand to rub it on his body, to know its strength and life. Then Adodarhoh was made straight and his mind became healthy."

The peace hymn finished, Dekanawida then addressed the throng of the three nations. The music of the hymn seemed to pass into the voices of the birds, into the wind, as Dekanawida spoke. "Each Nation," he said, "must now appoint a certain number of its wisest and purest men who shall be rulers, Rodiyaner. They shall be the advisers of the people and make the new rules that may be needful. These men shall be selected and confirmed by their female relations in whose lines the titles shall be hereditary. When these are named, they shall be crowned with deer antlers."

Then, say the legendkeepers, the Mohawk women brought forth nine chiefs who should be their Rodiyaner, and one man who should be war chief. So, too, did the women of the Oneidas and the Onondagas elect the Rodiyaner of their nations. "Each chief then delivered to Dekanawida a string of lake shell wampum, a span in length, as a pledge of truth."

This, Seth Newhouse tells us, was the beginning of the Great Binding Law. Here, in this quiet forest matriarchy, women were to share the burdens of state, and to be the Confederacy's final authority as the choosers of its statesmen. Before a council of all the Five Nations Dekanawida then published the full plan of the Confederacy:

"I am Dekanawida, and, with the Five Nations Confederate Lords, I plant the Tree of the Great Peace. I plant it in your territory, Adodarhoh and the Onondaga Nation, in the territory of you who are the Fire-Keepers.

"I name the Tree the Tree of the Great Long Leaves. Under the shade of this Tree of the Great Peace we spread the soft white feathery down of the globe thistle as seats for you, Adodarhoh, and your cousin Lords.

"There shall you sit and watch the council fires of the Confederacy of the Five Nations, and all the affairs of the Five Nations shall be transacted at this place before you, Adodarhoh, and your cousin Lords, by the Confederate Lords of the Five Nations. Roots have spread out from the Tree of the Great Peace, one to the north, one to the east, one to the south and one to the west. The name of these roots is the Great White Roots and their nature is peace and strength.

"Any man or nation may trace the roots to the Tree, and if their minds are clean and they are obedient and promise to obey the wishes of the Confederate Council, they shall be welcome to take shelter beneath the Tree of the Long Leaves.

"We place at the top of the Tree an eagle who is able to see afar.

"When there is business to be transacted, and the Council is not in session, a messenger shall be dispatched, either to Adodarhoh, or his brother Fire-keepers, or the War Chiefs, with a full statement of the case to be considered.

"If the Fire-Keepers think the case is of great importance, then shall they summon all the confederate lords to assemble beneath the Tree of the Great Long Leaves. Then shall the fire be kindled, but not of chestnut wood.

"You, Adodarhoh, and your cousin Lords, shall faithfully keep the space about the council fire clean and you shall allow neither dust nor dirt to accumulate. I lay a long wing before you as a broom. As a weapon against crawling creatures I lay a staff with you so that you may thrust them away from the council fire. If you fail to cast them out, then call the rest of the united lords to your aid."

The legendkeepers say that the council was to be divided into three groups, the third to listen only to the discussions of the first two. "If an error is made, or the proceeding is irregular, the third group is to call attention to the error or the irregularity." When the case had been settled by the two discussion groups, the third then referred it to the Seneca Lords for their approval. When the Seneca Lords "have decided in accordance with the Mohawk Lords, the case shall be referred to the Cayuga and Oneida Lords on the opposite side of the house." Because the Mohawks were the "Elder Brothers" of the Long House Confederacy, no council could take final action unless they were present.

Dekanawida's last words to the council were directions for its future openings; it is a forest poem that would make a magnificent preamble to any constitution:

"The Onondaga Lords shall open each council by expressing their gratitude to their cousin Lords, and greeting them, and they shall make an address and offer thanks to the earth where men dwell, to the streams of water, the pools, the springs, and the lakes, to the maize and the fruits, to the medicinal herbs and trees, to the forest trees for their usefulness, to the animals that serve as food and give their pelts for clothing, to the great winds and the lesser winds, to the Thunderers, and the Sun, the mighty warrior, to the moon, to the messengers of the Creator who reveals his wishes, and to the Great Creator who dwells in the heavens above, who gives all things useful to men, who is the source and the ruler of health and life.

"Then shall the Onondaga Lords declare the council open."

The Tree of the Great Long Leaves, the Iroquois symbol of aspiration, grew and perished. Dekanawida and Hayonwatha live beyond time beneath its shade. If they were ever real men, that fact was forgotten as the Five Nations carried on the ancient work of mythmaking. There may have been men of the Long House who dreamed of universal peace, of nations tracing the Great White Roots to the Tree of Peace itself. But there is that tragic speech of Ondaaindiont, the Huron, to the chiefs of the Susquehannocks which ended ". . . have pity on a land that is drawing to its end."

The warrior Iroquois, operating within the framework of the Great Binding Law, spread not peace but death and destruction. The Law, before the coming of the white man, served probably to keep the Long House from destroying itself. After the white man came, the Law gave the Confederacy a pattern of offense and defense for a new age. They, of all the Stone Age people of America, seem to have evolved a plan of organization capable of meeting for a time the insidious and constant threats to their survival.

The Great Binding Law failed at last before the infinite provisions and niceties of the white man's laws, adjustable always to the white man's ambitions. Indians still live by it, but they are reservation Indians, long gone from the Fireplace of the Onondagas, from the river on whose banks walked Dekanawida and Hayonwhatha, teaching the Hymn of Peace.

Their Great Binding Law was said to have inspired Benjamin Franklin's plan for a union of the colonies. Through him and those other political philosophers who knew the Iroquois well it may even have helped to shape the Constitution of the United States, in the morning of a new American Confederacy.

5

"To See If It Was True..."

THE surgeon's first entry began piously.

> Praise the Lord above all. . . . Fort Orange, 1634.
> December 11. First, the reasons why we went on this journey were these, that the Maquas and the Sinnekens very often came to our factor Marten Gerritsen and me stating that there were French Indians in their land, and that they had made a truce because the Maquas Indians wanted to receive just as much for their skins as the French Indians did.

Hermen Meyndertsz van den Bogaert, surgeon at Fort Orange, was probably the author of this first white man's report on the Mohawk Valley. The Dutch surgeon's reasons for the grim winter trip had nothing to do with healing the sick. He, and Jeronimus La Croix and Willem Thomassen, employees of the West India Company, tramped west on strictly political-commercial business.

The "Maquas," of course, were the Mohawks. The "Sinnekens" of the *Journal* were the Oneidas, although for a good many decades Sinnekens were members of any of the Indian nations lying west of the Mohawks.

But the fact that "there were French Indians in their lands" constituted the real problem at Fort Orange, in 1634. That was why the worried surgeon "proposed to Mr. Marten Gerritsen to go and see if it was true, so soon to run counter to their High Mightinesses."

The "High Mightinesses" were the States-General of the Netherlands, lords of the most progressive and tolerant country in Europe. The valley of the Mohawk and the lands of the "Sinnekens" were, according to their philosophy, part of the Dutch preserve that ran from Virginia to the St. Lawrence. "French Indians" in the beaver country back of Fort Orange were a serious threat to those ledger figures of the Dutch West India Company, charged by their High Mightinesses with developing fur trade, agriculture, settlement, and if convenient, an interest among the "wilden" in a Lutheran God.

That *Journal* entry "trade was doing badly" establishes the state of mind of Mr. Marten Gerritsen, in charge of Fort Orange activities. There, on the banks of the Hudson, almost 150 miles from Manhattan, the Dutch had maintained trading posts for twenty years. Business had been wonderful . . . "a great traffic in the skins of beaver, otters, foxes, bears, minks, wildcat, and the like."

In 1624 two ships had sailed for the Netherlands with 4,000 beaver and 700 otter skins in their holds. Two years later the company's ledgers showed that 7,257 beaver and 857 otter skins had been taken out of the New Netherlands. In 1628 the total rose to about 10,000 skins. The year before Surgeon van den Bogaert began his *Journal*, 33,000 skins went into the company's warehouses. And then, in 1634, the slump.

The reason for the slump around Fort Orange was clear. The French were moving in. What may not have been so clear was that beaver were being taken out of the lands of the Five Nations at an alarming rate. What neither the Dutch nor

the French understood at all was that trade goods that had
been going over their counters to the Iroquois were no longer
luxury goods. None of the Indian Confederacies could survive
now in the new world of guns and plows, axes, duffel cloth,
and cooking pots unless they, too, had them. The economics
of this new world were clear enough: no beaver, no trade
goods.

Surgeon van den Bogaert's employers, and the French,
were, without intending it, soon to put the Iroquois Long
House on the offensive. Now, in 1634, without Dutch or
French guns, knives and axes the Five Nations could not hold
the Mohawk Valley for long. If that privilege had to be paid
for in beaver skins, then they would find beaver skins. When
the local supply failed, they would try treaties with those who
had them. If the treaties failed, then . . .

So the Fort Orange surgeon "proposed to Mr. Marten
Gerritsen to go and see if it was true, so soon to run counter
to their High Mightinesses."

A great newspaper has no more resourceful or observing
reporter on its staff than had Mr. Gerritsen on his. Hermen
Meyndertsz van den Bogaert might just as well have been
heading toward Erewhon as toward the country of the "Sinnekens." There were as yet no maps of it that were not a com-
pound of wishful thinking and rumor. The frontier, in 1634,
was in hailing distance of the west wall of Fort Orange. Beyond it were the "wilden," savages stinking with bear grease,
hunting with stone axes through the forests of the Stone Age.
Little wonder the anxious surgeon wrote, as part of his first
day's entry, "May the Lord bless my voyage!"

On December 11, 1634, the three white men left Fort
Orange. They had five Mohawk Indians for guides, and, apparently, an unwelcome complement of Indian dogs. The
weather seems to have stayed above freezing until the night

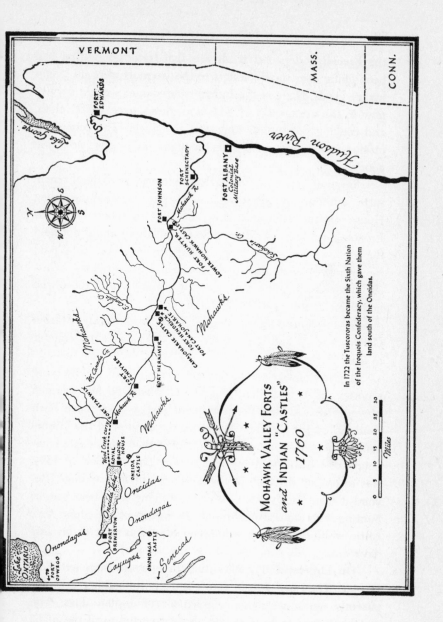

MOHAWK VALLEY FORTS and INDIAN "CASTLES" 1760

In 1722 the Tuscroras became the Sixth Nation of the Iroquois Confederacy, which gave them land south of the Oneidas.

VERMONT

MASS.

CONN.

Lake George

FORT EDWARDS

Hudson River

FORT SCHENECTADY

FORT JOHNSON

Mohawk R.

FORT ALBANY Colonial Military Base

Schoharie R.

FORT HUNTER

LOWER MOHAWK CASTLE

Mohawks

CANAJOHARIE CASTLE

FORT HERKIMER

FORT CANAJOHARIE

Mohawks

W. Canada Cr.

FORT SCHUYLER

FORT STANWIX

Mohawk R.

Mohawks

Wood Creek carry

ROYAL BLOCK HOUSE

ONEIDA CASTLE

Oneidas

Oneida Lake

FORT BREWERTON

Onondagas

ONONDAGA CASTLE

Lake ONTARIO

TO FORT OSWEGO

Onondagas

Cayugas

Senecas

Miles
0 5 10 15 20 25 30

51

of the 12th, by which time the dogs had eaten their meat and cheese, the guides had proved to be unreliable, and the Mohawk River was discovered to be so flooded they could not go up it in canoes.

Two days' tramping west on the narrow Indian trail had taken the Dutchmen past the flats of Schonowe, today's Schenectady, and on to what is now called Little Nose, on the south shore of the river. Here, overlooking Wasontha Creek, was the first of the Mohawk "castles," one of the Long House towns of the Five Nations.

"There," wrote the surgeon, "stood but 36 houses, in rows like streets, so that we could pass nicely. The houses are made and covered with bark of trees, and mostly are flat at the top. Some 100, 90, or 80 paces long and 22 and 23 feet high. There were some inside doors of hewn boards, furnished with iron hinges. In some houses we saw different kinds of iron work, iron chains, harrow irons, iron hoops, nails—which they steal when they go forth from here. Most of the people were out hunting deer and bear. The houses were full of corn—and we saw maize; yes, in some of the houses more than 300 bushels."

It was the "iron work," the hoops and harrows and nails that were important. These were trade items the Iroquois had to have. They got them with beaver skins, or they stole them. One old chief showed the Dutchmen "his idol, a cat's head, with the teeth sticking out." Van den Bogaert didn't emphasize the fact that it was dressed "in duffel cloth," another trade goods item the Indians were demanding in ever-greater quantities.

After presenting such gifts as "a knife and two awls, and a pair of scissors" to the surprisingly hospitable savages they left the castle a little after midday. Willem Thomassen was feeling better. Willem, the night before, his legs "swollen . . .

from the march, had a few cuts with a knife made therein, and after that had them rubbed with bear grease."

About two hours after dark they came into their second castle of importance, the village of Canagere, a little east of Canajoharie Creek. Van den Bogaert's roving eye again quickly picked out what was important to the distant High Mightinesses. In one of the sixteen houses that made up the village "we counted . . . 120 pieces of saleable beaver skins that (the owner) captured with his own dogs." "Every day," he wrote, "we ate beaver meat here."

The surgeon was interested in everything he saw. He looked into one house "containing a bear to be fattened. It had been there upward of three years, and was so tame it took everything that was given it to eat." On December 18 he wrote: "Three women of the Sinnekens came here with dried and fresh salmon; the latter smelled very bad." The fish must have been high indeed to affront noses inured to the filth that collected around an Indian village. He added as an afterthought the comment that the Sinneken women with their fish had been on the march six days.

On December 20 these hardy commercial travelers came to "Schandisse," the Middle Castle of the Bear Clan. "We were wet up to above the waist, and after going for another half league we came thus wet, with our clothes, shoes, stockings frozen to us, to a very high hill on which stood 32 houses, like the other ones."

You had to be hardy, too, in the Mohawk country in 1634 in your attitude toward the social amenities. "A good many of the savages were at home," wrote the ubiquitous reporter, "so we were much looked at by both the old and the young; indeed, we could hardly pass through. They pushed each other in the fire to see us, and it was more than midnight before they took their departure. We could not absent ourselves to go to stool; even then they crawled around us without any feeling of shame." The chief lent van den Bogaert "a lion skin" for a bed cover; in the morning he reported, "I had more than a hundred lice."

The next night they spent in the village of "Hulled-corn soup." Here the surgeon had his fears about the French confirmed. "I asked (the chief) whether there were any French savages there with the Sinnekens. He said yes; and I felt gratified and had a good hope to reach my aim."

December 22: "When the sun rose, we waded together through the stream; the water was over the knee, and so cold that shoes and stockings in a very short time were frozen as hard as armor." The Dutchmen arrived that day at Tenotoge, the largest castle of the Wolf Clan, and probably one of the largest towns in the New Netherlands, European or Indian. "There are 55 houses, some one hundred, others more or fewer paces long— The savages . . . crowded each other in the fire to see us." White men in the Mohawk Valley caused a good deal of commotion in 1634.

December 25: Christmas Day. There were no Christian sentiments recorded in the *Journal* for the 25th, nothing but the doleful note that as "it was snowing steadily, we could not go, because nobody wanted to go with us to carry our goods," the lament of the real salesman.

The weather apparently improved the next day. The surgeon, after accepting "two pieces of bear's bacon to take with us on the march," took to the trail west again, with Willem and Jeronimus. The savages who followed them some distance kept shouting "Aklesa rondade!" . . . "that is, to fire our pistols." The Dutchmen were too cautious, however, to empty their weapons, and so leave themselves open to attack.

By the 27th the snow was two and a half feet deep in some places. For the next three days they tramped through the bitter cold, getting precious little sleep in the Indian lean-tos where they spent the nights. But the observing surgeon never missed the important things. Here a great stand of beech trees, along this stream many beavers and otters were said to be caught; on the 29th "a good deal of flat land, with many oaks and handles for axes." Mr. Gerritsen, back in Fort Orange, was going to have a useful inventory, provided the Sinnekens of the next, and the most westerly, castle they planned to visit had not made fatal commitments to the French intruders.

December 30, and journey's end. "Without anything to eat, we went to the Sinnekens' castle . . . a woman came to meet us, bringing us baked pumpkins to eat." And then the inevitable inventory note: "This road was mostly full of birches and beautiful flat land for sowing." What emotion the surgeon felt as he walked by the "three graves, just like our graves in length and height," he doesn't record; he must have been a little disturbed, however, because he added, "usually their graves are round."

Four or five leagues of tramping brought them to the castle itself, "where the savages divided into two rows, and so let us pass through them by the gate . . . 3½ feet wide, and at the top were standing three big wooden images, carved like men, and with them I saw three scalps fluttering in the wind, that they had taken from their foes as token of the truth of their victory." Three graves and "three scalps fluttering in the wind"—hardly comforting omens to support the business in hand. On the way up to the castle the guides had pointed out "a large river . . . and tremendously high land that seemed to lie in the clouds . . . the savages told me that in this river the Frenchmen came to trade."

It was here, at the chief Oneida castle, on the banks of the upper Oneida Creek that these Dutchmen saw French axes, "very good axes to cut the underwood," French shirts and coats and razors. These things were like sparks in the forest, forerunners of the conflagration that would finally burn out the life of the Iroquois Confederacy. When guns and rum finally loosed the fire, the men of the Long House carried the ruin like a torch to every Indian tribe and nation that tried to interfere with their control of the trade channels.

The Oneidas played their first hand beautifully. "In the afternoon," van den Bogaert wrote, "one of the council came to me, asking the reason of our coming into his land, and what we brought for him as a present. I told him that we did not bring any present, but that we only paid him a visit. He told us that we were not worth anything, because we did not bring him a present. Then he told us how the Frenchmen had come thither to trade with six men, and had given them good gifts, because they had been trading in this river with six men in the month of August of this year . . . this member of the council said we were scoundrels, and were not worth anything because we paid not enough for their beaver skins. They told us that the Frenchmen gave six hands of sewan [wampum] for one beaver, and all sorts of things more."

"The savages," wrote the surgeon, "were pressing closely upon us so that there was hardly room for us to sit. If they had desired to molest us, we could hardly have been able to defend ourselves; but there was no danger."

The Dutchman knew his "Sinnekens." There was no real danger, for they wanted what Fort Orange had to offer. Few trade conferences are ever run with nicer finesse than was this one.

The Oneidas played the next card. On the following day "the chief of this castle came back . . . and one more man. They told us they returned from the French savages, and some of the savages shouted 'Jawe Arenias!' which meant

that they thanked him for coming back." Nothing like letting
the visiting delegation know that you are keeping in touch
with the competitor. That afternoon Jeronimus was put to
work by van den Bogaert, making a chart of the Oneida country on the basis of what they could pick up from the more
talkative members of the castle.

So far, things were at dead center. "We fired three shots
in the night in honor of the year of our Lord and Redeemer,
Jesus Christ." Firearms were still impressive adjuncts to any
trade argument, and besides, it *was* New Year's.

January 1, 1635: "Another savage scolded us. We were
scoundrels, as told before; and he looked angry. Willem
Thomassen got so excited that the tears were running along
his cheeks, and the savages, seeing that we were not at all
contented, asked us what was the matter, and why we looked
so disgusted at him."

The surgeon's next move took courage, but it was worth
the risk. "There were in all 46 persons seated near us; if
they had intended to do mischief, they could easily have
caught us with their hands and killed us without much trouble; when I had listened long enough to the Indian's chatter
I told him that he was a scoundrel himself and he began to
laugh, said he was not angry and said: 'You must not grow so
furious, for we are glad you came here.'"

The Dutchman had played the right card. Now they
could get down to the real business of the journey. Jeronimus distributed presents. That evening the Oneidas "allowed"
the visitors to sit in on the ratification of a peace treaty that
had been pending with the French Indians. How effective this
last bit of stage-setting was is not known, though there is
little doubt that Mr. Marten Gerritsen heard about it. In
any event, what all committeemen like to call "conversations"
could now go forward.

The next day the Oneidas began to practice the friendship formula. It was suggested that the Dutchmen stop at the castle "another four or five days. They would provide for all our needs and have us treated nicely," wrote the pleased surgeon, who immediately opened the dampers on this display of warmth by saying that he couldn't possibly wait that long. The Oneidas, now eager to get on with what was vital business to them, added another inducement to stay: they had sent for the Onondagas, the nation just west of them; weren't they good customers at Fort Orange? Van den Bogaert countered that the Onondagas had nearly starved him, though there is no evidence that he had ever been among them. The Oneidas were not easily discouraged: "Then they said that in the future they would look better after us, and twice during the day we were invited to be their guests, and treated to salmon and bear's bacon."

On the afternoon of January 3 the Oneidas finally stated the terms on which they expected to trade with Fort Orange. At the beginning of this session van den Bogaert had to submit to an odd test: "after consulting for a long time an old man approached me and laid his hand upon my heart to feel it beat; and then he shouted we were really not afraid at all." Marten Gerritsen's representatives had at last proved themselves. Graves and scalps and scolding savages and treaties with the French could not intimidate them.

The Oneidas seemed to think things might go better with a little gift giving first, on their part; after six more council members had listened to the surgeon's unafraid heart, they presented him with a coat of beaver skins. The council then shouted "Netho, netho, netho! [It is well!]" "and directly after that they laid five pieces of beaver skin at my feet, at the same time requesting me that in the future they should receive four hands of sewan and four handbreadths of cloth for every big beaver skin." Not six hands, as they were getting from the French, just four, plus the cloth.

This first trade conference in the Iroquois country, with its bid for higher prices, has all the familiar elements. The Oneidas pointed out that they were inconvenienced by the long trip to the Dutchmen's trading post. And then there was the old complaint about empty shelves: "very often when we come to your places," said the Oneida spokesman, "we do not find any cloth or sewan or axes or kettles, or not enough for all of us and then we have had much trouble for nothing, and have to go back over a great distance, carrying our goods back again."

Van den Bogaert's behavior, in the face of this pressure, was what an army man would call S.O.P. . . . standard operating procedure. . . . "I told (them) that we had not the power to promise that, but that we should report about it to the chief at the Manhatans, who was our commander, and that I would give him a definite answer in the spring, and come myself to their land."

The surgeon's next entry shows the Oneida chiefs realized, when they heard this speech, that the conference had produced all that could be expected of it. "They said to me *Welsmachkoo*, you must not lie, and surely come to us in the spring, and report to us about all. And if you will give us four hands of sewan we will not sell our skins to anyone but you . . ."

That last commitment must have been music in the Dutchmen's ears. Exclusive trading rights was what their High Mightinesses expected. . . . The Oneidas knew that four hands of sewan, and extras, from the Dutch were better than six hands "and all sorts of things more" from the French. The Mohawk Valley was their trade channel, not the long, cir-

cuitous, and dangerous route to the French by way of the
Oneida Lake and the Oneida River, to Lake Ontario, and
then east again down the St. Lawrence to Montreal. The
route to Fort Orange ran through the lands of "brother" Indians; the trails, land or water, to Montreal, ran through competitor "Nations" who in 1634 still looked down on the Confederacy of the Long House. So long as beaver were plentiful
in their own country, so long could the Iroquois maintain their
pre-eminent position astride the back of the Great Turtle.
When the beaver were to be found only in the lands of one's
neighbors, then neighbors were likely to become enemies and
such treaties of friendship as van den Bogaert and Jeronimus
and Willem had just seen the Oneidas arrange with such ceremony between themselves and the French Indians became of
less value than the strings of wampum which symbolised
them.

The conference was over. The surgeon had said he could
not stay as many as four or five days, but that was before the
air cleared and they had got down to business. The Dutchmen, loaded now with gifts—twenty-eight beaver skins, a
beaver coat, five salmon, and some loaves of bread—left the
Oneida castle for home on January 12.

On the 19th of January "a letter from Martin Gerritsen
(was) brought us by a savage that came in search of us." The
Fort Orange authorities were worried about the fate of this
trade conference. And then the last note: . . . "after eleven
leagues' marching we arrived, the Lord be praised and
thanked, at Fort Orange, January 21, anno, 1635."

Surgeon van den Bogaert was now ready to report to Mr.
Marten Gerritsen, factor, that "it was true," that things had
"run counter to their High Mightinesses." However, these
were now the new commitments: "We will sell to you for four

hands of sewan, and four handbreadths of cloth," the Oneidas had said, and "we will not sell our skins to anyone but
you." The difficulty was that the French were not going to
like these arrangements.

6

"The Narrow Way of Paradise'

"**A** HURON, to whom they had given his liberty in that country, having perceived us, exclaimed, 'You are dead, Frenchmen, you are dead; there is no liberty for you. Think no more of life; you will be burned; prepare yourself for death!' "

Frenchmen, in 1642, had little prospect of leaving the Mohawk Valley alive. Father Isaac Jogues, thinking back later on the day of his arrival there, wrote: "I had always thought that the day on which the whole church rejoices in the glory of the blessed Virgin . . . would be for us a day of pain." It was on this day that Father Jogues and his two donnés, René Goupil and Guillaume Cousture, were driven, naked, bleeding, half alive, down what the Father called "the narrow way of Paradise," an Indian gantlet of howling, club-swinging Mohawks, who thus ushered them into their "castle" of Osseruenon, where now stands the Shrine of the Martyrs, at Auriesville.

Seven years earlier, in 1635, three Dutchmen from Fort Orange had gone through the Mohawk valley, their thoughts grounded among the earthly details of the beaver trade, counting the skins they saw in the long houses, asking always about the Frenchmen they had heard were there bidding against the Dutch for the Iroquois trade.

In that seven-year interval Frenchmen, traders and priests alike, were forced to test their faith as they ran the Indian gantlets and died in the flames of the Iroquois pyres. What had happened? Why was this Jesuit priest greeted from the Huron captive with the shout, "You are dead, Frenchmen, you are dead . . . ?"

The answers are all in the ledger books of the times, Dutch and French alike, and in the letters and the *Relations* of the Jesuit Fathers of New France. The Dutchmen of the New Netherlands were of one kind and one mind. With a nice singleness of purpose they set out to exploit the resources of the Indian country. For them "resources" meant material things: furs, lands, forests, but chiefly furs. Around Fort Orange grew up Beverwyck—the beaver's town. The souls of the "wilden" they left to the shamans and the jugglers of the tribes.

But there were two kinds of Frenchmen who came to New France. The larger group, like the Dutch, thought also in terms of furs, and lands, and forests. The French governors, beginning with Champlain, saw the hazy outlines of a vast French-American empire which was to include not only the St. Lawrence country, but all of the New Netherlands, the valley of the Ohio, and the valley of the Mississippi. The presence of the Dutch and the English they looked on as a matter of temporary inconvenience.

The second group of Frenchmen were soldiers of the cross. The Society of Jesus, to which Father Jogues belonged, had their vision, too, of a new empire in America. The two French empires, these Jesuits knew, must, of necessity, have a common geography.

French Jesuits and French laymen both knew that to achieve their ends they must use each other. Their common enemy was the Devil. To the traders of Montreal, Three Rivers, and Quebec the Devil was a synonym for Iroquois. To men of Father Jogues's crusading spirit, the Devil was the thief of souls. A Jesuit's duty, as they saw it, was to convert every savage he could find, and then to police the wilderness at whatever cost, to deal with the Devil wherever he found him, in the camps of the Algonquins and the Hurons, or, if need be, in the long houses of the Five Nations.

Fighting the Devil is dirty business. If treaties and armed Hurons and Algonquins would not keep the Canadian fur trade open, then perhaps the cross would. For their part Father Jogues and the other members of his order were glad to see the guns of French soldiers open up clearings in the forest for their chapels. And the Iroquois, within the pattern of their own Stone Age thinking, were concerned with devils. Weren't the "blackrobes," the French priests, devils demanding submission to new gods, seemingly bringing with them disease and crop failures wherever they went? Hadn't the Dutch told them to beware of the sign of the cross?

Father Jogues's martyrdom in what he once called "the nation of devils" began in earnest on August 1, 1642. A young man, thirty-five, sensitive, a man of books and cloisters, he had already spent six years among the Hurons. Christianizing pagan Rome called for less endurance. The mission fields of the Apostles may have been rank with pagans but there were at least familiar things about: customs one shared with the unsaved, food, dress, houses, language frequently, patterns of thought and action common to the redeemed and the damned. The mission fields of New France, however, lay not only west of Europe, but backward by ten thousand years on the clocks of civilization.

Father Jogues knew, as he climbed into the lead canoe of the flotilla of twelve that was to carry him and his two donnés and the Huron traders back to the Huron villages, that all of the Europe there was in New France would soon vanish behind the river mists of the St. Lawrence. If they could avoid the Iroquois they would finally pull their canoes up among a people who had never known the wheel, who had no written language, who had never seen horses or cows or pigs. He was hurrying back to bring Christ to savages who were dying by thousands of Europe's imported diseases, wonder on their faces as they died of tuberculosis, in the epidemics of smallpox and measles against which they had no resistance. All this, if these Frenchmen could avoid the Iroquois, whose new Dutch guns now made them a scourge along the whole St. Lawrence.

But in 1642 there was no avoiding the Iroquois. Sometime during the second day out of Three Rivers several of the canoes were beached, the party suspecting there were Iroquois nearby. "We had not made half a league," wrote Father Jogues, "when the enemy, concealed among the grasses and brushwood, rises with a great outcry, discharging at our canoes a volley of balls. The noise of their arquebuses so greatly frightened a part of our Hurons that they abandoned their canoes and weapons, and all their supplies, in order to escape by flight into the depths of the wood."

Father Jogues could have escaped, too, but he didn't. "Flight," he wrote afterward, "seemed horrible to me. 'It must be,' I said in my heart, 'that my body suffer the fire of earth, in order to deliver these poor souls from the flames of Hell; it must die a transient death, in order to procure for them an eternal life.'" Father Jogues, knowing what captivity among the Iroquois meant, elected to stay with Cousture and René

Goupil, whom he had just seen surrounded, along with a number of Huron converts, by a band of painted Mohawks.

It had been seven years since Surgeon van den Bogaert had made his winter's trip to check on the Fort Orange trade slump, and look for Frenchmen. Guns were a novelty among the Long Houses in 1635. Now, in 1642, the Mohawks alone had about four hundred of them. Trade, Fort Orange discovered, was greatly improved when guns were made available to the savages. Converts, the Jesuits had observed, were more numerous when guns were allowed to pass into the hands of the new Christians.

As late as 1641 a deer could be bought at Fort Orange for the price of one Dutch pipe. Three years later there was bitter complaint because deer were bringing six and seven guilders. The deer had moved north to the hunting grounds of the Algonquins. The Five Nations were running out of beaver. They had tried to make trade treaties with the Hurons, but New France had interfered, sending out Jesuits to break up Indian accords which might divert the fur trade from Montreal and Three Rivers to the Dutch on the Hudson. Running through this turmoil of economic change were the old angers between Iroquois and Algonquins, Iroquois and Hurons, bad blood which the new frictions heated until nothing but spilling by guns and tomahawks would cool it.

Father Jogues, his donnés, and their Christian Hurons, on the morning of August 2, 1642, walked their first miles toward the "country truly foreign." Cousture, before he was captured, managed to shoot one of the savages. Immediately, "four other Hiroquois fell upon him with the rage of Lions, or rather Demons. Having stripped him bare as the hand, they bruised him with heavy blows of clubs, and tore out his finger nails with their teeth . . . crushing the bleeding ends, in order to cause him more pain." Father Jogues embraced him. " 'Courage,' I say to him, 'my dear brother and friend; offer your pains and anguish to God, in behalf of those very persons who torment you. . . . Let us not draw back; let us suffer courageously for His Holy Name; we have intended only His glory in this journey.' The Hiroquois, seeing us in these endearments, at first remained quite bewildered, looking at us without saying a word; then, all at once,—imagining, perhaps, that I was applauding that young man because he had killed one of their captains,—they fell upon me with a mad fury, they belabored me with thrusts, and with blows from sticks and war clubs, flinging me to the ground, half dead. When I began to breathe again, those who had not struck me, approaching, violently tore out my finger-nails; and then, biting one after another, the ends of my two forefingers, destitute of their nails, caused me the sharpest pain—grinding and crushing them as if between two stones, even to the extent of causing splinters or little bones to protrude. They treated the good René Goupil in the same way, without doing, at that time, any harm to the Hurons: they were thus enraged against the French because the latter had not been willing to accept the peace, the preceding year, on the conditions which they wished to give them."

The thirteen-day trip south to the Mohawk Valley was one of "torments almost unendurable." Wounds went undressed, became "putrid even to the extent of breeding worms." They met another war party of two hundred Iroquois—"at this encounter we were obliged to sustain a new shock . . . they formed a line,—a hundred on one side, and a hundred on the other, and made us pass, all naked, along that way of fury and anguish; there is a rivalry among them to discharge upon us the most and the heaviest blows; they made me march last, that I might be more exposed to their rage . . . they burned one of my fingers, and crushed another with their teeth, and those which were already torn they twisted and squeezed with the rage of Demons; they scratched my wounds with their nails; and, when strength failed me, they applied fire to my arms and thighs."

On the day of the Feast of the Assumption, naked, his body covered with dried blood, his wounds festering, Father Jogues looked for the first time on a Mohawk community as he passed again through the "narrow way of Paradise," a gantlet formed by the young men of the village "armed with sticks, and some with iron rods, which they easily secure on account of their vicinity to the Dutch." The Christians offered themselves with great courage, the Father wrote, "in order to be victims sacrificed to His good pleasure and to His anger, lovingly zealous for the salvation of these people."

"You are dead, Frenchmen, you are dead; there is no liberty for you . . ." had been shouted at them from the crowd of onlookers. For the next three days the Frenchmen must have wished many times that death would take them. They were placed on a platform in the middle of the Mohawk town. "A captain exclaims that the Frenchmen ought to be carressed. Sooner done than it is said . . . one wretch, jumping on the stage, dealt three heavy blows with a stick, on each Frenchman, without touching the Hurons . . . an old man takes my hand and commands a captive Algonquin woman to cut one of my fingers; she turns away three of four times, unable to resolve on this cruelty; finally she has to obey, and cuts the thumb from my left hand; the same carresses are extended to the other prisoners. This poor woman, having thrown my thumb on the stage, I picked it up, and offered it to you, O my God!"

There was seemingly no end to the nightmare. "Evening having come, they made us descend in order to be taken into the cabins as the sport of the children." After the prisoners had been staked to the ground, "the children, in order to learn the cruelty of their parents, threw coals and burning cinders on our stomachs . . . taking pleasure in seeing us broil and roast. Oh, my God, what nights."

Torture, with the Iroquois, was a convention of war. If captured, you taunted your captors for their clumsy attempts to break your spirit. You expected the gantlet and the flames, and were afraid only of being afraid. Sometimes your enemy, impressed with your fortitude, cut your bonds and initiated you into his tribe, gave you to some family who had lost a member in battle. Only the women turned away from the work of these artists in cruelty.

From Osseruenon the prisoners were dragged two miles up the south bank of the Mohawk to Andagaron and from there on to Teonontogen, the last of the Mohawks' three towns. Each time they stopped they were made a spectacle, the tortures repeated until the mind goes numb contemplating them.

That fall and winter Father Jogues spent at Osseruenon where he saw the devoted René Goupil brained for teaching the Mohawk children to make the sign of the cross. He became a servant, a carrier of wood and water. He marked his faith by cutting the name of Jesus on the trees in the groves where he worshiped when he could avoid his captors. He gave absolution to the Christian captives when he could, and carried on his work of trying to convert those savages who would listen to him. He watched with horror as his captors, on the occasions of their religious feasts to Areskoui, the Demon of the Iroquois pantheon, ate with apparent relish the arms, buttocks, and trunk of their victims, reserving to the royaneh, their chiefs, the head and the heart.

This monotony of horrors continued until the end of July, 1643. How this frail soldier of the army without banners endured is one of the mysteries of faith. Because he made no attempt to escape he was allowed to go freely among the three Mohawk towns, and to accompany fishing and hunting parties. It was at the end of a fishing expedition that Father Jogues was forced to make his decision—to stay and await the death he knew the Mohawks were planning for him or to escape.

To the Dutchmen of Fort Orange, where Father Jogues had been taken by his captors who stopped there to trade on their way home, there was something about this scarred and mutiliated man they could not understand. They offered to hide him on a Europe-bound vessel then at anchor off the fort, and, to their amazement, he thanked them, and asked for a night in which he hoped to receive God's counsel in the matter.

The following morning, convinced now that his usefulness in the Mohawk country was at an end, he accepted his Dutch friends' offer. Escape, however, was not easy. The Mohawks, enraged to find their choicest prisoner gone, ransacked the post and the cluster of farmhouses around it. Dominie Megapolensis, spiritual warder for the patroon of Rensselaerswyck, whose seven hundred thousand acres surrounded this West India Company trading station on all sides, and Arendt Van Curler, the patroon's cousin and a fiscal agent, now risked their profitable peace with the Mohawks. For six weeks they kept Father Jogues hidden in the garret of the house of one of their neighbors, a miserly farmer who thought nothing of withholding part of the food that had been provided for his "guest."

The Mohawks were bought off, finally, with goods "to the value of three hundred livres." A boat was sent up the river at last from Manhattan to bring the weary Jesuit down to the little Dutch capital of New Netherlands.

Manhattan must have seemed a noisy, money-makers' babel to Father Jogues. Eighteen languages, Director Kieft told him, were spoken in its crowded taverns. The Dutch, however, were generous. They found it hard to believe that the Father had not gone among the savages in the interest of the French traders. They gave him new clothes, tried to name one of the Hudson River islands after him, and finally put him aboard a "bark of 100 tons, bound for Holland."

France looked on him, it was reported, as "Lazarus raised from the dead." Because he had been disfigured, he was debarred by church law from saying the Mass. A special papal dispensation restored that privilege to him. Anne of Austria, Queen of France, on hearing of his return, made a fine, enameled comment: "Romances are feigned; but here is a genuine combination of great adventures."

Father Jogues, finding himself again on the broad highway of the world, soon begged permission to leave it. "He made no long sojourn in France," wrote the chronicler in the *Jesuit Relations;* "the Spring of the year 1644 having come, he betook himself to la Rochelle in order to cross back to the country of his martyrdom. . . ." Paradise, for Father Jogues, still lay at the end of the narrow way.

7

"The Secret of Their Country"

"When I speak of a mission among the Iroquois," wrote
Father Lalemant, Superior of the Jesuits in New France in
1646, "it seems to me that I speak of a dream, and yet it is a
truth. It is with good right that it is made to bear the name
of the Martyrs."

Father Jogues, in May of that year, went back again to
the Mohawks.

"It is judged necessary here," he wrote to a friend in
France, "in order to maintain it [the French-Mohawk peace of
1645] and to ascertain quietly what can be done for the in-
struction of these tribes, to send thither some Father. . . . I
have reason to believe I shall be employed therein. . . . I must
be responsible for all accidents between the Hiroquois,
French, Algonquins and Hurons."

His journey this time was obviously political as well as
spiritual. He would never have questioned that higher honesty which had brought about the new "peace." It was enough
for him that he was to establish a mission on the banks of the
Mohawk, the river into which the savages had thrown the
body of René Goupil. He looked on the Iroquois, wrote Father

Lalemant, "with an eye of compassion, as a mother looks at a child of hers, stricken with a raging disease; at other times he regarded them as rods which our Lord employed for punishing his crimes . . . it is incredible what ardor he felt for enduring the rage of the Hiroquois for the sake of the Hiroquois themselves."

Father Jogues had been at Montreal since his return from France. While there he "examined all the folds and recesses of his conscience . . . he asked in what manner he should offer prayer aright, and in what manner he should perform his act of thanks after holy Mass . . . through a belief that what proceeded from others was always the best."

For whom, though, was this "peace" over which he was to preside "best"? For Hurons? For one year only were they able to get their fur-laden canoes to the traders at Montreal and Three Rivers. The Oneidas, the Onondagas, the Cayugas, and the Senecas had refused "to have their ears pierced," to come into the peace agreement. For the Mohawks? They wanted the hunting grounds of the Algonquins. A Huron warrior had heard from them "the secret of their country," and the "secret" had to do with the treaty itself, and the private talks the Mohawk ambassadors had had with the French governor. For the Algonquins? By 1650 the Jesuit missions to the Hurons and the Algonquins were withdrawn, for these nations were dead, and their remnants had been "adopted" by the conquering Iroquois. For the French? They made the treaty and lost their Indian allies. For Father Jogues? Because of it he became the chief martyr of the mission he had been sent to erect.

It is possible that Father Jogues did not know about those "private talks" between the leader of the Mohawk delegation, "le Crochet," and Governor Montmagny, up from Quebec for the occasion of the peacemaking at Three Rivers. Father

Jogues attended the public councils, and listened to the pledges of the Mohawks and the Hurons and the Algonquins to honor an eternal and binding peace. Each party to the agreement wiped away the memory of past errors with innumerable strings of wampum. The Mohawks, not knowing Father Jogues was present, "regretted" his untimely departure from among them, saying that they had intended to release him. The Father whispered to the Jesuits sitting near him, "They had the pile laid to burn me. They would have killed me a hundred times, if God had not saved my life."

It was in the private talks that the real work of the conference was done. Father Lalemant, the Jesuit superior in 1646, chose to note what was said during them in Latin, not in the usual French of the rest of his report for that year. He begins his comment on these private talks with the significant statement that "what was surprising therein was that our Fathers sent us no word of all that."

"When these things were reported by us," he continues, "that is, by me and Father de Quen . . . to Monsieur the Governor, he himself disclosed to us the whole matter." The "whole matter," of course, was an explanation of the sensational story that had been spread by the Huron warrior of the secret agreement the French had made with the Mohawks at the conclusion of the public treatymaking sessions, held at Three Rivers in 1645. The Mohawk chief, at the conclusion of the public meetings, had insisted on further private talks and had, during them, demanded that the French abandon their Algonquin allies if they expected a binding Mohawk peace treaty with the Hurons, whose furs the French wanted. The private talks had been almost broken off by the governor's refusal to consider the demand. The Mohawk chief, Father Lalemant wrote, "was chagrined at this repulse, and from that time the peace seemed endangered."

"Monsieur the Governor saw this," the Father continues, "and both Father Vimont, the Superior, and Father Le Jeune thought that the difficulty might be smoothed over. In a second private conference . . . Monsieur the Governor said there were two kinds of Algonquins, one like ourselves, recognized as Christians; the other, unlike us. Without the former, it is certain we do not make a peace; as for the latter, they themselves are the masters of their own actions, nor are they united with us, like the others. This, as uttered by Monsieur the Governor, was, and for perhaps a worse reason, thus repeated by the envoy to his people."

The French could deny it, but to the Mohawks the governor's private statement on the "two kinds of Algonquins" was clear enough. Everyone was satisfied. The French would now get Huron furs, the Mohawks could hunt non-Christian Algonquins, and the Fathers had split hairs in the medieval manner.

Father Jogues seems to have been given an impossible assignment. How could he now be "responsible for all accidents between the Hiroquois, French, Algonquins and Hurons?"

Dressed as a civilian, his political commission clear, he left Three Rivers in May, 1646. With him were a French engineer, two Algonquins laden with gifts to confirm the peace, and four Mohawk guides. "One should," wrote Father Lalemant, "be all things to all men, that he may gain them all to Jesus Christ." Perhaps, when one goes forth to fight the Devil, double-dealing is justified, but the Algonquins, in the months that followed, must have been a little puzzled by the diplomacy of their French allies.

The party followed the usual trail south, down the Richelieu River and Lake Champlain and into Lake George, named by Father Jogues Lac St. Sacrement. They then crossed over to the Hudson, borrowed canoes from an Iroquois fishing party, and paddled on to Fort Orange, where Father Jogues' Dutch friends must have welcomed him with amazement. After a short rest the peace party headed west across the pine plains and on to the first of the Mohawk villages.

Instead of entering it through the "carresses" of the Indian ganlet, they came in through a curious and repectful crowd, a little awed by this delegation from the great "Onontio," Governor of New France. The parleys, as far as the French were concerned, were punctuated only by Mohawk grunts of approval. The two Algonquins had their gifts accepted, but the French "were answered with more pomp." How much of this Mohawk welcome was staged, made up of the theatricals and dissembling at which the savages were masters, is hard to say. Much was made, apparently, "of a little chest, which the Father had left as an assurance of his return; they imagined that some misfortune disastrous to the whole country was shut up in that little box. The Father, to undeceive them, opened it, and showed them that it contained no other mystery than some small necessaries for which he might have use." It was the "little chest," however, which gave the Mohawks their excuse later to break the peace they perhaps had never really thought they could keep.

The spring meetings along the Mohawk where concluded with a promise made by Father Jogues to the few visiting Onondagas present that there would be French delegations soon in their nation and the other nations of the Iroquois Confederacy. The Mohawk elders "manifested surprise at the proposition," but did not openly oppose it.

It was suggested, however, that the French embassy return to New France at once. The Mohawks pointed out that a band of Iroquois from the nations to the west were even then lurking in the woods, waiting to intercept the Hurons headed for Montreal: "We do not believe," they said, "that they will do you any harm when they meet you; but we fear for the two Algonquins who are with you."

"Such was the beginning of a Mission," wrote Father Lalemant later, "which must furnish an opening to many others among well-peopled Nations." The Jesuit superior could see, stretching before his eyes, that American Empire of God of which Jogues' Mission of the Martyrs was to be the cornerstone. Monsieur the Governor could hear the warm approval of the French "Associates" for whom the fur trade had such magic charm. The Hurons and the Algonquins had no reason to be sure of anything.

Father Jogues, "entirely attentive and devoted to this Mission, after having rendered an account of his commission, thought of nothing but undertaking a second voyage in order to return thither . . . he could not endure to be so long absent from his spouse of blood." Toward the end of September he was allowed to return to the Mohawks. "He goes intending to spend the winter there, and, on all occasions which shall present themselves, to influence the minds and the affections of the savages,—but especially to care for the affairs of God and the riches of Paradise."

South of Lac St. Sacrement, Jogues and his companion, a young Frenchman named Lalande, met a Mohawk war party. Forgotten were the wampum promises, the protestations of friendship, the cleared passage from "Onontio," Governor of New France, to the Mohawk River. The warriors seized the priest and the horrified Lalande, stripped them, and led them back to their castle.

The brutal rituals began again. Strips of flesh were cut from Father Jogues's back and arms. "Let us see," said the flailer, "if this white flesh is the flesh of an oki."

"I am a man like yourself," Jogues replied, "but I do not fear death or torture. I do not know why you would kill me. I come here to confirm the peace and show you the way to Heaven, and you treat me like a dog."

"You shall die tomorrow," the crowd yelled. "Take courage, we shall not burn you. We shall strike you both with a hatchet, and place your heads on the palisades, that your brothers may see you when we take them prisoners."

Two days later, on the morning of October 19, 1646, the head of Father Isaac Jogues was there, on the palisades, for his brothers to see. Alongside of it was the head of his donné, Lalande. There would be no more journeys for them down the "narrow way of Paradise."

In a letter the Dutch sent to the governor of New France telling of Jogues's death is an enclosure "from our Minister up yonder," giving the results of his investigation of the two murders. He had inquired "from the principal men of that canaille, concerning the reason of this wretched deed; but he could not obtain other answer from them, except that . . . the Devil in the 'Little Chest' which Jogues had left in their custody had caused their Indian corn to be devoured."

"For the rest," the Dutch wrote, "their desire and undertaking is to go away, three or four hundred men, that they may try to surprise the French . . ."

Father Jogues's death and the wars of extermination that followed had their origins outside the "little chest." In the unending struggle to stay alive in a changing world the Five Nations of the Iroquois were forced to challenge powers they little understood. These men of the Stone Age soon learned, however, the importance of the private talk, the subtleties of fur trade negotiations, and the economics of Christian salvation. When the confusion became too great, the savages were inclined to rid themselves of it by direct action. If their excuse of the "little chest" seems too naïve, it was at least straightforward. Was not "the Devil among some of the clothes?"

8

The Death of Maria Aukes

Maria Aukes was murdered in the general neighborhood of State Street, Schenectady. It was a good hour for treachery . . . somewhere between eleven and two in the morning, just as Saturday was ending and Sunday beginning. If you figure the time according to our "new style" calendars, it was Saturday, February 18, 1690.

The general view of the town from, say, the rise of ground that is now the front campus of Union College had nothing in common with the pattern of factories and houses seen from this well-groomed spot today. The shape of the hills was the same; the Mohawk spread over the Groote Vlachte, under the snow, undisciplined by the dams which curb it today.

Maria's Schenectady had perhaps forty houses in it, maybe a few more, but not many, although the French commander, after that Saturday night's blood bath, wrote that some eighty houses had been destroyed.

If you had stood on this rise of ground, knee deep in snow, that Saturday morning, and the sun had been behind you over your shoulder as you looked west, it would have

thrown deep shadows back into the town from the log stockade which shut Maria and her neighbors into a kind of do-
mestic pen divided by two streets running north and south.
Just inside the west stockade wall was a narrow lane running
north to the blockhouse where Enos Talmidge and his garrison of twenty-four Connecticut men held out against a wilderness that stretched to the Pacific Ocean.

The northeast gate opened out to the river road that
led east through Niskayuna to Albany. The other public gate
opened onto the road to the Mohawk country, a road which
decayed into a path soon after you crossed the river. Maria
went through the south gate when she wanted to buy flour
at the gristmill on the newly harnessed Mill Creek.

Maria's Schenectady was a cozy place: there was Dominie
Tessemaker's church near the south gate, and there were
many good neighbors; Reynier Schaats, who purged the body;
Jan Roeloffse de Goyer, son of Anneke Jans whose Manhattan real estate is still causing agitation among her thousands of heirs; there was Sweer Teunise Van Velsen, the
miller, whose house stood just east of Maria's husband's inn,
next to the church. Lieutenant Talmidge's soldiers were something else; they were Connecticut men, and you couldn't be
sure with Connecticut men.

There were Mohawks and Onondagas and sometimes a
Seneca or a Cayuga grunting around Douw Aukes's inn, and
there were Negroes who hated this Dutch lady's sense of
order.

This was the Dorp Schenectady in 1690.

There is this to be said about the violent death that came
to Maria—and to Jan Roeloffse de Goyer and Dominie Tessemaker and Reynier Schaats and most of the Connecticut men,
and Douw Aukes, who didn't trust them, and the Negroes and
the child of Engeltie Vrooman, whose "brains were dashed out

against ye wall," and the dozens of other neighbors—it would never have come to the streets of Schenectady if Louis XIV of France, the "Sun King," the Grand Monarch, had not planned to make England a ruin.

Look backward a moment. In 1688, two years before Maria Aukes of the Dorp Schenectady was to feel the backwash of great events, an English princess and her Dutch husband, William of Orange, were brought back to England on a flood tide of anti-Catholic sentiment, new sovereigns to preside over the Glorious Revolution.

James II, the Roman Catholic father of the new Protestant queen, now found France far more hospitable than England. He and Louis XIV saw eye to eye on all things political, their accord being particularly warm in the matter of humbling England.

The wars drummed up at Versailles echoed across the Atlantic into America. Louis XIV struck at England by sending French troops south out of New France into the wilderness of New York to the north and south gates of unprepared Schenectady.

Douw Aukes in his tavern next to Dominie Tessemaker's church may have served wine punch to the Albany men who came through the snows to urge special care through the days ahead. He had heard Captain Sander Glen talk seriously to the young men of the dorp's militia about duty to country and king. The Goopels and the Bradts and the Vedders said Captain Sander and young Ensign Glen were patroon's men, that they would do anything to oppose Jacob Leisler, the Manhattan German who had appointed himself to act as governor of New York until William and Mary, England's new rulers, should send over a replacement pleasing to the royal will. Sweer Teunise, the miller, said the Glens and Albany's Mayor Schuyler and the Albany Livingstons hated Jacob

Leisler because that pro tem governor's hand was getting too near their pockets. Sweer Teunise knew well enough that the Glens and the Schuylers and Van Rensselaers and the Livingstons feared Leisler's support of the little men of the Mohawk country whose right to trade among the Indian castles and to bolt their own flour had been strenuously denied by these landed gentlemen.

The Dorp Schenectady knew what was blowing downwind, all right. Douw Aukes knew a good deal, for Leisler had made him a justice of the peace along with five of his neighbors. They knew Albany's old tricks; they knew, too, that the landed gentlemen had abruptly turned down Jacob Leisler's offers of help in fortifying Schenectady against attack.

Attack, attack, everyone talked about it. Maria worried sometimes. She had wanted to leave Schenectady that last September, but she had been shamed out of it. The Leislerhaters in Albany, whose political fingers were deep in the Schenectady pie, had forbidden any of them to leave the dorp "upon penalty to be esteemed, pursued, and followed after as fugitives, cowards, runaways, and vagabonds."

Of course there will be an attack. The French will come down the lakes, down Corlaer's Lake Champlain and down Lac St. Sacrement (Lake George), but not now, to be sure; the February snows are far too deep; but they will come, and with them the "praying" Mohawks of Caughnawaga, whose Jesuit Christianity had not softened their rage against their enemies. They will come, all right. Douw Aukes and his fellow justices of the peace talked about it over hot punch. We must get ready, they all agreed. The Glens talked preparation, Dominie Tessemaker preached it, the Albany gentry gave it lip service, and they all did these things: They divided their strength to make a political holiday; the men of wealth and land against the growing horde of traders and millers and householders; the Albany lady in her carriage against a Maria Aukes in the pig tracks of Schenectady. They dignified the quarrel by blaming it on a change of English rulers, but down underneath, there it was, the uncertain voice of the people beginning the cry in the new world which had led them out of the old one; Douw Aukes and his Maria claiming rights the dorp's great-grandchildren were to get by renouncing all kings.

In 1690 Douw and the Glens and their neighbors were so busy quarreling over "rights" that they delayed preparing a defense against the common enemy.

The French attack would come, all right, but not now. The snow and the cold, you know, puts Montreal a world away.

Little did they know what Louis, the Sun King, and his ambitious governors of New France, who were not too concerned about rights, were planning for Dutchmen and Englishmen along the Mohawk and the Hudson.

Against a French plan to carve out an American empire the men of the dorp and of Albany pitted eighty-seven soldiers. Twenty-five of them had just plowed through the twenty miles of snow from Albany to occupy the Schenectady blockhouse and drink beer and wait for spring.

Leisler-hating Mayor Schuyler of Albany, thinking chiefly of his snug collection of Dutch houses, arranged with the Mohawk Indians to keep a watch of braves along the trails north. He sent out thirty or forty Indians to report on what happened in the thirty or forty thousand square miles of winter-bound wilderness.

And the upstart Governor Leisler's shot and guns and powder and troops were not wanted, thank you. "Thank you, thank you," ripe with displeasure, echoed north, east, south, and west of Albany. And so eighty-seven doubting and indifferent men, from Connecticut and the local militias, made ready to protect Maria Aukes and her neighbors from ugly death in the winter night, eighty-seven militiamen against a humiliated and organized and wrathful France. Women and children, Maria and the Engel baby were stirred into a burnt sacrifice for a dozen French failures to possess the Mohawk River country.

By that September, when Maria was considering quitting the dorp, and the rich man-poor man quarrel between the gentry and Jacob Leisler was ripest, a gentleman with a most impressive name, a devoted churchman, the most recent governor of New France, the Count de Frontenac, had put the finishing touches on a pretty plan of his king's. It was a scheme to take Manathe (New York City) by land and sea; two ships of war from Rochelle and a land attack on a grand scale against Fort Orange (Albany) and south through Rensselaerswyck, the patroon's country, to the happy junction on Manhattan Island. The French would expel, if the plan succeeded, the Dutch and the English from New York as completely as the Children of Israel were thrust out of Canaan.

It was a neat plan. It provided labor slaves out of the conquered population, huge ransoms and the everlasting chastisement of the Five Nations. Louis of France still looked for Iroquois warriors to fill the oarsmen's places in his galleys on the Seine. And Frontenac remembered his own fondness for beaver skins.

And so the long gash in the skull of Maria Aukes, and the incinerated body of Francyn, her Negro slave, and the unrecognizable corpse of Antje Jans, daughter of Jan Spoor, and all those others have a common and ugly history. The tragedy begins, really, no one knows where. It gets mixed up in the Mohawk Valley with Indians who wanted none of it. It twists into the schemes of Canadian Frenchmen who planned to please God by pleasing Louis XIV. It is mixed with the bio-

logical uncertainties of a queen's bedroom. It moves ineffectually through the querulous have-and-have-not arguments of
New York colonials and comes to a hideous climax at eleven
o'clock of a Saturday night in the brutal cold and the deep
snow, before the house of Douw and Maria Aukes and the
houses of their sleeping neighbors.

Of course they wouldn't come in February, through the
snow—but they did.

Two hundred and ten men: eighty "praying" Mohawks;
sixteen Algonquins, the rest Frenchmen, "couriers du bois,"
all but nineteen of them, Frenchmen as familiar with the
woods as wolves. Gentlemen with musical names led them
south from Montreal: Le Moyne de Sainte-Hélène and Dáille-
bout de Montet.

Snow often up to their hips; swamp water hell-fire
couldn't warm. The sick and the weaklings turned back within
a week.

The terrible twenty-two days' march south by way of
Lake Champlain and Lac St. Sacrement made a grim prelude
to the butcher's work Chief Kryn and his "praying" Indians
were waiting to do.

Butcher's work came soon enough. Frenchmen and Indians warmed themselves late that February Saturday afternoon over a fire kept by four squaws. These Indian women
told the gentlemen with the musical names how Schenectady
looked to see them later, perhaps in the spring, but not now.

Giguières and his scouts joined the column again a few
miles north of the town. The cold was paralyzing. The black
square of the dorp cut a hole in the white night. The attack
was set for two, and it was now eleven; and, thought these
Frenchmen, who but God and the Little Jesus could wait for
that three hours to pass!

There was the north gate, all right, just as the squaws

had said and, Most Holy Name! the Dutchmen had left it open! The only shadow of noise in the world was the velvet noise of buckskin legs plunging deep in fresh snow.

As silently as sleep and death come into the dark room, so the Frenchmen slipped through the open gate: Sainte-Hélène, de Montet, and their soldiers who had the smell of bear fat on them, Kryn and his Indians, as excited as children to be at a game. They divided their forces inside the gate, and met again at the south end of Cross Street, and then drifted like leaves in sixes and sevens up to the doors, up to the face of Reynier Schatts' house, of Jan Roeloffse de Goyer's, quietly, up to the blank windows of Sweer Teunise's house. They flattened like fog against the wall of the church, against Maria's door.

Then the Indian signal. It slipped like a knife up the seam of sleep.

Puncheon doors rocked off their hinges. Some died so suddenly that their dreams and this nightmare that now rushed in on them seemed one thing.

There were shadows everywhere. Fire drew a caricature of the fort on the snow west toward the river.

Noise of killing and dying and fire leaping up; the whimper of the Vrooman child and its thin scream as a Mohawk paid a manhood debt by dashing the child's brains out against the wall of its father's house; Engeltie Vrooman, its mother, dead at her husband's feet, and Adam Vrooman standing off a dozen Frenchmen until they cried quits and gave him his life.

West of Adam's house, in the blazing fort, Lieutenant Enos Talmidge and Sergeant Church and three more of the useless defenders were wetting down New York snow with Connecticut blood. The blockhouse gate had held for seconds

after Kryn's Indians tore the night with screeching, just for
seconds, long enough for those inside to know that they would
not see spring.

This is the way the record runs:

Barent Lause Van Ditmars killed and his sonne killed
Sweer Teunise shott and burnt his wife killed and burnt
Hend: Meese Vrooman and Bartholomeus Vrooman kild and
　　burnt
Two negroes of Hend: Meese the same death
Jan Roeloffse de Goyer burnt in ye house
David Christoffolse and his wife with four children all burnt
　　in there house.

The moon moved down toward the Helderbergs. The
Dorp Schenectady was a flaming, ugly square in the deep
snow and cold.

Peter Tessemaker, the minister, lay waiting for immola-
tion on the wet floor of his house; no one would have known
him, for he had been hewed down with swords.

The moon vanished. East of the stockade a wounded
horse fought through the snow on the Niskayuna road. Symon
Schermerhorn, as the noise of killing became fainter and
fainter behind him, rode through the night to tell his neighbors and Albany of the end of their world. On that ride he
was sure half the men of New France were spreading south
and east on a war of extermination.

In the darkness and the cold, on the floor of Douw
Aukes's inn, lay Maria. She had never concerned herself with
birth and marriage and death beyond the cleared lands of the
Mohawk. But death, brutal and ugly as savagery could make
it, had come down to her, hand over hand, from Louis XIV to
the "praying" Mohawk who drove his stone ax through her
long hair. . . .

After daybreak Chief Kryn and Sieur d'Iberville went alone to Captain Sander Glen's house across the river in Scotia and assured that beleaguered landlord that the French had had specific orders to spare him and his property, largely because of the kindness the Glens had shown to the French on other occasions. Captain Sander immediately laid down his arms and took the two men into what they called his "fort" and there "entertained them."

Following breakfast, Kryn and the Frenchman and Glen returned to the wreck of the town and to the miserable huddle of terrified and broken families, and the shells of houses, blackened cellar holes, and the mutilated bodies of his neighbors. Glen must have been struck dumb by the misery of the scene. The story goes that Glen, "Coudre," the French called him, was asked to pick out his own relatives from the crowd of men, women, and children who had survived the previous night's destruction. How many "relatives" he was able to claim we don't know; but it was said that the Indian allies of the French complained of the sizable number of Schenectadians who were "cousined" that morning.

What had Albany been doing while sixty inhabitants of the dorp were giving their lives as a memorial to official stupidity? Symon Schermerhorn, "shott threw his Thigh," arrived at five o'clock that Sunday morning. "Ye fort fyred severall guns" to warn farmers beyond the stockade; few apparently heard. All that day refugees from Schenectady, frost-bitten, twenty-five of them with their limbs frozen, came into the enclosure in twos and threes; all of them seem to have agreed that the attackers were going to head for Albany. Letters went down the Hudson posthaste for assistance; to "Sopus," to "Skackook," to Kinderhook and Claverack.

The first small company of horsemen sent out to "Discover ye Enemie's force" had to return because of the deep

snow; the second attempt to get to Schenectady was success-
ful. It was not until the next day that enough men braved
the journey to the wrecked town to permit burial of the dead
and some sort of stock-taking.

There was little enough left: sixty dead; twenty-seven
men and boys, those able to march back through the February forests, had been taken by the raiders. Of the town there
was little but rubbish. The widow Bradt's house was left
standing because it had been used to shelter a wounded
French officer, and a house belonging to the Glens went
untouched. Dead cattle littered the place; the horses were
gone; it was said that fifty of them were necessary to carry
off the loot.

The Albany burghers did what neighbors have always
done; they took in the "Refugees of Schoonechtede." Deacon
Johannes De Wandelaer of that weighty Dutch town kept
a list of the goods he and others distributed to these frightened and broken families:

2348½ Dutch ells Osenb: Linen (Osnaburg Linen)
3 Prs Serge
13 pairs Stockings
72 ells pennestont (Penistone, a coarse woolen cloth)

The Mohawks came down from their upriver castles and
made eloquent speeches. Belts of wampum were given to
wipe away tears. ". . . we cannot account it a great Victory
for it is done by way of Deceit. The Governour of Canada
comes to our Countrey . . . and speaks of Peace . . . but
war is in his heart, as you find by woeful experience."

Mohawks, Dutchmen, and Englishmen learned by woeful experience. Maria Aukes in her shallow grave among the
ruins of the Dorp Schenectady was by way of being a sacrifice to the blind discipline of tradition. New men and new

ways were needed to secure the vast Mohawk country and all it was key to against the ruthlessness of an empire-minded France. This latest attack lost its force in the destruction of Schenectady; but the intention was to fight on until the ownership of North America was decided.

A BALLAD

"In which is set forth the horrid cruelties practised by the French and Indians on the Night of the 8th of Last February. The which I did compose Last Night in the space of one Hour, and am now writing, the Morning of Fryday, June 12, 1690."

Walter Wilie

God prosper long our King & Queen,
    Our lives & Safties all,—
A sad misfortune once there did
    Schenectady befall.

From forth the woods of Canada
    The Frenchmen tooke their Way
The People of Schenectady
    To captivate and slay.

They marched for two & twenty dais
    All thro' the deepest snow;
And on a dismal Winter Night
    They struck the Cruel Blow.

The lightsome sun that rules the Day
    Had gone down in the West;
And eke the drowsy Villagers
    Had sought and found their reste.

They thought They were in Safetie all,
    And dreampt not of the Foe;
But att Midnight They all awoke
    In Wonderment & Woe.

For They were in their pleasant Beddes,
    And soundelie sleeping, when
Each Door was sudden open broke
    By six or seven Men.

The Men & Women, Young & Olde,
    And eke the Girls & Boys,
All started up in great Affright,
    Att the alarming Noise.

They then were murther'd in their Beddes,
    Without shame or remorse,
And soon the Floores and Streets were strew'd
    With many a bleeding corse.

The Village soon began to Blaze,
    Which shew'd the horrid sight,—
But, O, I scarce can Beare to Tell
    The Mis'ries of that Night.

They threw the Infants in the Fire,
    The Men they did not spare:
But killed All which they could find,
    Tho' Aged or tho' Fair.

O Christe! In the still Midnight air,
    It sounded dismally,
The Women's Prayers, and the loud screams
    Of their great Agony.

Methinks as if I hear them now
    All ringing in my ear;
The Shrieks & Groans & Woeful Sighs
    They uttered in their Fear.

But some ran off to Albany,
    And told the dolefull Tale;
Yett, tho' We gave our cheerful Aid,
    It did not much avail.

And We were horribly afraid,
    And shook with Terror, when
They told us that the Frenchmen were
    More than a Thousand Men.

The news came on the Sabbath morn
    Just att the Break of Day,
And with a companie of Horse
    I galloped away.

But soone we found the French were gone
    With all their great Bootye;
And then their Trail We did pursue
    As was our true Dutye.

The Mohaques joynd our brave Partye,
    And followed in the chase,
Till we came upp with the Frenchmen
    Att a most likelye Place.

Our soldiers fell upon their Reare,
    And killed twenty-five;
Our Young Men were so much enrag'd
    They took scarce One alive.

D'Aillebout Them did commande,
    Which were but Theevesh Rogues,
Else why did they consent and Goe
    With Bloodye Indian Dogges?

And Here I end the long Ballad
    The Which you just have redde;
I wish that it may stay on earth
    Long after I am Dead.

9

"The Promised Land of Scorie"

THE blow fell on September 12, 1712. When Jean Cast finished telling the "list keepers" that the commissary was closing, he could read fear and anger in the German faces around him. It wasn't Cast's fault that Governor Hunter's fine project to make naval stores in the crown colony of New York had failed. He was a Frenchman, assistant commissary agent for the governor, doler-out to the Germans of ship's beer, salt pork, bread, sleazy clothing, and tools to girdle the pine trees for the turpentine that had barely run.

Cast might have said, privately, "Blame Livingston!" But the fault wasn't really "Lewenstein's"—that's what the German redemptioners made out of Robert Livingston's name. Livingston had seen a good thing in the naval stores project. Hunter was a new, ambitious, overeager colonial governor with two thousand Germans in tow. He was out to prove to the English Lords of Trade that he could break the Swedish naval stores monopoly with these bound laborers. For a man like Livingston, an old hand at manipulating crown agents and a late colleague of Captain Kidd, Robert Hunter was— well, Hunter was a tyro in the business of exploiting a colony.

and Livingston could make a profit on the governor's ignorance.

John Conrad Weiser, late corporal of the Württemberg Blue Dragoons, baker of Gros Aspach, was now a "list keeper" of Annsdorf, one of the seven Palatine towns on the Hudson. He had become a girdler of pine trees, subsisting on the "queen's bounty." He must have hated Livingston. Weiser and his neighbors knew, perhaps not the details, but certainly the crooked outline of the whole Livingston arrangement. How Livingston, afraid of losing his great barony, 16 miles long and 24 miles broad, had attached himself to Governor Hunter, sold him six thousand acres of sandy pitch-pine land on which the governor's Germans were to live as serfs, making tar to float the queen's navy. How Livingston had got the contract to feed and provide generally for the redemptioners. How not only Livingston, but the whole pack of administrators of the naval stores project were to get their salaries out of the profit on the tar, and ships' spars the Palatines were to wring out of Livingston's acres. What was left, if anything, would go to canceling the Germans' debt to the crown.

Jean Cast had pointed out the errors in Weiser's thinking on their agreement with the Lords of Trade. The forty acres the Palatines were to have were to be granted *after* they had worked off the costs of their transportation to New York, *after* the charges for their subsistence had been cleared, *after* Livingston and his assistants had been taken care of, *after* the expense of the coffins for the ships' dead had been discharged.

So there they were on September 12, 1712, behind them two years of serfdom and misery uglier than any they had left in the Rhine and Neckar valleys of the Old World, nothing for their pains but Governor Hunter's "permission" to ask for tickets of leave to quit the Hudson, to look for subsistence jobs within the two provinces under his jurisdiction,

New Jersey and New York. Jean Cast told them they were to stand ready to return to the tar boiling at the governor's pleasure. And further, anyone daring to leave Livingston's domain without first getting that ticket of leave would have a hue and cry raised after him.

John Conrad Weiser could remember when Governor Hunter of colonial New York had "in a passion stamp'd on the Ground & said here is your land (meaning the almost Barren Rocks) where you must live and dye." The Palatines were a stubborn lot, however, and never allowed Hunter to forget the acres they were sure the queen had promised them, the wonderful acres in the "land of scorie."

"Scorie" had become a challenge to Governor Hunter's pride, his purse, his sense of the fitness of things. How many of these Palatines had there been in London, because Queen Anne had a woman's heart, and Germany was disgorging Protestants faster than ships could ferry them across the Channel? Some said thirty thousand. Others scaled the numbers down to ten thousand. Eighty pounds a day they were costing the shaky Whig government. These refugees from famine and Louis XIV's armies explained why Englishmen saw their own wage scale go down from 18 pence to 15 pence per day. Ungrateful German dogs, the lot of them.

Robert Hunter, by 1712, felt very sorry for himself. His whole naval stores project had wisped out to thin air. Here he had generously taken his Palatines out of the dirty tents at Blackheath, brought them to America on queen's bounty to sweat out his government's first real make-work program. And what happened? Not a pence had come from England Very Important Persons in the colonies were saying the government should get out of tarmaking, out of competition with private enterprise.

And there was Robert Livingston and the whole crowd

of New York land-grabbers. Their kind made up the New York legislature. Unless Governor Hunter came to terms with them on certain matters concerning title guarantees to their princely holdings he couldn't even collect his salary. Van Rensselaers and Schuylers, Bayards, Kipps, Cortlandts, the Nine Partners, singly and in association, they had first carved up the New Netherlands, and then subdivided it as though the future of the colony was theirs alone.

And as for private interests, before and since England had nudged the Dutch out of New York in 1664, they had been largely a matter of furs and the "extravagant grants." The Lords of Trade were now suggesting that the New York legislature annul the worst of the grants. Poor Hunter. It was his job to make peace with the private interests, who had been asked to turn back to the crown some of the little kingdoms they had set aside for themselves with the help of a few of Hunter's venal predecessors. Palatines on one side of him, demanding food, demanding clothes, demanding all the things that cost money, demanding those damned lands at "scorie" no one of importance, not even the queen, had ever said they could have. And there on the other side a phalanx of gentlemen colonists ready to defend their acres against him, Parliament, the crown, anyone who thought to cut in on their take. Robert Hunter, on September 12, 1712, was a bitter, disillusioned man who could easily be put in a passion when anyone, particularly a Palatine, mentioned "scorie" to him.

John Conrad Weiser at first wanted only the queen's forty acres. That's what the contract called for. Forty acres didn't seem like much when Robert Livingston had a grant of land 16 miles long by 24 miles broad, at a yearly cost to him, when it pleased him to pay it, of 24 shillings, current money. Weiser and his neighbors did not intend to live and die on Livingston's "Barren Rocks." Not when Queen Anne, of blessed memory, had accepted on behalf of her "poor Palatines" a broad, rich valley some forty miles west of the Hudson, in the "Maquas" country.

"The lands at scorie" had become a challenge, too, to the Palatines. The valley of the Schoharie, whose river drains north out of the Catskills into the Mohawk, was to them a Promised Land, and John Conrad Weiser seems to have elected himself to be a kind of Moses to lead his now-abandoned people out of bondage into the freedom they had been told they would find in the New World. *The Golden Book*, with Queen Anne's picture on it, had circulated throughout the Palatinate, touting the opportunities waiting for Germans in the English colonies. Pamphlets, and recruiting agents from Pennsylvania and the Carolinas, had for years been advertising free or cheap lands to these dispossessed people. If, to get land, you had to make tar for a while, well and good, but now Hunter was through with them.

That's the way Weiser and his neighbors saw it. On October 31, 1712, the irritated Governor Hunter wrote to the Board of Trade that "some hundreds of them took a resolution of possessing the lands of Schoaree & are accordingly march'd thither have(ing) been buisy in cutting a road from Schenectady to that place . . ."

No one, not even the Mohawks, remembered any "queen's gift." Certainly the Board of Trade didn't. They remembered "Schoaree" as one of the "extravagant grants" the crown had managed to annul. Nicholas Bayard had bought the valley in 1695/6 "from Six Idle drunken People" of the Mohawks, a tract "of so large an extent that a Young man has enough to doe to run over it in a day's time, and that for the value of thirty beaver skins in Rum and other goods." No one could say the quitrent was exorbitant: two shillings, or one otter skin, payable yearly to the crown.

How, then, had Weiser and his neighbors got the notion that Schoharie was theirs? "The lands given them by the Queen," Weiser's son, Conrad, wrote years later. The Palatines liked to talk about a Mohawk Indian delegation to London, touched to generosity, deeding a lush wilderness valley to them. Unfortunately that Indian delegation, off to London to publicize the need for British forts in the Iroquois country, didn't arrive until the Palatines had been herded into their little fleet and left to ride the tides off the English coast.

True enough, the Board of Trade had talked, back in 1709, of at least three possible sites for gathering naval stores. Governor Hunter was to decide which of them was best for the purpose. There was the Hudson Valley, and the Mohawk Valley, and there was that vacated grant of Bayard's along the Schoharie. Hunter had all three sites checked, and then decided on settling his redemptioners on the Hudson, chiefly on property purchased from his helpful friend Robert Livingston.

Perhaps Weiser, prime mover in the hegira to the Schoharie, had heard of the talk of the Mohawk chief, "King" Hendrick, with Governor Hunter in August, 1710. "We are told," said Hendrick, "that the great queen of Great Brittain had sent a considerable number of people with your Excy to settle upon the land called Skohere, which was a great surprise to us and we were much Disatifyd at the news, in Regard the Land belongs to us. . . . Nevertheless since your Excell'cy has been pleased to desire the land for christian settlements, we are willing and do now Surrender . . . to the Queen . . . for Ever all that tract of Land Called Skohere. . . ." Perhaps Hendrick had the Palatines in mind. Perhaps Weiser had had a few campfire talks with him. Perhaps the sachem thought to make capital of a bad situation and give the land to Hunter before the crown took it for another barony-minded colonial.

In any event, Hunter accepted the land in the queen's name, and who's to say the Palatines didn't get wind of it? From then until they were told by Jean Cast, the commissary agent, to get their tickets of leave hundreds of them thought their forty acres or more were to be carved, not out of Mr. Livingston's "Barren Rocks," but out of the rich soil of "scorie."

John Weiser and the 150 families who went with him to the new valley didn't concern themselves about the governor's tickets of leave. They knew Hunter was in no mood to issue them to help along the purpose they had in mind. First to do then, after Jean Cast had called a halt to tarmaking and Hunter's soldiers had gone off, was to send a delegation to the Schoharie Valley "to consult the Indians about it who allowed them to occupy schohary." "My Father," wrote Conrad Weiser, "was the First of the german deputies."

If the frontier of New York in 1712 had been marked by a taut cord, it would have stretched up the Hudson to Albany, bent northwest to Schenectady, rebuilding after the French and Canadian Indian massacre of 1690, and then frayed out west and east along the Mohawk into little knots of farms that depended on Albany for help. With the migration of the Palatine families to the Schoharie Valley the frontier moved west thirty miles. "They will be a good barrier between Her Majesty's Subjects and the French & their Indians in those parts," the Board of Trade had hopefully recorded when the several sites for the naval stores project were under discussion, "and," they continued like good husbandmen, "in process of time by intermarrying with the neighbouring Indians (as the French do) they may be capable of rendering great Service to Her Majesty's Subjects there."

John Weiser and his six fellow deputies, looking for the first time down into their "promised land," had no plans to propagate the wilderness with German-Iroquois stock. Jeptha Simms, one of that devoted band of mid-nineteenth century antiquarians who gathered fact and hearsay with equal enthusiasm, has left a record of that first sight of the promised land which is helpful and which it would be unkind to question. "The German messengers," writes Simms, "deputed to Schoharie, were conducted by an Indian guide over the Helleberg (the Dutch term "Helderberg" is now the common name for the Catskill spur that runs south of the Mohawk River), and on the second day they gained a commanding view of the flats along Fox's Creek. They proceeded down that stream, until, from one of the hills which skirt its lowlands, they gained a prospect of the Schoharie Valley, at the place where Fox's Creek runs into the Schoharie. There their vision was delighted by one of the most beautiful and picturesque scenes with which nature has decorated the earth. They beheld the green flats of Schoharie, spread before them like a beautiful, though neglected garden. . . . Off to the right hand of the deputation, as they stood on the summit of the hill, near where it descends into the two valleys, on the north side of Fox's Creek, they were able to catch a view of the great bend in the river, where it takes a more easterly course, immediately after receiving Cobel's kill."

The deputies were satisfied, and so were the Indians, who had now disposed of the valley for the third time. As far as Governor Hunter was concerned, the migration that now took place was unauthorized, illegal "madness," to be handled, as soon as feasible, with "an extraordinary severity." The "Pitch and Tarr" project had loaded him with a £20,000 debt which his government was never to honor; because of its failure, he knew his enemies would raise their own kind of "hue and cry" against him which would finally bay him out of public life. Illogically, but humanly, from now on he was to think of every Schoharie Palatine as a whipping boy on whom he could heap his own sense of frustation and defeat.

The whipping was to begin soon enough. The return of the seven deputies from Schoharie "put the people in heart. All hands fell to work, and in 2 weeks' time cleared a way thro' the woods of 15 miles long, with the utmost toyle and labour." The first fifty families pushed their way west of Albany, across the wilderness of the Helderbergs, down their new road, down Fox's Creek to a small brook where tradition says they stopped for "a general purifying." The Palatines left behind them not only the grime of their journey but also a name for the stream where they had bathed; it is still known as "Louse Kill." They arrived that day in the beautiful, though neglected garden, the land of "scorie," to throw up shelters on the open, treeless flats which the Schoharie Indians turned over to them.

Then Hunter's arm reached out. "Being arrived and almost settled, they received orders from the Governour not to goe upon the land, and he who did so should be declared a Rebel . . . having seriously weighed matters amongst themselves . . . they found themselves under the fatall necessity of hazarding the Governor's Resentment, that being to all more eligible than Starving."

They didn't starve, but that first winter in the Schoharie Valley is reminiscent of another winter an equally determined band of emigrants had spent among the sand dunes of Cape Cod almost a hundred years earlier. The "barbarous people showed them no little kindness," and shared their Indian maize and the roots and ground nuts which they knew how to find. "Many of our feasts were of wild potatoes and ground beans."

In the spring of 1713 the hundred families who had wintered in Albany and Schenectady joined their more eager friends. Their quarrel with Hunter now began to take on a Biblical tinge: "the remainder of the people (tho treated by the Governor as Pharaoh treated the Israelites) proceed on their journey, and by God's assistance travell'd in (a) fortnight with sledges thro' the snow, which there covered the ground above 3 foot deep, cold and hunger, Join'd their friends and countrymen in the promised land of Schorie."

The settlers put down roots as fast and as deep as they could. Seven towns, "dorps," named after the seven deputies who had first bargained with the Indians for the valley, took shape immediately. Weiserdorf, the most southerly of the first settlements, was named after John Conrad Weiser, and soon grew into a crude huddle of some forty earth and log huts, with skins for doorways and bark for roofs. The quiet, elm-shaded town of Middleburgh today covers whatever there is left here of "listman" Weiser's "forty acres." Hartmansdorf was next, two miles to the north. Then followed Brunendorf, two and a half miles north of that, Schmidsdorf, or Smith Town, and Fuchsendorf, later called Fox Town; all three of them within less than a mile of each other, are now a part of the town of Schoharie. Gerlachsdorf, of which nothing is left today, was two miles south of Kniskerndorf, the most northerly of the Palatine settlements. It stood opposite the present village of Central Bridge, at a point where the Cobleskill enters Schoharie Creek.

Weiser and his Palatines had taken the "queen's gift."

10
Pharaoh's People

W<small>HAT</small> happened in the "land of scorie"? The stage was set and the actors ready to play out a regional drama whose implications were never fully comprehended by producers or players. Governor Hunter, in spite of himself, was scheduled for the villain. John Conrad Weiser played out the part of an elderly and difficult hero ready to defend "the queen's gift" with any rough-and-tumble device the frontier offered. In the background were the supernumeraries necessary to any large production; for this historical drama there were Indians in a state of bewilderment at the white man's viciousness, the men, women, and children of the seven dorps who moved across the stage at the direction of voices they barely understood.

There was first the incident of Nicholas Bayard. A good director would play it as straight "historical romance," Bayard as the villain ready to make a nefarious deal with the outraged citizens of the frontier settlements. Never mind the unconventional character of the frontier, in this case only forty miles west of the Hudson River, or the fact that its villain and citizens lived a hundred fifty years before the

West of Hollywood's bandits and stagecoaches. It merely took those years for the new line, a segment of which the Palatines had established along the Schoharie, to move west to the buttes and mesas beyond the Pecos River.

Bayard was the grandson of that Nicholas Bayard whose "Lordship or Mannour of Kingsfield," whose "Courts Baron and Leete" on the Schoharie had all been dissolved when the "extravagant grants" had finally reverted to the crown in 1708. What grandson Nicholas's real scheme was has never been clear. He arrived one day at the house of Han-Yerry Schmidt which served also as Schmidsdorf's hotel and there set himself up as the patron and friend of every Palatine in the valley.

The news of Bayard's coming got around fast enough, spurred by the notice he promptly published. First he said he was an agent of the sovereign. Then he began to bluff in the best "badman" tradition. He supposed that every householder there was interested in keeping his land. Bayard couldn't have been very bright, or he would have changed his tactics. Any of the Weisers who heard him mention "land" must have got restless. Nicholas continued his bluff. He would guarantee any Palatine title, he said, if the landholder would make known to him the boundaries of the land he had occupied. That was all that was necessary. No fees, no charges, just a statement giving the name of the prospective owner and the dimensions of the property, and a clear deed would be forthcoming, issued in the name of Queen Anne.

An ace falling out of a gambler's sleeve in the midst of a high-stake game could have produced no more violent effect. If Bayard had been Governor Hunter in person, the Palatines could have been no more convinced that this offer was crown villainy.

What happened from here on is pure Red Gulch melo-

drama. The Palatine ringleaders, John Weiser probably at
their head, resolved that Bayard was too dangerous to leave
the valley alive. Jeptha Simms gives us the action sequence:

> . . . the honest burghers of Schoharie, armed with guns and
> pitchforks, with many of the softer sex, in whom dwelt the
> love of liberty, armed with broad hoes, clubs and other mis-
> siles, surrounded the hotel of Smith, and demanded the per-
> son of Bayard, dead or alive. Mine host, who knew at that
> early day that a well-managed hotel was the traveler's home,
> positively refused to surrender to his enraged countrymen
> his guest. The house was besieged throughout the day. Sixty
> balls were fired by the assailants through the roof, which was
> the most vulnerable part, as that was straw, and as Bayard
> had, previous to his arrival, been by accident despoiled of an
> eye, he ran no little risk of returning to the bosom of his
> family, if fortunate enough to return, totally blind.
>
> Bayard was armed with pistols, and occasionally returned
> the fire of his assailants, more, no doubt, with the desire of
> frightening them, than killing them. Having spent the last
> round of their ammunition, hunger beginning to gnaw, and
> the sable shades of evening to conceal the surrounding hills,
> the siege was raised, and the heroes of the bloodless day
> dispersed to their homes, to eat their fill and dream on their
> personal exploits . . . the invulnerability of their foe, and the
> mutability of princely promises.

What can the Wild West writers do with sagebrush and
stagecoaches that old Jeptha Simms has not done with "broad
hoes, clubs and other missiles"? Bayard decamped, "under
the cover of night," for Schenectady. From that safe distance,
and in a spirit of unrivaled forgiveness, he sent back a mes-
sage that he would still give the queen's deed to any Palatine
who should appear there "with a single ear of corn." There
were no takers.

Hunter actually was not backing Bayard, who probably
thought to lay the groundwork for an appeal to have his

grandfather's Kingsfield patent restored. But Hunter, never forgetting his naval stores failure, soon came on-stage. As far as he was concerned the Germans were squatters, and worse, they were subject to the sheriff's "hue and cry." If he couldn't dislodge them one way, perhaps he could another.

On November 3, 1714, the land on which the seven Palatine towns stood was officially patented to the "Five Partners," including Robert Livingston, Jr., son of the grasping lord of the tar acres. The next year the Palatines were ordered to purchase the land, to take leases on it, or to quit it. As far as the Palatines were concerned, the Partners were the trespassers. Ownership of the Schoharie Valley, according to Weiser's thinking, was strictly a matter between the settlers and Queen Anne, and Queen Anne by now was dead.

Then Peter Vrooman, the son of Adam Vrooman, survivor of the Schenectady Massacre, moved into the valley, on land his father had secured from the Indians in 1711 and later purchased from the Partners. The climax in the bitter controversy then came to a head, or perhaps several heads. In the first place, Adam Vrooman made the mistake of taking his thousand acres out of the land across the creek, or "kill," as the Dutch have it, from John Conrad Weiser's house. Weiser, by now, was easily moved to action where intruders were concerned.

On July 9, 1715, father Vrooman wrote from Schenectady "in hast," he says, to Governor Hunter. The governor was now to have the dubious pleasure of reading again about his favorite villains. "The Palatines," Adam wrote, "threatened in a rebellious manner, if I should build or manure the Land at Schore that your Excellency was pleased to grant me a Patent for." Adam and Peter were made of sturdy stuff, and had no intention of leaving those rich acres under Corn Mountain if they could help it. Adam continued bitterly that he was

building a stone house 23 feet square and so high, so I had
Layd the Beames of the Chamber, they had a contrivance to
tie bells about horses' necks and drive them to and fro. In
which time they pulled my house Stones and all to the
Ground. . . . They used such rebellious expressions that was
never heard of . . . John Conradus Wiser has been the Ring
Leader of all the factions. . . . They made the Indians drunk
to that degree to go and mark off land with them. . . . I am
no ways secure of my life. They went and pulled my son
off of the waggon and beat him and said they would kill his
father or anybody else who came there so that my son was
forced to come away. . . . Likewise they say they care for
nobody. . . .

The windows must have been rattling by the time Hunter
had finished Adam's letter: "likewise they say they care for
nobody"—the governor knew all about that. "Wiser . . . Ring
Leader of all the factions . . ." From what followed, it looks
as though Hunter played his scene strong enough to reach the
back of the galleries. He sent out an order at once to every
justice of the peace in Albany and Dutchess counties to arrest
on sight "one John Conrade Wiser a Covenanted Servant of
His Majesty, who has been Guilty of Several Mutinous Riotous
and other disobedient & illegal practises is now skulking in your
County to avoid punishment . . . and to cause him to be sent
down in safe Custody to the City of New York. That he may
be proceeded against as the Nature of his Crimes shall require."

The phrase "skulking in your County" offers a rare in-
sight into the governor's thinking about John Weiser. Events
had now come to such a pass that neither Weiser nor Hunter
could ever think of the other in anything but cloak-and-
dagger terms. Each of them would have agreed that there
wasn't enough pitch and tar on all of Livingston's Manor to
copy the blackness of the other's soul.

The trick now was to catch Weiser. Sheriff Adams was

sent down to Weisersdorf to apprehend this "Ring Leader" who apparently was thought to be doing his skulking at home. The sheriff should have come with troops and cannon. Under the direction of one Magdalene Zeh, the women of the settlements took the matter into their own Amazonian hands. Simms tells it all:

> . . . sharing with their husbands the belief that they were the objects of oppression . . . they took the sheriff . . . and dealt with him according to his deserts. . . . He was knocked down by a blow from the magistrate (Magdalene Zeh), and inducted into various places in that young village where the sow delighted to wallow. After receiving many indignities in the neighborhood of Weisersdorf, some of which he was conscious of receiving, and some not, he was placed upon a rail and rode skimington through most of the settlements.

After a trip of some six or seven miles on the rail, Sheriff Adams was finally deposited on a log bridge on the road to Albany. Magdalene "then seized a stake which she carelessly laid over his person, until two of his ribs made four, and his organs of vision diminished by one half." After a final, and unmentionable, indignity, "she called off her compatriots, leaving him for dead."

Thus was Sheriff Adams "prevented." For the Palatines, though, it marked the end of their happy frontier freedom, when, according to the diary of young Conrad Weiser, "each one did what he thought was right." Governor Hunter swore he would hang John Conrad Weiser.

From then on, according to tradition, "the Schoharie people got very shy to go to Albany . . . made the practise to send their wives for salt, or not to enter Albany but on Sundays, and then out again." The Albany officials played a waiting game. In time the Palatines got so "tame" that groups of the men began to visit Albany as they had before Sheriff

Adams and Magdalene Zeh tangled in the matter of the queen's gift. Then the blow fell. One day the sheriff, accompanied this time by a posse, charged out and "took everyone of them and clapped them to jail. The most notorious were put in the dungeon, among them was young Conrad Weiser."

But not John Weiser. He had done all he could to secure for himself and his neighbors the forty acres and the "queen's gift"—made so long ago that even he probably believed in it now. He must have heard with bitterness, wherever he was "skulking," of the capitulation to authority of his son and neighbors, who, in order to get out of jail, were forced to agree to buy or rent their lands from the Albany Partners. "The land of scorie" was slipping beyond his control.

In 1717 Governor Hunter ordered three men from each of the villages, including the elder Weiser, to appear before him. Needless to say, Weiser was not available. The whole valley was ordered to come to an agreement with the patentees. The Palatines, stubborn to the end, refused to buy or rent land they said was theirs. The governor then ordered them to stop plowing and sowing until they came to their senses.

The harried Germans now turned to the last and only hope they had left. Perhaps the king and the Lords of Trade would listen to their grievances. In 1718 John Weiser and two of his neighbors slipped out of the valley to Boston. From there they shipped for London, where, though they pleaded with all the eloquence of men asking for their lives, they found only deaf ears. Governor Hunter had made his own case too strong.

After five years of heartbreak, John Weiser returned empty-handed. The Schoharie Valley he had left was a changed land. Many of his neighbors had knuckled under and purchased title to their lands from the Albany Partners. Others had taken up grants offered to them by Pennsylvania. Among them in 1729, was young Conrad Weiser, who became one of the great Indian interpretors and mediators in the quarrels between colonists and savages.

In 1722 a number of Palatine families extended the Schoharie frontier by moving into the Mohawk Valley, where Governor Burnet, Hunter's successor, gave them permission to purchase land so long as it was at least eighty miles west of Albany. Inasmuch as it was the Lords of Trade who directed Governor Burnet to open the Mohawk Valley to the Palatines, it is possible that Weiser's pleading and that of his fellow traveler, William Scheff, had struck home.

Stone Arabia and Burnetsfield patents were the first official grants made in behalf of a long-suffering people. The new governor offered one hundred acres of land to each German who wished to move onto the tract that stretched twenty-four miles along the Mohawk River north of Little Falls. Takers were few because of the factions which had grown up among the Palatine families. Those who believed Governor Burnet's huge patent could not hold the quarreling groups who wanted to move petitioned for an additional grant, which was made by Burnet in October, 1723, and became known as the Stone Arabia Patent, an area of 12,700 acres between Cayadutta Creek and Garoga Creek, lying a few miles north of the river, behind the Depeyster and Van Sluyck grant.

By 1735 the Mohawk River was a German river, an American Rhine, between Fort Hunter on the east and the settlement of Frankfort on the west. There was a new rush of German immigrants in 1723, many of whom took up land in the Mohawk Valley patents, and, of course, on the government's terms. Although much of the land along the river had long been patented, they were sterile patents, held by colo-

nial speculators on terms which kept them closed to settlement. John Conrad Weiser and his Palatines who tramped
across mountains to a promised land, tramped also across the
barriers to settlement which a blind government and a host
of rapacious colonial gentlemen had set up against tides
stronger than they knew.

Robert Hunter, the governor, and John Conrad Weiser,
the Palatine, are types who live in every generation. In 1712
their quarrel was over pitch and tar and forty acres of land.
In 1690 their names were different, but the contest between
them was the same; one of them was fighting for the right
of Schenectady's farmers to bolt their own flour and trade
with the Indians for their own profit; the other was holding
out for the rights of absentee landlords and trade monopolists.
Such quarrels usually end in personal disaster, but the heat
they raise seems to burn away some of the fog through which
men grope.

Perhaps the bitter contest over the "land of scorie" was
not frontier melodrama, after all. Perhaps it was a problem
play, good for as many conclusions as there were members of
the audience to see it. Weiser, we know, escaped his arch-
enemy, the governor, to find sanctuary after years of unre-
warded land hunting, with his son Conrad, in Pennsylvania.
Robert Hunter, his purse empty, out of favor with a Tory government in England, retired to private life. The Schoharie
Palatines, ironically enough, had the last word in Hunter's
affairs with Parliament. In order to recoup the money he had
expended on the naval stores project he was required to get
certificates from the Palatines stating that they had received
all that their contract called for from Robert Livingston.
Hunter got his certificates back, unsigned.

The play, whatever its type, closes as such plays must,
on a rising note. Because of the Schoharie migration the fron-

tier, in Governor Burnet's words, "was much extended." By 1727 these settlers would break the back of the Albany monopoly of the fur trade, and its profits would go as far west as the Germans, or any other colonials, were able to travel. A new bulwark against any threat from New France had been thrown up. Jeptha Simms's "neglected garden" was slowly brought to such a state of cultivation that, by the time of the American Revolution, the Schoharie and Mohawk valleys were among the granaries of the revolutionary armies, and their German farmers an army in themselves. It's a long remove from the gangs of German Palatines girdling pine trees for the naval stores project to General Herkimer's militia fighting the British at Oriskany, but the line of descent is clear.

11

"Brother Warra"

"Where's the High Dutch girl?" Lewis Groat wiped the Schoharie beer off his mouth with the back of his hand and looked around the untidy cabin. "I thought you were going to have her four years, Alex. You paid her indenture money, didn't you?"

Alex Phillips poured himself a tankard full of beer. As the suds rolled down its pewter sides he said, "Johnson, that damned Irishman, came the other day and offered me five pounds for her, swore he'd horsewhip me if I didn't sell her. I thought the five pounds were better than a flogging, and took it. He got Katy."

William Johnson got Katy Weisenberg, all right. If she had lived she would have become Lady Johnson of Johnson Hall, wife of Sir William Johnson, Bart., Major General of Militia, Superintendent of Indian Affairs for North America, the victor of Lake George, a member of the council of his Excellency the Royal Governor of New York, and owner of a Mohawk Valley barony as big as an English shire. Katy, the indentured servant, the "High Dutch girl," was the mother of Sir John Johnson, Kt., whose surly manners and Irish-cum-

117

London speech covered a capacity for revenge that is still a father-to-son tale along the Mohawk. Katy died, however, soon after the last of her three children by that "damned Irishman" was born. The plain gold wedding ring on her finger, inscribed on the inside "June, 1739. 16" was transferred by her husband to his own strong hand.

William Johnson, a half inch under six feet, big shoulders that carried a fine head—"there were auburn lights in the hair," wrote one woman—an open, Irish face that smiled invitation on many women, came into the Mohawk Valley in 1738. A quarter of a century earlier John Conrad Weiser had helped wrench the "queen's gift" of the Schoharie Valley out of Governor Hunter's hands. Both Weiser and Johnson were immigrants. Where Weiser's Palatines, however, were willing to settle for homesteads as they looked west toward "scorie," William Johnson the Irishman would settle only for acres by the tens of thousands.

But, then, Weiser was an ex-corporal of Würtemberg, with no connections that counted. Johnson's uncle, Peter Warren, an adventurous British naval officer, married the daughter of the chief justice of New York. Young Johnson had fine connections. As manager of Peter Warren's patent, "Warrensbush," on the south side of the Mohawk and east of the mouth of Schoharie Creek, he really didn't need the advice Peter Warren gave him as he took up his duties there as storekeeper, farm manager, and fur trader. "Keep well with all mankind," wrote the future Admiral of the Red, "don't be notional . . . and don't say anything of the badness of the patroon's horses . . . he is a near-relation of my wife, and may have it in his power very much to serve you."

Johnson, after a boyhood among the closed fields of Ireland, must have been amazed at the vast, shadowed wilderness that closed around him in the Mohawk country. And the

patroon—a Van Rensselaer, and a "near-relation of my wife,"
Peter Warren had written—how many acres did he own? Better than a half million, a feudal domain surrounding Albany
on which the Van Rensselaers lived with all the rights and
privileges of nobility. This America was a proper place for a
young man with broad shoulders, good connections, no desire
to be "notional," and with an accommodating morality that
endeared him to his Iroquois neighbors and wrote "Johnson"
on the features of many an Indian child.

With Katy the "damned Irishman" lived at Warrensbush
for four years at least. He put in an orchard of "the best trees,"
as his uncle had requested, planted Indian corn and grass on
the farm he laid out for himself, and measured off the acres
for his uncle's tenants. During these first years he sowed also
an invisible crop whose harvest was to yield him his Mohawk
Valley barony and England and the colonies their final victory over New France.

William Johnson began at once to cultivate the friendship of the Six Nations as though he were a parent determined to win the love of his fractious children. By the time
Katy had given him an heir he was "Brother War-ragh-i-ya-
gey" to his Mohawk neighbors, "Brother Warra" in the familiar address of some of his Indian correspondents.

When the braves of the lower castle at Fort Hunter came
to trade with him at his Warrensbush store, they found, to
their amazement, that they got an honest deal, not only the
first time they threw their packs of skins on Johnson's counter
but every time. This was something new from a white trader.
Word of it went up to the Mohawks' middle castle on Prospect Hill, and on west to the upper castle at Canajoharie. And
then they found that this man was learning to speak the
Long House language. When he visited their castles he ate
the bear's bacon and the baked pumpkins, outwrestled the

braves, danced their war dances in the firelight, and slept with their women.

William Johnson, glints of red in his hair and laughter in him all the time, came to Warrensbush on the Mohawk as a man might come to a high tower: from his vantage point he was able to survey two wildernesses. West of him he could see limitless America, a pattern of river and forest and savages he was determined to understand and exploit. East of him he saw another kind of wilderness: a political jungle in which New York colonials were sharpshooting at their royal governor and the agents of the crown, protesting every possessive gesture England made toward her colonial offspring.

The young manager of Warrensbush could not have traveled the Iroquois trail up the Mohawk River through Fort Hunter and Canajoharie, through the Oneida country, to the English trading post at Oswego a half dozen times without becoming aware of what was bothering the Iroquois. "We come to you howling," their sachems had said to Governor Burnet eleven years before Johnson moved to the Mohawk country, and the howling had never stopped. Why, they said, did the English allow their French enemies to build a fort near the Falls of Niagara, and set up a trading post there to lure the Huron and Ottawa and "far Indians" away from the trading post at Oswego? Why, the sachems asked, did the governor allow the old covenant chain to rust? Could the governor not stop the Albany merchants from selling English goods to the Montreal traders? Such trade was putting Oswego out of business! And, chorused the Iroquois, were the English soldiers women to let the French build Fort Frederick at Crown Point, on the southern end of Lake Champlain? The Iroquois complaints were endless and bitter. Why did the English let the Jesuit blackrobes preach holy wars against

England to the chiefs and the tribes outside the Six Nations Confederacy?

Johnson listened, and traded, and bought land and grew in stature as "Brother Warra." In 1742 his heir was born to Katy, and the "bush" was left for a new home on the north shore of the Mohawk, a square mile of land on both sides of the Kayderosseras Creek, a few miles west of the present city of Amsterdam. Here he erected a grist mill and a frame house, and later, in 1749, a solid stone house which he called "Fort Johnson" in 1755, after the Battle of Lake George.

Katy died soon after the move across the river, leaving three children, John, Ann, and Mary. Taking seriously his role of Brother Warra, Johnson soon brought home a "housekeeper," this time Caroline, the niece of the Mohawk chief, King Hendrick, and, in due time, the mother of three "breeds," a boy and two girls.

His Indian neighbors, Johnson soon learned, were not the only ones who "went howling" to the royal governor. In 1745 he accepted an appointment as justice of the peace for Albany County, and so began his public service. He was soon aware of the clamoring going on in New York politics: Assembly versus the crown, the people (the landless and voteless "mob" of the rapidly swelling colonial towns) against their tax collectors and the recruiting gangs of his Majesty's navy. The "Liberty" theme was already growing uncomfortably loud as the mob caught the beat.

Johnson had every chance to get into the quarrels that swirled around the head of Governor George Clinton. The New York Assembly during these mid-century years was made up of colonials who were big men largely because of their land deals and their trade with Canada and the Indians. They lived in terror that the crown would find some way to cut up their marches along the frontier and their great Mohawk and Hudson River patents. The big merchants feared the governors would discover a way to end the illicit Albany-Montreal fur trade that was pauperizing the Iroquois and putting guns into the hands of the French Indians.

Johnson soon learned that these untitled barons had the governor where they wanted him, for the year after he arrived on the Mohawk the New York Assembly won for itself, in the name of the people, the right to vote the province's maintenance funds on a yearly basis; not only that, but also the right to tell the governor for what those funds were to be used. Funny, in a way, to see *Democracy* being italicized here in New York by a group of landed aristocrats who hated the word and despised the people for whom it stood. In order to get their way these landlords had to speak in the name of the people. But in doing it, they were saying "Sesame!" before a door which hid a waiting giant.

William Johnson grew on the diet of confusion. He was perfectly in joint with the times. Painted, plumed, dressed in the deerskins of a Mohawk war chief, Brother War-ragh-i-ya-gey strode into Albany in August, 1746, at the head of a band of angry Mohawks, who with the other members of the Confederacy wanted to know what England intended to do about the French, now at war with England. Johnson had already so coupled the Mohawks to him that they were committed without reserve to fighting. The rest of the Confederacy, jealous perhaps of the Mohawks' possession of Brother Warra, came to the conference surlily to hear what the do-nothing English had to say; but they came. The sachems drank wine with Deputy Governor Colden, who drew bloody pictures of French outrages against a practically undefended frontier. Johnson, remembering his twenty thousand bushels of stored grain and the ease with which the French were taking scalps among his Dutch and German neighbors along the

Mohawk, talked French scalps and hatchets and ancestral bravery until the Confederacy could hardly wait to roast the first blackrobe who dared to come out of the forest. The meeting broke up with the usual distribution of presents and a solemn declaration by the Six Nations that they were ready to join England in throwing New France out of her strongholds along the St. Lawrence.

Johnson filled his days with the kind of activity he had come to love. He was now a colonel in charge of the Six Nations. Will his Excellency please urge the Assembly to vote money for the payment of bounty on female scalps? Are the trails open to Oswego, for he must see that the garrison receives provisions? And those fat-cat Albany merchants—the colonel knew they wanted to keep the Six Nations neutral in order to pass their own goods north to Montreal—would the Assembly never wake up to that kind of treason? Was the Assembly going to appropriate money for the barest kind of defense, let alone attack?

Mt. Johnson was no place these days for a man with a sensitive nose. Bear fat and unwashed buckskin and raw Indian tobacco left a stench in Johnson's house that was never dissipated, for he was meeting delegations of worried chiefs, counting out the scalps of the returning war parties, talking to the Palatine lieutenants from Fort Hunter and German Flats and Burnets Field on militia matters, talking to everyone about the great plan to wreck Crown Point, the French fortress at the south end of Lake Champlain.

The Iroquois, crowding back and forth to Mt. Johnson, were convinced for sure now that the English were women. There was a good deal of bitterness among the Indians, for whom war was not the casual affair it was for the white man; they pointed out to Johnson that once they took up the hatchet it was not easily buried. They had no stomach for these lady-wars.

England blandly announced in 1748 that she had made peace with France, a peace which gave every colonial alum-mouth. Five years of border alarms and one mighty victory at Louisburg, and nothing to show for them; Louisburg now given back to the French, Crown Point not even mentioned, and all the frontier wounds left to fester. The Mohawk Valley had braced itself for siege, collected its Indians and farmer-militiamen for attack, and the only thing that happened along the river was the bloody battle of Beukendaal, a few miles west of Schenectady, in which the town's militia lost twenty of its young men to French bullets and thirteen more to the raiders as prisoners. "King George's War," as the colonies called it, was about as effective as wet powder in a broken flintlock.

At Mt. Johnson on the Mohawk, however, the powder was dry and the aim of its owner unblurred by events. He was now the most important man in the Mohawk Valley. He was in full command of the whole northern department of New York's militia establishment, busy interviewing and ap-pointing new officers, writing the old ones minute instructions on how to discipline their men, worrying about supplies for the troops on duty in the valley forts, all of which were "badly contrived and tumbling down," as Governor Clinton was com-pelled to admit.

"Brother Warra," or Colonel Johnson, depending on whether you were looking west or east, by January, 1750, was living in a new stone house, one of the finest houses on the river. Molly Brant, known to the valley gossips as the "brown Lady Johnson," was with him, a "housekeeper," if the lan-guage of her vigorous employer's will is enough, a wife, ac-cording to the evidence of biology and tenure. Following the death of Caroline, there was probably a succession of comely and able Indian "housekeepers" at the new Mt. Johnson. That is, until Molly took charge. The story goes that Molly, a niece of Caroline's, and only sixteen, caught the young colonel's eye at a regimental militia muster. Tired of being a spectator, she wheedled permission from one of the field officers to mount behind him as his horse pranced along the line of spectators. Before the officer could laugh at the girl and ride on, she had leaped onto his frightened animal's back. The spectators forgot the review as Molly, her black hair and Indian blanket blowing in the wind, clung to her red-faced gallant, whose horse, half out of control, raced with them across the parade ground. The young colonel with the new house and the six children for whom he admitted responsibility, liked the show. He soon "connected himself," as the peripatetic Mrs. Grant wrote in her *Travels* after a visit to Fort Johnson, "with the daughter of a sachem, who possessed an uncommonly agreeable person and good understanding." Molly not only tended the new house, she added new inmates to it, bright half-breed youngsters who helped to strengthen the bonds between their Irish father and his Long House "brothers."

What a household it must have been! If Brother Warra got half the things on his "Memorandum for Trifles" which he ordered from London at this time, Mt. Johnson surely impressed its Indian visitors as much as Rome did her junketing "allies" from Gaul. There was "a good globe to hang in the hall with light." There were eye-filling pictures: Titian's "Loves of the Gods," Le Brun's "Battles of Alexander," and "pictures of some of the best running horses at New Market." There was a good beginning at a gentleman's library, the sort of reading that would have pleased Benjamin Franklin. The boys of the house must have loved the "good, loud trumpet," and the "French horn."

The New York frontier, by a mighty heave of the land-hungry Palatine Germans, had long since been pushed forty miles west of Mt. Johnson, though the dull war just finished had kept new settlers from coming in. Albany County had more than ten thousand people on the rolls at the end of the war. By the time the fighting was under way again, in 1756, the population had jumped to better than seventeen thousand, and a good part of that increase had moved into the Mohawk Valley west of Johnson's stockaded house.

There were orchards, now, of cherry trees and apples. Pears, it was said, "did not succeed here." Some of the settlers were still experimenting with peach trees, but they learned that the winters which rolled down the valley from the Great Lakes killed all unhardy things, trees and men alike. From a half bushel of seed the river farmers got back a hundred bushels of corn. Twelve bushels of wheat from a bushel of seed was the ordinary harvest, though with luck, and good soil, some farmers reaped as much as twenty bushels. "Albany flour," which was largely Mohawk Valley flour, was popular in Manhattan, where it brought several shillings more per hundred pounds than flour from the Jerseys.

Johnson's Palatine neighbors and his own tenant farmers came to his gristmill on the Kayderosseras in homespun made out of their own flax, and took their flour home in sacks bound up in hemp they grew themselves. They were having trouble with their "pease," for the beetles that had wrecked the Pennsylvania and Jersey crops had moved into the Mohawk Valley by 1749. They were having trouble with "Bermuda potatoes," which seemed to rot out in the winter, and there was a controversy under way as to the best method of keeping them through till spring: some said sand was best to bury them in, others swore by ashes. Cooks were told to put ashes into the pot with their peas, "when they will not boil or soften well."

There was lots of river traffic, bateauxmen poling their clumsy sharp-ended boats through the many rifts and shoals to Fort Hunter and on to the portage at Wood Creek, where goods for the Indian trade at Oswego were carried from the Mohawk to the shallow little stream that flowed west to Oneida Lake.

From the windows of Mt. Johnson one could see, from year to year, the wheel ruts of the King's Highway deepen. Cleared land and cabins and their kitchen gardens were making patchworks of light in the dark shadows of the hunting grounds. If, however, the colonel's house had been on a mountain, and the mountain had been high enough, one might have seen, on the chessboard of land between the St. Lawrence on the north and the Great Lakes and the Ohio and Mississippi rivers to the west and southwest, chess moves in a giants' game.

12

Win or Draw?

It was at the Albany congress of 1754 that King Hendrick, the Mohawk sachem, delivered himself of a blast at the English which must have been heard in London. "Look about your country," he said to the assembled governors and generals, "and see; you have no fortifications about you . . . no, not even to this city. 'Tis but one step from Canada hither, and the French may come and easily turn you out of doors. Brethren, you were desirous we should open our hearts and minds to you; look at the French, they are men . . . they are fortifying everywhere; but, we are ashamed to say it, you are like women, bare and open, without any fortifications."

Like women, bare and open, the English now began to fight. In 1755 came the tragic four-way campaign of General Braddock, one prong of which he was to lead against Fort Duquesne. Louisburg was to be taken by a naval expedition. Governor Shirley of Massachusetts was charged with leading an army against Fort Niagara by way of the Mohawk Valley and Oswego. Brother Warra, now Major General Johnson and superintendent of Indian Affairs by command of General Braddock, at the head of a mixed army of militia and Indians, was to take Ticonderoga and Crown Point, and so remove those ancient French thorns from New York's side.

Schoolboys all know what happened to General Braddock, who died with most of his redcoats as they marched into a French ambush in the Pennsylvania wilderness. It might not have happened if Braddock hadn't been so top lofty with young George Washington and with the "half-king" and his Indians who had been sent by William Johnson to act as guides and scouts. A few days of Braddock and his parade-ground posturing, and the Indians slipped back into the forest where they were safe.

The news of Braddock's defeat took the courage out of Shirley's men, organizing at Schenectady and Albany. But Shirley intrigued his way through the Mohawk country, damning Johnson, hoping to engage as many of the Iroquois as possible for his own undertaking against Niagara. Shipbuilding and fort reinforcing at Oswego, storms and dallying, however, wrecked Shirley's plan for that year, and he returned to Albany, a sorry figure of a commander.

Johnson half won his battle. Between Shirley's intrigues and the success of the French in winning away his Indians, the new major general arrived at Lac St. Sacrement late in August with no more than three hundred of the eleven hundred Iroquois who had just drunk the king's health with him by the Mohawk, at Mt. Johnson. A few days after he arrived, he changed the name of Father Jogues's Lac St. Sacrement to Lake George, "not only," he wrote, "in honor of his majesty, but to ascertain his undoubted dominion here."

The new general played everything safe at the Battle of Lake George, to the disgust of most future historians. The French escaped after the drubbing he gave them, but Crown Point was never attacked, and the expedition was disbanded that November, after the levies had turned into carpenters and put up Fort William Henry at the south end of the lake.

William Johnson and his farmers, his summer soldiers, however, had won the only success in the whole fourfold plan of campaign. The colonies were glad to make it an excuse for victory bonfires, and processions, and toasts to the Mohawk Valley general. The New York frontier and Albany were safe. New England farmers felt a little freer to go about their harvesting. And Johnson went back to his stockaded fine house a baronet, Sir William Johnson, now richer by a title and £5,000, the gift of his king and a grateful Parliament.

But a stupid war! Two years of dawdle, and the curve of colonial fortunes turned down to a new low. Imported English generals sniffed at colonial levies, and made Albany and New York City over into rioting army towns. Oswego went by default to the French, as did the carrying place at Wood Creek, where the personnel holding out at Fort Bull were massacred for lack of a relief. The Iroquois, disgusted by this kind of war, sent peace delegations to Canada, and all of them except the Mohawks, Oneidas, and Tuscaroras swore they were done with fighting for either side. Johnson, in council after council with his charges, managed at least to hold the sourest of them from attacking the defenseless Mohawk farms.

Abercrombie and Loudon, the imported generals, were too busy planning textbook campaigns to follow up William Johnson's pleas to build forts and garrison the stockaded farmhouses already in the valley. And so on November 12, 1757, forty Germans were scalped or burned to death in a French sweep into German Flats. Sixty houses were leveled, five blockhouses destroyed, and one hundred fifty frightened settlers dragged north to captivity. Johnson again saved the Mohawk country from a worse disaster by preventing the stupid Loudon from marching against the Six Nations, who, said Loudon, were to blame for it all. The French had now, for all practical purposes, pushed the frontier east down the Mohawk Valley, almost to within gunshot of Sir William's house.

The next year the English curve went up. England had Pitt for premier. Loudon went back to England and his drill-yards. Amherst and Howe, men of sense, arrived for the new campaign. The French line of forts, stretched thin for more than three thousand miles, began to crumble. First Louisburg, and then Fort Frontenac, guarding the line to the Ohio, fell to England's new command. The St. Lawrence and the Ohio country were now divided. The bungling Abercrombie, with a huge British and colonial army, failed to take Crown Point, but the fine seam the French had sewn down the colonial frontiers was beginning to give, in spite of Abercrombie.

On the upper Mohawk, England finally got around to building a real fort at the vital carrying place between the Mohawk River and Wood Creek. Fort Stanwix, £60,000 worth of fort, was completed, to the astonishment of the Iroquois, who began to revise their thinking about the English. With the fall of Fort Duquesne the Ohio lands long claimed by the Six Nations were again clear, and the covenant chain took on renewed luster.

Sir William Johnson, baronet, was still "Brother Warra"; he was now officially superintendent of Indian Affairs by order of the crown and independent of any colonial control. Until the French were ousted from all of the St. Lawrence, however, and their pretensions to an American empire ended, he was wholly a military man, a war chief around the Six Nations' council fires, and a general of militia among his neighbors.

But the end was in sight. By the end of 1759 Fort Niagara had fallen to General Johnson and General Amherst had

driven the French back to the St. Lawrence from Ticonderoga
and Crown Point. Storms and planning for the final assault
on Montreal gave the French an uneasy respite until the
spring months of 1760, when Amherst mobilized his main
army near Schenectady. Brother Warra was busy with delegations of the Six Nations, first at Fort Johnson and then at the
upper castle of the Mohawks at Canajoharie. Rumors were
flying up and down the valley that Quebec had been recap-
tured from the English, and the Iroquois, like weathercocks,
were about-facing with every shift in the news.

Schenectady must have been a minor kind of Bedlam.
On "the Camp" in Scotia, across the Mohawk River from the
town, Amherst had assembled the greatest army the Mohawk
Valley had even seen: six thousand colonials and four thousand British regulars. Letters were hurried between Fort
Johnson and Amherst's headquarters. When the two leaders
moved against Montreal, everything useful in the valley would
move with them. The Mohawk Valley forts were to be emptied, not even a corporal's guard left to polish brass.

On June 22 the final nutcracker squeeze against New
France began. The Lord Jeffrey whose "name was known to
fame in days of yore," according to the Amherst College boys,
rode west along the Mohawk River, stopping overnight at
Fort Johnson. The plan called for one British army to march
against Montreal from Quebec and another to push north
from Crown Point. Amherst was to meet these armies before
the city after a grueling march up the Mohawk Valley to
Oswego and rough boating back down the St. Lawrence, cutting off any possibility of a French retreat.

The squeeze play came off without a hitch. True, many
of Johnson's Indians, excepting the Mohawks, went home, an-
noyed because they were not permitted to massacre the
French garrison of Abbé Picquet's little mission school of

Oswegatchie, which fell to Amherst as his army moved down the St. Lawrence. But on September 8 it was all over. Appropriately, a Mohawk Valley boy, Captain Jelles Fonda, recorded the final act in the long bloody drama that had begun with the Schenectady Massacre some seventy years earlier. His spelling isn't notable, but the event is clear enough. "Septr 8th in the morning," the captain wrote, "as we laid before Moreial ye French Sent a flag of Truse to Jenral amhost that theay would Capetelate and give op all the Country to ous. agreed open and the graneders Marched in Montereial this Day and placed centrys Round the Cetty."

The stockades could come down now. Bateauxmen on the Mohawk could leave their guns behind the cabin doors. The problem of how to cook "pease" was again important, and muster days for the militia could be holidays. The French, Captain Fonda had written, "would . . . give op all the Contry to ous."

How many of them, villagers in Schenectady, farmers seeding the Groote Vlachte, the Episcopal minister who served Fort Hunter, the Palatines who had spread out their landholdings west of the "promised land of scorie" as far as Fort Herkimer and beyond, how many of the militiamen home from Montreal, and the great sachems of the Long House, realized what had really happened on September 8, 1760?

Well, what happens when trunk-line switches are thrown? When old highways are closed? Traffic moves in new directions. The collapse of New France ended the traffic patterns that colonials and Indians had followed since Henry Hudson dropped anchor off today's Albany, and Champlain had set up the standard of France on the St. Lawrence. One hundred fifty years of one kind of competition for a continent were over.

In 1634 Surgeon van den Bogaert made his winter's trip

west from Fort Orange into the then unknown land of the Mohawk country, looking for Frenchmen who had gone there to divert the fur trade to the St. Lawrence. That problem was settled now.

Father Jogues, twelve years later, died near the mouth of the Schoharie, hoping to save Iroquois souls after the French manner. The "Jesuit problem" was concluded, and the Six Nations would from now on be taught meekness according to the formulas of England's Society for the Propagation of the Gospel, with help from the Dissenters of New England.

The frontier was now where you chose to mark it. Land was the thing. The French were ousted, and only the Indians stood in the way of acres, and townships, and counties, and colonies of empty, wonderful land.

The death of New France was a signal for the end of the Six Nations Confederacy as anything but a nuisance to the west-marching parade of settlers. The patentees along the Mohawk River now came to life. Surveyors tramped the woods looking for unpre-empted gores of land the earlier land-grabbers had missed. Exploitation of the land was in the air, and it ran like a fever through the colonies.

With the end of New France there came also a new tempo in the democratic dissonance the colonial governors had been hearing in their legislatures, and in deeper tones in the streets of the cities. The "Liberty" theme began to lose its chamber music quality. It quickened and roughened, in the throats of "Yorkers" and those other colonials who had, until Montreal fell, been marching for England to the camp-fire song of "Yankee-Doodle." It would grow, now, as men turned to tax protests, to dealing with crown interference with local manufacturing, as they began trespassing on Sir William Johnson's great Fort Stanwix boundary line, which he would soon set up between white men and Indians hoping to hold

back the crowds pushing up every available route to the un-
plowed and defenseless west.

Along the Mohawk River, and to all those colonists who
knew what Johnson's long control of the Iroquois had meant
in the breakup of New France, there was a growing belief
that Sir William Johnson, Bart., was the biggest man in British
America. Many hoped he was also the kind of man who
would frown on such mob-music as "Yankee-Doodle."

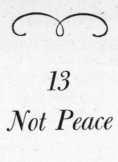

13
Not Peace

ONE WONDERS how Katy Weisenberg, the indentured servant, would have liked the coat of arms of her Mohawk River baronet: "Argent, two lions counter-rampant," the College of Heralds proclaimed, "supporting a dexter hand, gules; in chief, three estoilles of the last, and in bas, a salmon naiant in water, proper."

She would have understood the motto, at least: *Nec aspera terrent—*"Boldness wins."

He was home now at Fort Johnson, back from Montreal with great plans in his head. He had earned the years of peace he saw stretching ahead of him. Samuel Fuller, General Abercrombie's engineer-architect, would be put to work on "Johnson Hall" at once. The site was a good one, north and west of Fort Johnson about ten miles, on high ground four miles back from the river and the muddy King's Highway. The Indian trails stretching north from the Long House castles ran by the site; figuratively, of course, every Indian trail east of the Mississippi would end here at Sir William's front door.

Around him he would soon have his new tenants, the hundred Scotch families he was bringing in to settle on his vast Kingsborough estate, and there would be his new town, with an Established Church, a potash works, shops, a tanner, a carding mill, gristmill, blacksmith shop, a wagonmaker, and a tavern. In time there would be a free school, and in front of it the public stocks and the whipping post.

With William Johnson, the dream was simply the beginning of the deed. It all came to pass. Two years after the French collapse he had moved into the "Hall," close to his new town. Young John was twenty and soon living with Clara Putnam, his mistress, at Fort Johnson. Ann and Mary were cloistered with their governess on the second floor of the new house. The "brown Lady Johnson," Molly Brant, and the first of her brood of half-breeds, were there to welcome relatives from the Canajoharie castle or the bigwig nabobs from Albany and New York, who more and more came up the river to bargain for land and talk about the distressing evidences of leveling that were showing themselves among the lower classes.

Sir William, moving a little more slowly these days because of the French bullet in his side, found the world almost exactly to his taste. His lands now ran into the hundreds of thousands of acres. He wrote in his will that they "were all of my own acquiring." In that boast he was an American. In his thinking, however, he was a baronet of England. Young John must go to London, "to wear off," as it was expressed, "the rusticity of a country education." He was delighted when the boy came back with London manners and a knighthood from George III. He was blind to the fact that John was a most un-American young snob, thoroughly disliked by his Dutch and German neighbors whom he never tired of trying to impress.

There was a summer place now for hot weather entertaining, built on the edge of the Great Vlaie, where the town of Broadalbin stands today, and four miles northeast of it was a rustic lodge on the Sacandaga River known as the Fish House, where Sir William and his friends, in their lustier moments, could shed their responsibilities and many of the conventions.

Peace had come to the Mohawk, after almost a century of backwoods butchery. A skull cap would be worn for life by many a Mohawk farmer or his wife who had managed to survive the scalping knife. When Johannes Roof put up his squatter's house and barns at the carrying place at Fort Stanwix the year the war ended he moved the settlers' frontier to a point one hundred miles west from Albany to the very end of the navigable Mohawk. Plow and reap now, buy and sell. Let Sir William, the mighty neighbor, worry about the western Indians who were taking up the hatchet against unlicensed white men moving in on the hunting grounds. It was exciting to go up to the Hall, nevertheless, to see Sir William haranguing the sachems, and giving wampum belts to guarantee the promises of the colonial governors that they would keep trespassers at home. The talk at Tice's Tavern, in Johnstown, was that there was no boundary the settlers wouldn't cross, and if the Indians didn't like it, send the redcoats in to teach them what's what.

It wasn't "Johnstown" officially until 1770, but the streets were laid out, and the half dozen yellow frame houses Sir William ordered went up soon after the Hall was occupied. Farmers trudged up from the river to see the baronet's blooded horses, and the first sheep to be introduced into the valley. On Fair days there were sack races, greased pig chasing, and see-who-can-make-the-worst-face contests. Down by the river, on the best straightaways of the King's Highway, there was a good deal of horse racing, which was moved onto the river in winter.

Johnson now had time to worry about the "Mohawk Dutch," his neighbors, and their stubborn resistance to change. ". . . neither will they," he wrote in 1765, "hazard the smallest matter for the most reasonable prospect of gain, and this principle will probably subsist as long as that of their equality, which is at present at such a pitch that the conduct of one neighbor can but little influence that of another." "Equality" was one of that universal trinity of which "Liberty" and "Fraternity" were the other parts. The Mohawk farmers would accept change only when the line between Whig and Tory was clearer, when men like Sir John Johnson began to push them around, and when Sheriff White would dare to shoot one of the local "Sons of Liberty."

Until then, however, Sir William had time to worry about the overproduction of wheat along the river, the high cost of labor, and the terrible roads, "which would be still worse did I not take care that the inhabitants labored to repair them according to law." Sir William, himself, was down on the tax list for an annual nine days' work on the King's Highway, and young John was on it for six.

The peace meant holidays again. The Mohawk Valley Christmas Day was a great surprise to the missionary Samuel Kirkland, who liked the New England way best. It was "very affect'g and strik'g," he said. "They generally assemble for read'g prayers or Divine service . . . but after that, they eat, drink, and make merry. They allow of no work or servile labour on ye day, and ye following . . . their servants are free . . . but drinking, swearing, fighting, frolic'g are not only allowed, but seem to be essential for ye joy of ye day." Whit-sunday was a sort of slaves' holiday, when the valley Negroes would dress up in their best and, with bunches of "pinkster-bloomies" in their hands, go calling on their friends. The fiddles came down from the walls, and between dances at the

Hall one gossiped about John and Clara, exchanged courtesies with Molly Brant, and frightened one's partner with talk about the latest witch scare in the Schoharie country.

In the Long House, the peace turned sour very quickly. West of the Confederacy the bitterness was intense. "Englishmen!" stormed a Chippewa chief to an English trader at Michilimackinac, in the Great Lakes country. "Although you have conquered the French, you have not yet conquered us! . . . We are not your slaves! These lakes, these woods, these mountains . . . we will part with them to none!"

The loud anger rolled like a ground swell from Schonowe, the "gate" at Schenectady to the Long House, west along the Seneca Trail, onto the plains of the Illinois; it rolled north to the Lakes and south along the river channels of the Ohio and the Tennessee and the Mississippi.

To the Mohawk Valley came Johnson's excited deputies, George Croghan, from Fort Pitt, and his son-in-law, Daniel Claus, from Canada, with letters from the post commanders, all of them reporting the same story. The Indians feared the British forts were to be used in a war of extermination against them. The Indians were complaining because they were cheated right and left by the unlicensed traders who had rushed into the newly opened wilderness. Now that the French were out of the way, the English no longer wanted to sell guns to the Indians. Settlers were moving into the hunting grounds without even the farce of treatymaking.

There was no real peace. Towering head and shoulders above the crown officers and the men of the bickering colonial assemblies, Johnson, almost singlehanded, tried for the rest of his life to save the lands for his Indian "brothers." He had got his own bargain barony by open trading, at least. But he knew what little chance the Indians had when the rum-bottle speculator descended on them. "Get a few Indians drunk" was the formula, then, unbeknown to their tribe, have them sign a deed for a "little farm," pay them off with trade junk and small cash. Then, if you are a Yorker, hurry back to New York, pay the governor's fees, arrange for a crooked survey, and emerge from the deal with a crown patent for a "little farm" of one hundred thousand acres.

Sir William knew the worst of the patents along the Mohawk River had been obtained in this way. The Kayderos-seras Patent, for instance, to seven hundred thousand acres of land lying between the north bank of the lower Mohawk and the Hudson River began, in 1708, as a deed for a "little farm." The sachem Abraham, sixty years later, looking at his "Brother Warra" during the council called by Sir William to salvage what he could for his charges, said what was in the mind of every Indian tribe in the Mohawk Valley, and west of it, beyond the Alleghenies to the Mississippi: "We assisted the English to conquer the French, thinking that when that people had been brought to reason we and our young men should sit down and enjoy peace agreeably to what was told us. But, brother, to our very great sorrow, we understand . . . that some of our brethren are determined to deprive us of the chief tract of hunting land we have left . . . which we never could learn had been sold by our nation. Wherefore, we must say, if that is to be the case, we are much deceived in the opinion we ever entertained of our brethren's honesty."

What could he save of the opinion the Indians once had of English honesty? The oysters and Lisbon cheese, the Taunton ale and the limes and lemons sent up regularly to Sir William at the Hall must have lost a little of their flavor as the peace soured.

The smell of new paint and fresh, fine paneling was hardly out of Johnson Hall before the land anger flamed into savage border warfare along the whole Allegheny-Great Lakes frontier, led by the Ottawa firebrand, Pontiac. Drive out the English! Drive out the English! Through most of 1763 Johnson Hall echoed to the solemn oratory of Indian peace councils. The farmers on the upper reaches of the river at German Flats and Burnets Field wondered when the Senecas would begin to add their scalps to the eighty bloody hanks of English hair they brought back from a massacre staged at Niagara. Out of loyalty to Sir William, however, all of the Confederacy, except the Senecas, refused to join Pontiac. By fall the Ottawa chief, sure now that promised French help would never come, raised the siege of Detroit and, with his warriors, slipped back into the shadows of the forest. South and west of the Mohawk Valley Pontiac's allies, dejected at Colonel Bouquet's success along the Ohio, slowly gave up the dream of independence which their leader had given them.

At the Hall, the good strong Georgian house designed by Sam Fuller, the boundary-line plan now took final shape. There would be no peace, Sir William was certain, until a boundary line between settlers and Indians was drawn so clearly down the whole length of British America that not even a moonlight surveyor would trespass on it.

At Fort Stanwix, William Johnson drew his boundary line. Here, at the carrying place to the west, in the late fall of 1768, was held the greatest Indian congress America was ever to see. It was also the most tragic. Here, like King Canute, the government of George III said "No farther!" to a tide of land-hungry white men as deaf as the waves of the sea.

For months letters of preparation went out of the Hall. Three years earlier the Six Nations had agreed that a boundary line, a permanent frontier behind the northern colonies, was the only way to cool the frictions between Indians and settlers. The Lords of Trade agreed. That September, before the great congress opened, Governor Penn came to Johnson

Hall for preliminary talks. Virginia sent representatives, men who hoped to persuade the Iroquois to give up their title to land between the Ohio and the Tennessee. Benjamin Franklin's son, Governor Franklin of New Jersey, came. The great land companies sent their representatives, and the followers of Eleazar Wheelock were there, urging on the Indians a grant of land for the support of religion. Wheelock wanted his Dartmouth College west of the boundary line. Sir William himself would represent New York's interests.

All that summer Johnson had pulled on a yoke of work that would have strangled an ordinary man. He left the labor of rounding up the tribes for the meeting to his nephew, Guy Johnson, while he tried to bolster his failing health by bathing in and drinking sea water on the Connecticut coast. The French bullet in his side kept him from riding horseback. But the correspondence! There was the poor scholarship report of his half-breed son, William of Canajoharie. There were his letters pointing out the need of an American episcopate; he was anxious to have episcopal missionaries among the Six Nations to combat the work of New England Dissenters. He was asked his opinion on the Lake Superior copper mines; he forwarded papers in the matter of the trial for treason of Major Rogers of "Ranger" fame. He paid for Indian prayer-books, deplored the rioting in Boston, and took the purges ordered by his Albany doctor.

But the great problem was the congress. Thomas Gage, now commander-in-chief of His Majesty's forces in North America, was cynical about the whole business. In May he wrote to the baronet: ". . . all the good I can forsee from the . . . Boundary is, that it will stop the Clamors of the Indians for a short time . . . if means are not found to protect the Indians in their Persons and Property, it matters little where the Boundaries are fixed." But, then, Gage was the man who wrote to a military friend that "the Jealousys should be kept up amongst the Indians, by which we may be umpires in their disputes, and probably they will be fearful of attempting anything against us as long as they continue distrustful of Each other."

The cynics, the preachers, the land agents, the bargain hunters of the colonies were getting ready to move up the Mohawk to Fort Stanwix that summer. The 100,000-acre operations of the patentees along the Mohawk River seem pitiful when one remembers that the agents of the Ohio Company, the Susquehanna Company, and the lobbyists for religion were then planning a piece of land surgery elsewhere on the continent which would give them millions of acres.

Bateauxmen sweated through July and August, poling the congress supplies upstream. "Bowsmen up!" and then "Second men up!" echoed from Schenectady to Fort Stanwix, as the captains gave the rhythm to the men shoving their clumsy boats against the current. Six Flats Rift, a little west of Schenectady, was easier for the three-handed scows than it was for the two-ton bateaux, laboring west with the hogsheads of pickled meat and the bales of "red shallom" cloth and "Christian blankets" Sir William wanted to pile up on the tables of presents he planned to have prominently displayed during the negotiations. Beyond Little Nose Hill, Keator's Rift demanded help from shore. The towlines were thrown out and, between the men at the poles and those on the lines, and a wind of Dutch curses, the boats were edged on into deeper water. Boats and supplies had to be hauled out of the river at Little Falls, freighted around the better than half mile of rapids, and then reshipped.

The "Trow-Plat," as the Dutch called the carrying place, was ready by the middle of September. Flour, pork, and rice were under cover at the fort, ready for the hordes of Indians who, according to the baronet, could be expected to eat twice as much as an equal number of white men. A "good tight boat" was sent upstream from Schenectady to carry Sir William and Governor Franklin to the congress grounds, where they arrived on the 19th. The commissioners from Virginia were already there. Two days later John Penn arrived. Soon Fort Stanwix took on the appearance of a Fair Ground.

Not all the cash was on hand yet, but Sir William was expecting £10,000 of crown money to pay for whatever land the sachems could be persuaded to give up. The silver lace for coats and hats, the aurora, fuzees, and the black and white wampum were ready. But where were the Indians? More than three thousand were expected, but the lean-tos set up for them were almost empty.

Most of the Mohawks soon arrived, as well as a large body of Oneidas and a few Susquehannas. The Mohawks, to Sir William's annoyance, had invited eighty Stockbridge Indians from east of the Hudson to come along. By the 30th he had got rid of the Stockbridge Indians and was complaining bitterly that the provisions were fast disappearing. Where were the Delawares, and the Shawnees, and the northern Indians, and the Mingos from Ohio, and the rest of the Six Nations?

"I am in hopes," the baronet wrote to Commander-in-Chief Gage, "that the Whole will be here in 5 or 6 days." In the meantime he and Governor Penn and Governor Franklin could try the barrel of oysters that had been sent up the river for Sir William's use. There was plenty of wine to make the waiting less tedious. And there may have been other pleasures. One of Johnson's New York friends, unable to attend the meeting, blames Fortune for depriving him of "the Honour you designèd me & perhaps of being encircled in the Ivory arms of some Lovely Princess of the Woods." As Brother Warra, William Johnson could involve himself in matters which were of no concern to Sir William.

But where were the Indians? Days slipped by. Only four hundred had arrived at Fort Stanwix by the first of October. Twelve days later the number had grown to about nine hundred. Rumors to explain the delay began to settle on the congress grounds like evening mist on the river. The "Upper Nations," explained Johnson to the restless John Penn and to his correspondents, "are still behind, occasioned by the death of a Seneca Chief, on which account they halted to perform the ceremony of Condolence."

There were rumors that the French and the Spaniards were planning a rival congress of all the southern Indians, spreading promises of a great French army soon to land and destroy the English. The rumors, unfortunately, did not reduce the appetites of the Indians already on the scene. The upper Mohawk River settlements were scoured for cattle on the hoof and local corn was bought to replenish the failing commissary. Cattle prices, of course, skyrocketed.

Lieutenant Governor Penn finally fidgeted himself into believing that he was needed more in Philadelphia than he was here in the wilderness, and so went home. If he had waited a few days he would have seen more than two thousand warriors, some with their women and children, move out of the forest into the clearing at the Trow-Plat. Governor Franklin, for whom oysters and Madeira and the cool nights of late fall on the upper Mohawk were no inconvenience, estimated that there were about thirty-four hundred Indians present on the 24th of October, when Sir William formally opened the "Boundary Line Congress."

Katy Weisenberg's husband was heavier now, and there

were jowls, and the big Irish face showed suffering not even drinking the Saratoga Spring waters could erase.

"Brethren!" The strong, familiar voice, however, could be heard to the outer edges of the huge circle of Indians. The tables of presents set out for their inspection had put them in a receptive mood. "I take you by the hand and heartily bid you all welcome to this place where I have kindled a council fire for affairs of importance."

Always the forms must be observed. Chief Abraham, the Mohawk, had been appointed to translate Brother Warra's words. No matter that the speaker knew their poetic Long House language well, the tribal ceremonial called for an interpreter.

The big voice began the ceremony of condolence. "With this String of Wampum I do on behalf of his Majesty and all his Subjects wipe away the Tears from your eyes which you are constantly shedding for your late deceased Chiefs . . ."

Abraham, brother of King Hendrick, father of Caroline, the dark-skinned "housekeeper" who had succeeded Katy, rolled out the ritual words after Sir William. Here the forest and the river made the presents of silver lace and red cloth and Governor Franklin and Eleazar Wheelock's gospel chanters and the blank-faced commissioners from Virginia and Pennsylvania all seem one with the smoke from the Indian pipes that drifted high into nothingness on the October wind.

"With this String I clear the Passage to your Hearts . . .

"With this last String I wipe away the blood of your friends off your Births, that you may, on your return, rest with Peace and Comfort on them . . ."

Secretary Guy Johnson kept a careful record of the words and a strict account of the belts of wampum his uncle-father-in-law gave to the chiefs as a pledge of his sincerity.

The ceremonials continued the next day. An Oneida chief paid Governor Franklin a forest compliment by bestowing his own Oneida name upon him. The tribes then condoled with the English for their losses, "cleansing their hearts that they may be able to attend the important affairs which were to be transacted."

The third day of the congress saw the last of the condoling and compliments. Governor Franklin discovered that his new name meant "doer of justice." Sir William gave a large belt of wampum "in the name of your Father, the Great King of England . . . to renew the covenant chain subsisting between us . . . rubbing off any rust which it may have contracted . . . that it may appear bright to all Nations . . . so long as Grass shall grow or waters run."

The best of Sir William was Brother Warra. He, too, could think like a Long House poet. "I do now by this Belt," he continued, "clear the Rivers and Paths through your countries of all obstructions, removing Trees out of your Creeks & Logs, Briars and Rubbish out of your Roads, that our Canoes may pass along without danger and that our People may travel freely by Night or by Day . . ." Guy Johnson carefully noted that the Covenant Chain belt was a large one: "fifteen Rows with human figures at each end."

Two days later, "The weather being cold, Sir William clothed the old Chiefs of Every Nation for which they returned many thanks & told them that he now enabled them to meet and consider the Great Affair before them with pleasure." The boundary-line work could now begin.

Late that afternoon Brother Warra and the Iroquois chiefs stood in front of a map in the former's quarters, "on which the Country is drawn large and plain which will enable us both to judge better of these matters." Sir William's official finger pointed to the place on the map where Fort Pitt was indicated, and then moved north. "It remains to me," he said to the watching sachems, "to obtain a continuation of that line . . . which will be secure to you and advantageaus to us . . . the piece of Land in the Forks of the Susquehanna is very much desired by the Commissioners from Pennsylvania and would be more advantageous to them than to you."

The official finger moved north from Fort Pitt up the Ohio to the Mahoning River, and then to the west branch of the Susquehanna, and up to the east branch of that river to Owego, in southwestern New York. Sir William's finger continued on like a knife . . . "from thence," he said, "the line can be run eastward to the Delaware River, which is very near it at that Place, for that part of the additional Cession which will fall to Mr. Penn, you will receive a large and handsome consideration over and besides his Majesty's Royal Bounty."

All of New York waited nervously to see how far Sir William could push the frontier west of Fort Stanwix. He was tact itself as he presented the problem. "I expect," he said to the doubtful sachems, "that your Resolution will be advantageous to us, and that you will make proper allowance for the increase of our People."

The Iroquois had had enough for one day. "Brother . . ." said their spokesman, "we thank you for your advice, which we believe is well intended, but this is a great Cession of Land which will require much thought . . . therefore we shall defer consideration of it until tomorrow."

"That night," the faithful secretary of the congress wrote, "Sir William had a private conference with the Chiefs of the most influence with whom he made use of every argument to bring matters to an agreeable issue." The Mohawk Valley patentees would have trembled could they have heard the chiefs' proposal. "We think," they said, "that the Line should run up the Delaware to the Swamp [Oriskany] and from there run across to the Governors [the Cosby Manor, surrounding modern Utica], and then go away to Lake George, which we cannot think but a fair offer." If Sir William's arguments hadn't prevailed, the New York frontier would have moved east instead of west.

The next day the representatives of Eleazar Wheelock infuriated Johnson by trying to persuade the Indians to reserve lands for religion, and to oppose any important change in the frontier. The Iroquois were also scolded by Sir William for not hurrying things along; they were told "that the security of their lands depended on their despatch and the freedom of the Cession."

Bribes were offered to those chiefs who would persuade the procrastinators to accept the official version of the line. There would be "five hundred dollars and a handsome present" for each of them. Sir William, hopefully believing it himself, pointed out to all the sachems that only enough land was wanted to "give the People room on the Frontiers . . . that with the help of proper Laws it would not be liable to intrusion."

The Oneidas were difficult. They suddenly decided they wanted to go into business at the Trow-Plat, carrying boats and goods between the Mohawk and Wood Creek. "By keeping horses and carriages there . . . they might earn somewhat for the support of their families." For an extra $600, "besides the several fees which were given in private," they agreed, however, to move the line west of the carrying place to Canada Creek.

Tuesday, the 1st of November, the line was settled. "We have given him [the King] a great and valuable country, and we know that what we shall now get for it must be far short of its value." There, on the banks of the Mohawk, for less than it costs New York City to clean up the streets after a single light snowstorm, the Iroquois and their allies traded off the lands out of which western Pennsylvania, West Virginia, and Kentucky were formed. For $1,000 Spanish, the Penns got their western lands. The rest of this empire, including a cession of millions of acres in the Ohio country, went for £10,000 and the trade goods piled up on the tables at Fort Stanwix.

Sir William did as well as he could for New York, but the Iroquois refused to give up anything west of Canada Creek at the place where it joined Wood Creek. Bargaining for the land north of Wood Creek to the Great Lakes was put off until a "more appropriate time."

On November 5 the deeds were ready for signing. The presents were on display in the buildings of the fort. After the signatures and tribal signs had been affixed to the parchments, the chiefs received their cash, "which was piled on a table for that purpose . . . (they) then proceeded to divide the Goods amongst their People which occupied the rest of that day."

"That night," wrote Secretary Guy Johnson, "Sir William took leave of the Chiefs, recommending it to them against any committing any Disorders at their Departure, but to pack up their Goods & return home in peace and Good Order."

By Sunday night Sir William was far downstream on the Mohawk, heading for the carry at Little Falls and Johnson Hall. The boundary line had been drawn. One could hope that it meant peace at last. If he laughed a little self-consciously, in the darkness, it may have been because he was remembering his last official act at the congress he had just closed. In order to pay the full £10,000 to the chiefs for the vast land cession to the crown he had had to go to the Mohawk sachems and borrow $3,000 from them. Their cash, he knew, had just been received as payment for the "little farm," the vast stolen Kayderosseras lands.

14

...But a Sword

"Joseph, control thy people, I am going away."

Joseph Brant, the young Mohawk chief, could only nod. Through the open windows of Sir William's library, now his sickroom, drifted a hot July wind and the evening sounds of the Iroquois delegations camped outside the Hall: the barking of dogs, the voices of squaws bent over their cooking pots, men's talk, pitched low. The shadows in the room seemed still as sachems waiting for the answers he knew now others would have to give.

Between the fits of suffocation against which he fought with the desperation of a drowning man he remembered his compromises and his promises. The chiefs of the Six Nations were out there in the night, patient friends, wondering why he had been unable to explain the broken promises.

What was it he had written after the land cessions at Stanwix? "I have staked my reputation with the Indians that the Several Articles they have made shall be observed"? Nothing he had promised had been observed. Perhaps he had known all along that the boundary line would be a fiction. Without laws and without soldiers to enforce them no frontier had ever held back the lawless mob that always gravitated toward it. How could he tell these savages that that was the way the white men wanted things?

"Joseph . . . I am going away." Perhaps it was time. The boundary lines of his own world were breaking up. "No taxation without representation!" That cry was getting louder. He had heard it in the colonial assemblies, around the liberty poles in New York City, and even in Tice's Tavern, below the Hall. He had had to beg the Sons to Liberty to pass shipments of his Indian supplies through their blockade of English goods.

"Unless they alter the Stamp Act, we shall all be Republicans." Had he meant that? The Whiggish rage against England was worse now: protesting committees springing up everywhere; riots against the crown's tax collectors in New York and Boston; Boston people dumping tea into their harbor and calling themselves "Mohawks." Talk was ugly among the Palatines after the news came in of what people were calling the "Boston Massacre."

Would John never come? They said they had sent down to Fort Johnson for Sir John. It had all been written out, but he wanted to say it to John again. Never sell lands out of the royal patent. The Mohawks had given them to him, and the king had confirmed the gifts. Be kind, John, to Molly and her children, be lenient, John, to your needy tenants . . . be of upright conduct, John . . . afford more satisfaction . . . more pleasure . . . noble, generous mind . . .

It was bitter cold the day he signed the will. July was such fine council weather. Outside the library door there were hushed voices he couldn't understand . . . was John coming?

Sir William Johnson, Bart., his Majesty's superintendent of the Northern Indians, died on the night of July 11, 1774,

at Johnson Hall. Less than two years later the Hall was looted
by men who had been his neighbors, American officers who,
with their soldiers, marched up the old King's Highway in
an attempt to capture Sir John, his son, then the Mohawk
Valley's most dangerous Tory.

The revolt against England was on. Men's loyalties, the
least stable of boundary lines, shifted overnight. "Lady Washington" and the "Long Nine Pounder," two cannon from the
old fort in Schenectady, were set up in the dorp's streets to
guard the main stockade gates leading into the open country.
For the slow-wits who didn't understand what was happen-
ing in Boston and New York it was enough to whisper that
Johnny Johnson and his damned Scotch tenants would come
down the valley soon, burning and shooting. That was one
way to get the taproom soldiers to clean their guns and come
to musters.

For two years after Sir William's death the Revolution in
the Mohawk Valley was largely a war of correspondence. Like
angry hackles, the feathered quills were raised to Tory and
Whig inkhorns alike.

At Adam Louck's tavern in Stone Arabia six weeks after
the baronet was buried the Whigs of Tryon County gathered
to pen their say about George III. Tryon County was largely
Sir William's domain. It had been broken off two years earlier
from Albany County at Sir William's pleasure, complete with
its county seat at Johnstown, complete with its jail and courthouse and its Tory judges. The high ground north of the river
was full of his Roman Catholic club-swinging Scotch tenants,
hundreds of them, fanatically loyal to the Johnsons who had
inherited the barony and the king's authority.

The men who sat among Adam Louck's alepots and blue
Holland punch bowls, however, were mainly men from the
river farms west of the Hall. They were the Palatines whose

resistance to change had once worried Sir William. They were ready for it now, as they listened to Christopher Yates read out the resolutions.

First, there was a paragraph viewing with alarm the late acts of the British Parliament: "abridging the privileges of the American Colonies and blocking up the Port of Boston." It was solemnly agreed that George III was still the rightful ruler in the Mohawk Valley. No one doubted that he should have "true faith and allegiance." "We will," Christopher Yates wrote, "with our lives and fortunes support and maintain him."

There was a good deal more of that sort of thing, and then they took their tongues out of their cheeks and talked plain and clear: ". . . we think it is our undeniable privilege to be taxed only with our own consent . . . we will join and unite with our brethren of the rest of this country in anything tending to support and defend our rights and liberties."

Christopher Yates was a lawyer, and knew how to write it out. By the time the meeting was over and the ale mugs emptied, the Whigs of the Palatine District had approved New York's delegates to "a general Continental Congress" and had agreed to persuade the eastern districts of Tryon County to join them in setting up a Committee of Correspondence for the whole county.

There had been little enough excitement along the Mohawk River since the French wars and Pontiac's Rebellion. One wonders, though, if these farmers and inland lawyers would have been so busy with their resolutions and hot letters if they could have looked ahead just a little. Sir John was still in the Hall. Guy Johnson was at Guy Park, and was now King George's Indian superintendent, and there was certainly no one in Adam Louck's tavern who would dare say how the Six Nations would behave if and when the inkhorn was put by for powder horns. .

By the middle of May, 1775, Schenectady's freeholders down the river from Tryon County had chosen a Committee of Correspondence of their own. Revolutions, all these committees soon learned, are not romantic. There were brave decisions, but few shouts of "Hang that spy!" even though the neighbors saw villains everywhere. In Schenectady there was the problem of Wouter Dann and Henry Miller "who entertained Negroes in their House." Does Francis Haworth have a pass to be away from the Schoharie District? "Resolved that said John Monier be permitted to remain here for his health." How, they wondered, were they to keep horses in the neighborhood as long as the enemy's General Burgoyne "would give 20 guineas for each"? Who stole militiaman Lafferty's watch? The committee listened to complaints "against soldiers selling their Cloaths for liquor." And there was the sad case of "Elis'th Mabb . . . against Abr'm Brown [who] . . . came to her House and sat down to play Cards and Brown cheating, said Hall, a Quarrel arose and Brown got down a gun and said he would shoot Hall who had went out of the House a little before."

But Lexington and Concord had been fought. During May the Second Continental Congress met. George Washington would shortly take charge of the angry men laying siege to Boston. The Revolution was well down now out of its heaven of high sentiment to the mill lanes and the river road where Tom, Dick, and Harry were beginning to look around the cabins for the gear their fathers had used "in the last war."

A ghost walked at the third meeting of Schenectady's committee. The six members nervously pored over a letter from Albany, acquainting them that one "Daniel Campbell,

Esq. had a quantity of Gunpowder in store at Albany, which he wanted to take out, but they refused him that liberty until they acquainted this board of the same." The committee, "forseeing the Evil Consequences that may attend the powder falling into the hands of our Enemies . . . will purchase the said Powder from Daniel Campbell for the use of the Inhabitants of this Township."

At the next meeting, on May 20, the ghost became flesh and blood. "Rec'd a letter from William Petrey, at the German Flatts," the secretary wrote, "informing this board that the bearer of the said letter, Adam Perse, had heard Colonel Guy Johnson desire some Indians to rise in armes and cut of [sic] the Inhabitants."

"Our enemies" as far as the local Committees of Safety and Correspondence were concerned, were the Johnsons and their supporters. During May, 1775, the chief villain was Guy Johnson. Schenectady was "informed by good authority that one Mr. Fletcher, a schoolmaster of this Town, (said) that Colonel Guy Johnson would Com down the river with five thousand Indians, and cut us all of [sic]. And further said that it would be right, and if he had it in his Power he would do the same, for we were all rebels."

Schenectady stirred with rumors, keyhole spies, and a constant flow of suspicions and tattling from one committee to another, and shivered under the shadows cast over the Mohawk Valley from the Hall and Guy Park. All the local patriots had at least a walk-on part in a huge drama whose climaxes were fast being readied off-stage. Campbell's 338 pounds of gunpowder were bought for three shillings the pound. Schoolteacher Fletcher was sent for twice, but never showed up to explain his loose talk.

Whigs and Tories alike made their plans. The Schenectady inhabitants were ordered to meet in the forenoon of

Saturday, May 27, to show "how they are provided with arms and ammunition." And more ominously, on the same morning, they were ordered "to raise three companies of minutemen in this Township for its safety." If the Johnsons decided to take things into their own hands "Lady Washington" and the "Long Nine Pounder" might have work to do yet.

In late May the center of excitement moved up the river again. The Tryon County committee was in an uproar. A mysterious letter, picked up on the highway where it was thought to have been lost by an Indian carrier, called on the Oneidas to come down to Guy Park at once so that they and the Mohawks who signed the letter could save Guy Johnson from "the Boston People." Guy Park was being fortified. There were armed men around the buildings constantly, "stopping and searching travellers upon the king's highway and stopping our communication with Albany."

The committee sent a hysterical letter to Albany by a roundabout route through the Schoharie Valley: "we have not 50 pounds of powder in our district and it will be impossible for you to help us any till the communication is opened not a man being suffered to pass, without being searched. Tomorrow . . . we . . . propose the question whether we will not open the communication by force. . . . We are, Gentlemen, perhaps in a worse situation than any part of America is at present."

The Albany committee, being farther away from the Johnsons, was less anxious for direct action. Instead, they sent a letter back to Guy Park three days before the delegations from the Schenectady and Albany committees met the Mohawks there; Guy Johnson was told what the Mohawks were later assured was only rumor; the Boston people were not

coming, and, Albany added, the committees wanted nothing but "peace and friendship" with him and the Indians.

Peace and friendship were now, however, only letter writers' passwords. Guy Johnson continued to bully. It was probably Guy who drew the first blood of the Revolution in the valley. Shortly after the news of Lexington some three hundred local patriots gathered at John Veeder's house in Caughnawaga, now Fonda; they were full of talk, but un-armed, and peaceable enough. Something more tangible than talk was needed, however, to show their enthusiasm for the whipping the Boston redcoats had just taken. Before their liberty pole was up, Sir John Johnson and his two brothers-in-law, and a pack of their tenants, the "Johnson dogs," the Palatines called them, rode into the middle of the gathering. There was a good deal of sword waving and pistol brandish-ing as Guy climbed on a high porch and began to curse the patriots.

Young Jacob Sammons took all he could from the red-faced, squat cock-o'-the-walk. Unable to contain himself, he yelled out from the crowd that Johnson was a liar. He was a liar and a villain! The speech about the virtues of George III stopped abruptly, and Guy, who wasn't used to interruptions from these peasants, sprang down from his platform and grabbed Sammons by the throat.

In the middle of the scuffle one of the Tories swung on Sammons with a loaded whip, knocking him out for a mo-ment. When his sight cleared he found one of Johnson's Highlanders seated on his chest. A blow in the right place got rid of the Highlander, but by now the unarmed Whigs had beat a quick and inglorious retreat, and young Sammons was left to fight the valley's first battle by himself. The odds were unfair. He couldn't do much with Johnson pistols cocked and pushed into his face. The loyalists now went to work on him in bullies' style, knocking him down, and beating him with their clubs. When they had proved the virtues of the king the whole Johnson party decamped, and Sammons, thoroughly beaten up, was left to consider Liberty in a new light.

By the end of May, Guy Johnson had had enough of the Mohawk Valley Whigs and their committees. With his family, and what he would have called his "retainers" and most of the Mohawks of the Upper Castle at Canajoharie, he moved west up the Mohawk to Cosby's Manor, beyond German Flats, to what he said was to be a friendly conference with the Six Nations. Here he received his last broadside in Tryon County's brave paper war. General Herkimer, whose name the Johnson's were soon to have real cause to dislike, delivered the letter and took back the answer.

The Tryon committee's letter must have made Guy gag a little. All the stock phrases were there: "we are oppressed by the mother country . . . avowed design of the ministers to enslave us . . . save our devoted country from ruin and devastation . . . with the assistance of divine providence." Could these lawbreaking, disloyal Whigs really believe all this? The letter was clever. It closed with reassurances of good will, a plea to keep the Indians out of the swelling mother country difficulties, and a bid for Johnson's sympathy because "your family possess very large estates in this country." He must have smiled wryly at that one. These farmers weren't using threats, by any chance? Lawyer Christopher Yates could write a good letter—that touch about property must have been his.

The letter General Herkimer took back with him was up to anything Christopher Yates could turn out. The whole quarrel, Guy loftily pointed out, "is viewed in different lights according to the education and principles of the parties affected . . . it is not viewed in the same light in a country which admits of no authority that is not constitutionally established." He then defended the fortifying of Guy Park and swore that the only people he ever stopped from traveling west on the King's Highway were "two New England men." He ended with warm regards to the people of the county and assurances that "they would have nothing to apprehend from my endeavours." "I shall alway be glad," he wrote, "to promote their true interests." A few days later he and his family, and most of the Mohawks, were on their way to Canada, where, the Tryon County committee was soon to discover, Guy would busy himself promoting the Whigs' "true interests" according to his Tory kill-and-scalp recipe.

And Sir John? The Tryon committee learned quickly enough that Indian messengers were slipping north to Canada, to Guy, and back again to the Hall, the Lord knows what plots wrapped around the heads of the messengers' tomahawks. The anxious letters continued to flow; the price of powder to the committee had gone up two shillings a pound since Daniel Campbell's powder had been taken over by the Schenectady Whigs. Lead was forty shillings a hundredweight, and things were "deplorable."

Then came the affair of Sheriff White. White was Sir John's man, and a violent Tory who had officiously played the royal watchdog too long. The sheriff lighted a slow fuse to some highly combustible tempers when, late in July, he marched patriot John Fonda off to the Johnstown jail. The original sin was small enough, a quarrel between Fonda and a servant of Sheriff White's over the latter's trespassing on Fonda's land, but, like original sin, it spread fast. A mob of angry Whigs soon staged a jail delivery, and then marched on Tice's Tavern, where the frightened sheriff was waiting for them, guns cocked. The few shots he fired as the mob bore down on the tavern opened the gunpowder stage of the Rev-

olution in the Mohawk Valley. Apparently nobody was hurt.
Sheriff White made an inglorious retreat into one of the inn's
big chimneys, sat out the Whig search parties, and then
scurried off to the Hall.

Fonda and his Whig friends were determined to have
White. They sent a delegation to Sir John which got nowhere.
Christopher Yates wrote the whole story down for the Schenectady and Albany committees, pointing out that Tryon
County was all through fooling with the sheriff, and that, in
spite of Sir John, they were going to take him out of the Hall,
provided, provided . . . "we understand," said the letter writer,
"their [sic] are field pieces in Schenectady we request you
would send us a couple with all the implements necessary."

The five hundred or six hundred men ready to take the
Hall must have cursed at the reply they got from Albany.
"It gives us pain," the cautious old-lady's letter ran, "that we
on this head differ in sentiments with our Brethren to the
westward." There was more about the laws and feeling better when "Passion and Resentment . . . subside." The sheriff
himself probably kept their tempers from exploding by de-
camping the next day, presumably for Canada.

Sir John now played the hurt but understanding neighbor, assuring General Philip Schuyler, in command of the
northern department of the American forces, that he would
take no further part in the colonial-home government quarrel.
The role convinced no one, and Sir John soon gave up playing it. By the end of October, 1775, he had told the Tryon
committee that he would sooner have his head cut off than
lift his hand against his king. As for the Johnstown courthouse and jail, they were his property until someone paid him
£700. He would guarantee that his tenants would join no
militia run by Whigs, who, he said, had already forced two-

thirds of the county to sign the papers of association against their will.

By Christmas he was fortifying the Hall, as Guy had done earlier, and people along the river heard that as soon as the work was done he would garrison it with three hundred Indians in addition to the "Johnson dogs" young Jacob Sammons had such good cause to remember. That done, they'd start teaching the countryside loyalty to the king.

General Schuyler, early in January, decided he would do the teaching. With musters from Albany and Schenectady, the general moved quietly up the river as far as Major Fonda's house, facing the Mohawk, and not far from the Hall. General Herkimer ordered out all the Tryon County militia. The show promised to be good. By the time Sir John had had a chance to read General Schuyler's letters demanding all his arms and stores, and a promise from him that he would try to persuade his neighboring loyalists to behave, there were three thousand men parading up and down the frozen Mohawk. Robert Crouse, the strong man of the valley, was keeping himself warm and astounding his fellow militiamen by waving the big standard of the Canajoharie District Regiment with one hand.

Sir John found the three thousand militiamen convincing. He and his Highlanders dumped their arms into a pile in front of the Johnstown courthouse. Days later Sir John gave his parole. The road north to Canada, however, running past Sir William's Fish House and the Sacandaga River, continued to be a Tory highway. Rumors of impending Indian massacres became so numerous by May that General Schuyler decided to break up the whole Tory nest at Johnstown, and have the ringleader locked up.

If the Tory merchant, Alexander Campbell, hadn't passed word up the river to Sir John that Colonel Dayton and his men were on their way to arrest him, much of the later bloodletting in the settlements west of Schenectady might not have taken place. Sir John, however, got the news in time to bury his family plate, round up his tenants, and take off for Canada through the Adirondack wilderness. Lady Johnson, whose pregnancy made travel impossible, was left to meet the colonel.

The Johnsons, father, son, and nephew, were gone from the valley at last. Brother Warra's people were scattering. Sir William's barony was overrun by Whigs, who had established a new political frontier against which he had prepared no adequate defenses. A new kind of boundary line had been drawn, and the Johnsons were on the wrong side of it. Colonel Dayton's men wandered through the Hall now, pocketing what they pleased: "some fiddle strings, a large seal, some silver lace." The valley was theirs.

15

The Field of Nettles

"WHERE in the world," wrote Mr. S. to the editors of *Time* magazine, "did the Navy get the name *Oriskany* as the name of one of the new aircraft carriers? I have several histories of the Navy, not one of which mentions any *Oriskany*."

Time gave him the right answer, though they couldn't do much in a hundred words. The editors suggested he read the account of the battle in *Drums Along the Mohawk*, by Walter Edmonds, and that was a good suggestion. I don't believe, though, that Mr. Edmonds expected to tell his readers why "Oriskany" is a very special name to Americans, one that would do honor to a flagship of the fleet, or that Mr. S. and the editors of *Time* realized that we might still be British subjects if some eight hundred Mohawk Valley farmers hadn't answered the muster call on that Sunday morning, August 3, 1777.

Revolution is the same in any age. Nameless thousands move through bloody quadrilles, leaving, individually, no more impression on the record than a dancer's feet leave on a ballroom floor. Not that the men who tramped west to Oris-

kany for the new Republic were the sort who ever danced
quadrilles. They weren't. They were, with few exceptions,
farmers, heavy-shouldered from lifting their plows out of the
ends of furrows. Though they were born to be anonymous, a
deep passion for their land, rubbed to heat by fear, gave
those who didn't run that August day unforgettable names.

There wasn't as much money in the Mohawk Valley in
1777 as the navy spent for the engines of the aircraft carrier
Oriskany. The real money had vanished with the loyalist supporters of King George III, Tories who were rank happy and
privilege conscious, or who thought men were servants of the
state. These men, and the crowds of retainers and sympathizers who went with them, were in Canada that summer,
planning a return trip to the Mohawk Valley to take back
their estates and farms. They were looking forward to beating
their kind of sense into their old neighbors who had stayed
behind as citizens of a new Republic they expected to smash.
The English had a master plan that year to bring all this to
a quick, happy English conclusion.

General Burgoyne—"Gentleman Johnny" Burgoyne—
thought he could end the American Revolution in a month,
and make a summer holiday out of the business to boot. According to some, there were three parts to the plan. First,
Burgoyne himself would cut a nice swath from Montreal to
Albany, through patriot forts and the Saratoga wheatfields.
There would be ladies in the party, and wagonloads of wine,
and an easy schedule which would get them to Albany before the roads turned muddy. Part two called for Admiral
Lord Howe to break north out of encircled Manhattan, sail
up the Hudson River, and join the general and the ladies.
Part three would include Oriskany, though Burgoyne hadn't
scheduled it. Barry St. Leger—lieutenant colonel, brigadier,
what you will, his titles never seem to be the same as you read

the record—was to go up the St. Lawrence from Montreal, turn east from Lake Ontario into the Oswego River, and continue through Oswego Lake and up Wood Creek until he came to the head of navigation on the Mohawk River. With him would be five hundred or six hundred king's regulars, Butler's Rangers, and "Johnson's Greens," the Tory militia made up of Mohawk Valley men who had a very special interest in the expedition.

Once on the Mohawk River, St. Leger should find the rest of the journey east to Albany a happy jaunt through towns decked out to welcome their liberators. The idiots who had raised liberty poles, and supported something called the Continental Congress, and cheered a so-called General Washington would change their tune when they heard the roll of king's drums echoing down the river. Then it would be Burgoyne, Howe, and St. Leger in Albany, and a happy time of mutual congratulation, posses chasing the last of the rebels into the hills, and the old order once again.

It would have been that way, too, if it hadn't been for men like Nicholas Herkimer and Robert Crouse, men like John Gardinier, who mustered with the Tryon County militia when the news came through of what St. Leger was up to. They didn't like being diverted from their black cattle, from clearing the land, planting, harvesting, barn raising, but they came when old Honikol said they had to.

Nicholas Herkimer, "Old Honikol" to most of the men who came to the musters, was a big man horizontally, but not tall. Like most of his Mohawk Valley breed, his speech was full of gutturals, for he was a second-generation German, born into one of those Palatine families that had been pioneers along the flat lands of the Schoharie and the western Mohawk River.

The way he and his neighbors saw things in August, 1777,

is worth noting. First, they were badly frightened. You could have told that by the way they were patching up and adding to the Tryon County forts and palisaded farmhouses; there was a string of them down the Schoharie and along the Mohawk as far west as the huge log-and-mud pile of Fort Stanwix, at the carrying place to Wood Creek. Herkimer and his neighbors had tried to call it Fort Schuyler, but the old name stuck.

They were scared because they knew what kind of fighting they could expect from Johnson's Greens, those old neighbors, king's men now, waiting for the word to come down from Canada to come home again. They knew, too, there'd be Senecas and Mohawks with St. Leger. What with the English offering $8 for ordinary farmers' scalps, and $10 to $20 for the scalps of militia officers and members of the patriot Committees of Safety, the fighting, when it came, would be ugly.

All that July the Tryon County farmers divided their time between their fields and the drills ordered by Brigadier General Nicholas Herkimer. The title didn't fit Old Honikol on the white horse that moved as though it were pulling a plow. His rusty blue officer's coat and the black clay pipe, however, were symbols of home-grown authority. The musters were ragged and there were plenty of slackers; but fear at least was directed into oiling boots and cleaning guns.

In 1777 a medium-good cannon might blow a ball three hundred yards. A man's fighting equipment, in the Mohawk Valley, consisted of a flintlock, a pound of powder, lead, a scalping knife, and bread and cheese in his knapsack. Orders to strike the enemy may cross continents and oceans now in less time then it took Old Honikol to breathe deep as he read the letter from Fort Stanwix that announced its defenders had positive information the Tories were marching home.

The fort at the carrying place was the only barrier worth talking about between Albany and St. Leger. Burgoyne's squeeze plan to end the Revolution may have been an academic matter to the men of Tryon County, but Colonel Marinus Willett's letter acted like a match touched to dry leaves. Johnson and Butler were sending Indians, Willett said, "to cut off communications between this and German Flats. . . . I hope this will not discourage you, but that your people will rise up unanimously." Johnson was expected to follow with perhaps a thousand of his Greens to finish what the Indians left undone.

That was to be it. Neighbor fighting neighbor. Brother fighting brother. Old Honikol's own brother and his nephew were Tory militiamen with Sir John.

Orders went out for every man from sixteen to sixty to gather on Sunday, August 3, at Fort Dayton across the river and about ten miles west of the big red-brick Herkimer house. The general's order said they were to come "ready to oppose the enemy with vigor." The old and the sick were to gather behind the stockades in their own neighborhoods. Everybody knew, though, that if St. Leger and the Indians got through to the women and children the war in the valley would be over. What they didn't know was that probably the war in America would be over.

Colonel Cox, a blowhard and a one-time drinking friend of Sir John Johnson's, insisted on leading the march the next day with his Canajoharie Regiment. Behind him was the Palatine Regiment, and then the regiment from the Kingsland and Palatine districts. Behind the wagons came Colonel Fisher, the troublemaker with the polished boots, whose Mohawk Regiment was detailed to guarding the supplies. The line of march, better than two miles long, looked like a county fair about to take to the road. There was little discipline.

Only a few of the officers wore uniforms. For the rest, the best that could be said for them was that they carried guns. You could have mustered the whole eight hundred of them on the USS *Oriskany's* flight deck, and still had room to park planes. No ship, however, and no body of men was ever charged with a greater task than was Old Honikol's Tryon County militia.

By the morning of August 3 the British Regulars with St. Leger were lobbing shells into Fort Stanwix. They would have laughed themselves sick if they could have seen the noisy mob starting west on the 4th to stop them. The drought was expected to break. The heat was bad. Oxen bellowed. The farm horses and the oxen strained against the traces of the supply wagons. Somewhere west of the dust and the stink there was thunder. General Herkimer and a knot of colonels, Veeder, Paris, Klock, Bellinger, Campbell, rode between the Canajoharie and Palatine regiments. Colonel Fisher was back and forth, yelling "Way to the right!" as the wagons edged his horse off the road.

They made camp that night at Stirling Creek, ten miles west of Fort Dayton. The drought hadn't broken, and the night air was heavy with the smell of the Mohawk and the smells of army and animals. The general and his colonels argued late over which road they'd take the next morning. The north-side wheel ruts would get them to Stanwix quicker, but they'd have to cross the river right at the fort, in the face of the enemy. Colonels Cox and Paris were all for speed. Herkimer, in his bent English, suggested the road along the south bank of the river. True, there was swampy land that way. But Colonel Gansevoort, in command of the fort, had laid a corduroy road across the worst of it. Better the south side, and avoid crossing the Mohawk in the face of St. Leger's guns. The meeting broke up in anger, the hotheads

like Cox sure the general was showing up as nothing but a
scared old man. Maybe even a disloyal one.

Tuesday morning was clear and August-hot. The best of
it was taken up in getting the horses and oxen over the ford
at Deerfield, to the south shore. Some of the county-fair
bounce was gone, for the men had seen burned-out cabins
in the clearings the day before.

That night the Tryon County militia bedded down between the Sauquoit and Oriskany creeks. The Mohawk was
on their right across a half mile or so of flat marshland. The
low Oriskany bluffs stretched west, though you couldn't see
much of them through the trees that crowded against the
road on both sides. There had been no rain yet. For a long
time, as the fires burned out, the general talked to some of
the Oneida Indians who had just arrived with intelligence to
report.

St. Leger had put a ring of regulars, militia, and Indians
completely around the fort. The Senecas were there, invited
by the British to sit on the side lines and watch Fort Stanwix's
seven hundred defenders beaten into a quick surrender. Johnson's Greens were there, waiting for permission to sweep down
the valley.

Old Honikol must have wondered how well his neighbors
out there in the night were going to stand up to British regulars. The older men remembered the fight at Niagara, during
the last of the French and Indian Wars, but the colonels, like
Cox?

Gansevoort, at Stanwix, would have to send out a relief,
when the fighting started. In order to get word to him, Herkimer sent for three men he knew could get through St. Leger's
outposts. He told them to tell the colonel to fire three cannon
shots to let him know when they got into the fort. If the
colonel heard small-arms fire east, down the river, he was to

send out that relief fast. The messengers took off into the night.

That next day, Wednesday, August 6, 1777, was the day the drought broke, when most of Old Honikol's men mixed their blood with the rain and made American independence possible.

None of them wanted it to happen the way it happened. Cox saw himself leading his Canajoharie Regiment to easy glory past St. Leger and into the drill yard of Fort Stanwix, with cheers from the bastions. Colonel Paris and half the rest were all for that.

The general's tent, Wednesday morning, was crowded with his officers. Cox and Fisher of the fancy boots protested violently when the general told them he thought it would be best to squat where they were, and wait for Gansevoort's three cannon shots from the fort. Wait! Wait for what?

There was more temporizing in that bent English. Honikol said he was not only a general leading troops. The men outside were old friends and neighbors, farmers, not British regulars. It would be better to wait.

Cox put on a boy-colonel scene, said he wouldn't wait for a coward. Paris and Fisher caught the glory fever. Someone shouted that Old Honikol was half Tory anyway, and never intended to march.

"Vorwaerts!" The clay pipe came out of the general's mouth as though it were a part of the command. There was a rush from the tent for the horses. The county fair was back on the road, and Cox was at the head of the line. You can't be sure what Herkimer was thinking as he swung onto his white horse, and moved up to join Cox. He could never have fitted his English to it. "Forward!" echoed back of them, until the command was lost behind the wagons and yelling drivers, back among Fisher's men.

They were on their way to the field of nettles. "Oriskany" is the Oneida Indian way of saying it, and the "Oriska" was the creek they soon waded through on their way to Fort Stanwix, seven miles beyond.

If you're laying blame for what happened next, put it on the colonels who were very cocky, very brave, and on Herkimer, who was first a good neighbor, and then a general. Two miles west of the creek their road dipped into a nameless fold in the hills. It then crossed a small stream draining through the ravine north toward the Mohawk. Logs had been laid across the stream and over the worst of the marsh.

Cox and his regiment and the general first, then Klock and Bellinger's regiments. Then the wagons, and, two miles back, Fisher's rear guard, pushing on the tailboards. The road went ahead, through the forest and down the ravine like an aisle in a dark temple. Honikol's men crowded along it as though they were a mob on a holiday, heading for the altar, and the priests preparing the sacrifice.

They were the sacrifice. St. Leger had sent out an ambush of Indians and troops in the early hours of Wednesday morning. Senecas were waiting behind the trees on both sides of the corduroy road through the ravine. Just beyond the west rim were the Rangers and the Greens, waiting.

One hopes Colonel Cox lived long enough to know what portion of that day was really his. He went down in the first crash of guns, as he and the general topped the west bank. A ball killed the white horse, and then smashed through to shatter Herkimer's left leg six inches below the knee.

Men who had fallen on their knees along the stream to drink never got up. Wagons just starting down the east slope rolled over their wounded and screaming horses, snarled in the traces. South and north, back and forth across the ravine the Senecas stitched shots into the torn army. Fisher and his

men, still east of the ravine, turned and ran, swarms of Indians after them.

Nobody else ran, and there's the glory of the field of nettles. Six hundred fifty men of the Tryon County militia made their own Thermopylae there in the woods of the western Mohawk Valley. Gun butt and knife, clubs, fists—they soon found out they had no use for the drill tricks the colonels had taught them.

Jan Van Eps, age thirteen, volunteer from Schenectady, helped carry the wounded Herkimer to the base of a near-by beech tree. Men said later Old Honikol hoisted himself up against his saddle they had found for him, got out that black clay pipe of his, and spent the whole of the five hours of Oriskany rallying and directing those who could hear him. When they tried to move him to a more protected spot, he thanked them and said, No, he'd face the enemy.

Some kind of defense formed. Captain Seeber got his men into a circle. Others did the same thing. The British Rangers and Johnson's Greens tried to break them up with a wild bayonet charge from west of the ravine. Tom, the patriot, recognizing Dick, the Tory, ripped him up with his hunting knife. Neighbors of last year died as they blasted each other's faces off at short range.

Then the drought broke. The rain washed war out of their powder and drove the English and Indians back into the woods for cover. It swelled what is still called Bloody Creek, and gave the defenders an hour to help the wounded and rally on the higher ground west of the ravine. Herkimer now ordered his men to double up behind the trees they were picking out for defense. He had noticed earlier that the Indians had waited for a man to fire, and then as he reloaded they would leap out from cover to shoot or knife him.

At eleven o'clock the signal cannons at the fort went off.

Some kind of sally would be made. The rain moved on down the valley.

Johnson's Greens now tried a trick. They turned their campaign coats inside out so that they would look something like the expected relief, and took the hats the Indians had brought back from the dead and wounded they had been scalping during the lull. Then they marched toward the defense lines. Captain Gardinier, one of Fisher's Mohawk men who hadn't run, yelled out, "Don't you see them green coats?"

From then on anything went. Gardinier was knocked down as he tried to save one of his own men who had been taken in by the trick; both of his thighs were pinned to the ground with bayonets. Adam Miller brained one of the Greens who tried to shove his knife through the captain's chest. Gardinier, in spite of the bayonets skewering him to the ground, was able to grab a spear and run it through one of his attackers who had turned now on Miller.

The Bayonet Tree got its name when one of Herkimer's men was crucified on it. George Walter lay beside a spring, pretending to be dead while an Indian ran a scalping knife around his skull, tearing off, finally, hair and skin from the bloody head. The Senecas captured Robert Crouse, the tallest and strongest man in Tryon County. They trussed him up, and then, in order to cut him down to their size, they whittled his legs off below the knees, cut the ropes holding him, and told him to walk.

For two hours or more it was every man for himself. Old Honikol's militia was still fighting Greens and Rangers when they heard the Senecas' retreat cry of "Oonah! Oonah!" echoing through the woods. The Indians, who had only come to watch the British show, had had enough. "Oonah! Oonah!" faded west, toward the fort. The English followed fast enough, when they realized the Indians were quitting.

By midafternoon the Battle of Oriskany was over. In the ooze of Bloody Creek, among the flyblown horses and shattered wagons were almost four hundred Tryon County dead. There were about two hundred fighting men on their feet, and forty or so walking wounded. They held their positions long enough to be sure the field was theirs, and then they went to work making stretchers out of anything they could find. By late afternoon they had gathered up the wounded and started back over the road they had come down that morning like a holiday mob. The dead they left along Bloody Creek and in the field of nettles were never buried.

That night Herkimer was taken downriver, to Fort Dayton. The rest of the men followed the next day, silent, bitter, and, as far as they knew, defeated.

Terror soon made its own invasion along the Mohawk. Old Honikol, though his neighbors didn't know it then, was dying. There was little left of the county-fair army that had gathered at Fort Dayton three days earlier.

And that was the Battle of Oriskany. It was ugly, and stupid, and, in its agony, a theme for poets. Old Honikol's men thought they were defeated because they had not got through to the fort. St. Leger, however, whose eye was on Albany, never again put troops east of Bloody Creek. And because he failed, Burgoyne's whole plan collapsed at the Battle of Saratoga.

It was as though the navy's USS *Oriskany* had, by some miracle, stopped a conquering fleet, and, by her own death, given the victory to others.

16

The Bright Deception

Iᴛ ᴡᴀs Han Yost Schuyler, a Tory half-wit, and General Benedict Arnold who raised the siege of Fort Stanwix. The two of them put on a game of bluff that must have made Barry St. Leger wish he'd never been born. It was St. Leger who started the bluffing, but the game soon passed out of his hands.

After the fighting at Oriskany, the British and their Indian allies found themselves stalled before the picket-filled ditch that surrounded the fort. The shells St. Leger's junior-size cannon threw into the drill yard killed a few men, but made no dent in the ramparts. His Indians screeched in the dark beyond the glacis and the moat in the hope of intimidating the garrison, but Gansevoort's men had heard that sort of thing before.

What to do? If you can't blow an opening in a fort, bluff it open. St. Leger must have worked out his plans among his wine bottles, for certainly no sober man could have believed anyone but an idiot or a coward would fall for them.

Two days after the Tryon County men had failed to raise the siege Colonel John Butler of the British Rangers, paymaster for the bloody scalps the Indians brought in, and two other officers, strode across the treeless parade in front of the fort, bearing a flag of truce. Colonel Butler knew most of the officers inside; they were old neighbors in better days. After the preliminaries were over, and there had been comments about the weather, Butler presented St. Leger's demand for an immediate surrender. It was so bombastic that Colonel Gansevoort and his officers hardly knew how to treat it. The British, St. Leger thought, could still save the garrison from the enraged Indians who had recently suffered unfortunate reverses. The British, St. Leger thought, might even save the lower valley from a horrible massacre; but it was all conditional, of course, on surrender now. The insult was compounded by a letter Colonel Butler now delivered, written under duress, it was perfectly obvious, by two of Herkimer's officers who had been captured at Oriskany.

Poor Bellinger! He and Major Frey must have writhed as they wrote it. General Burgoyne, they had been made to say, was already in Albany. Fort Stanwix's communications, of course, were cut off, and the enemy "had a large parcel of fine troops, and an excellent park of artillery." If that last remark was true, what were those tennis balls St. Leger was lobbing over the parapets? The surrender demand ended on quite a high note: "as an act of humanity and to prevent the effusion of blood, (they) begged (us) to give up the fort."

Fort Stanwix's commanding officer was twenty-eight years old, but he had learned to say "No!" in fine, clear English. ". . . it is my determined resolution," he wrote to St. Leger, ". . . to defend this fort at every hazard, to the last extremity, in behalf of the United States who have placed me here to defend it against all their enemies."

A man who wrote that was not going to open his gates to anyone less than Gabriel. St. Leger was discouraged. The

futility of banging away with his undersize cannon must have
given rise to his next move, a piece of bravado that should
have been done to music. The general knew he couldn't send
a real force down the Mohawk Valley while Fort Stanwix
acted like a stuck stopper in a wine bottle. But did the people
of Tryon County know that? If they could be made to think
they were about to be put to the sword, what would they do?
If someone could go down there among them with propa-
ganda material and a good noisy proclamation, the results
might be very interesting. Enough Tories might come out of
their hiding places to swing the whole Mohawk Valley back
into the old orbit.

Ensign Walter Butler was the man to try the bluff. There
had been few more rabid supporters of the Sir John Johnson
way of life in the valley than young Butler. He and his father,
Colonel John Butler, who hadn't done well with the flag of
truce, had risen to power with the Johnsons, fattened themselves on outsize land grants, and were quite ready to risk
anything now to restore George III's authority.

St. Leger didn't know it, but the night before Ensign
Butler and some dozen men started down the river for German Flats, Lieutenant Colonel Marinus Willett and a companion slipped out of Fort Stanwix, through the British lines,
and started downriver also, heading for Albany to speed up
the expected relief. St. Leger's bluff would pass into far more
capable hands when young Butler and Colonel Willett met
six days later.

The ensign must have thought he had on the armor of
the Lord, or that there were no more patriots in the Mohawk
Valley. The slaughter at Oriskany, he knew, would bring into
the open any number of Tories who had been mouthing
loyalty to the Continental Congress in order to hold their
lands. He could count on their help. Being a lawyer, however,

he tried to give a faint legal sanction to his hare-brained expedition by carrying what he called a flag of truce, though no one had agreed to it but St. Leger.

Sometime Tuesday or Wednesday he arrived at Shoemaker's Tavern, a known Tory hangout about two miles above Fort Dayton, on the south shore of the Mohawk. There he set up a kind of recruiting office. In spite of the fact that a north wind would carry the smell of the fort's mess into Shoemaker's windows, Butler put out a call to the German Flats farmers to be on hand after dark. For pure nerve, Butler's recruiting call in the middle of enemy country would be hard to beat.

Needless to say, Colonel Weston, at Fort Dayton, heard about it. That night, when his soldiers surrounded Shoemaker's, they could hear snatches of Walter Butler's oratory, as full of heat as the still air in the valley. The blinds were closed, and the rooms were jammed with Tories and weathervane patriots.

". . . if they do not surrender the garrison," he was saying, "the Indians will put every soul to death, (and) the whole country without regard to age, sex, or friends . . . you cannot hesitate a moment . . ." Colonel Weston's troops broke down the doors and took Ensign Butler and Han Yost Schuyler prisoners.

St. Leger, it seemed, could neither blow Fort Stanwix's gate open nor bluff it open. While he loaded and fired, and waited for the rush to the king's colors in the Mohawk Valley, other men were moving on-stage, better fitted to confuse and mystify.

General Benedict Arnold and eight hundred men were detached for the Stanwix relief from the rapidly swelling army that was gathering to block Burgoyne from Albany. When Colonel Willett arrived from Fort Stanwix, Arnold's expedition was already on its way up the valley. By the 16th of

August they were at Fort Dayton, and busy with the court-martial proceedings against the brash young Ranger who thought the men of Tryon County didn't know their own minds.

Ensign Butler turned lawyer quick enough when he saw the gallows' shadow. He hung his defense on the thin fiction that he was a flag, not a spy. Arnold's prosecutor said Butler had been at Shoemaker's Tavern for only one purpose: "to seduce the inhabitants." The defendant then neatly confused the issue by saying that no law but king's law had any application, implying that everyone in the courtroom but himself was a criminal. When asked why he hadn't made himself known to Colonel Weston at Fort Dayton, if he had come down as a flag, he replied that "he knew no Colonel Weston nor Fort Dayton."

The ensign was sentenced to be hanged by the neck. Too bad, in a way, that higher authority interfered and had him shipped down to Albany for further examination. Because he was able to escape from the Albany jail, that winter the Cherry Valley Massacre took place in which the frustrated young Ranger had a major part.

The next case for consideration was that of Han Yost Schuyler, the half-wit who had come down the river with Butler. The procedure was routine. The boy had deserted from the Tryon County militia months before, and gone off to Canada with his Tory neighbors. No one seemed to know why Butler had brought along such an unprepossessing specimen. General Arnold knew a traitor when he saw one, and only agreed to the mild penalty of one hundred lashes because Han Yost had no sense.

Then someone, no one knows who now, thought up the bright deception. Han Yost's mother and brother had come up to the fort from the Little Falls neighborhood in the hope of getting General Arnold to turn Han Yost over to them. Tears and pleading had got the mother nowhere. But, someone suggested, perhaps Han Yost could be used.

St. Leger was now going to learn something about bluffing. The Indians, it was pointed out, had always held Han Yost in considerable awe. Half-wits, the Indians said, spoke in riddles, and could see into a world closed to ordinary men. Fine. Now, suppose Han Yost could see, say, two thousand soldiers with General Arnold instead of the eight hundred who were with him? And suppose he could be counted on to report to St. Leger's Indians that the two thousand soldiers were on their way up the Mohawk to the relief of the fort? It was an interesting idea.

Benedict Arnold liked the idea. In fact, it wouldn't hurt to add a few touches. Odd schemes were quite at home in his mind. An Oneida Indian was found around Fort Dayton who was glad to have a hand in making the Senecas and Canadian Indians look foolish. He agreed to start out for Stanwix soon after Han Yost "escaped" from the guardhouse. Then, after Han Yost had finished telling his story to the Indians, the Oneida would come into their camp from another direction, and tell them all over again about the two thousand soldiers coming up the river road.

Han Yost was delighted with the plan. He would have no trouble seeing any number of troops they wanted him to. Tory or Whig, it made no difference to him; but one hundred lashes did. His mother offered to stay as a hostage for the boy, but Fort Dayton's officers would not agree to that. They finally accepted Nicholas Schuyler's offer to remain in the guardhouse until his brother completed his agreement.

That night Han Yost slipped through the sally port as the guard looked the other way. His slow wits, turning like the wooden wheels in the clock as he hurried up the river road,

counted off the landmarks. He fingered the fresh bullet holes
in his dirty campaign coat. Arnold's officers had thought of
everything.

St. Leger's Indians were in just the right mood to listen
to someone like Han Yost. Nothing had gone right for them.
While they were filling Bloody Creek at Oriskany with Old
Honikol's men, Colonel Willett and his troops had burst out
of Fort Stanwix, stormed through the Indian camp and Sir
John's camp, picking up everything in sight, to their last pot
and blanket. They'd gotten nothing from Oriskany but a poor
haul of scalps, and they'd lost their best chiefs in the fighting.
They had turned away from St. Leger's excuses and promises
to their own councils, and from them to a powwow in the
hope the Great Manitto might have words of wisdom for
them. As the Indians waited in awe for the ancestral voices,
Han Yost came out of the forest.

There were frightened looks toward the river, as Han
Yost tried to get his tongue back. The audience was tuned
and ready, and Han Yost didn't let them down. First there
was a rush of questions. Men with guns down there, Han
Yost? How many men, Han Yost? Have they started up the
river yet, Han Yost?

How many men? Wild-eyed, Han Yost lifted his hands
toward the beech and elm branches over his head. How many
men? As many as there are leaves! See the bullet holes! He'd
been caught with Butler . . . they all knew Butler, who paid
for the scalps? His son! Han Yost had been caught by the
soldiers, but he had run away, and the bullets had zinged
through his coat! They were going to kill him!

Han Yost had found his tongue. St. Leger had him
brought to his tent, where the half-wit repeated his tale, em-
broidering it with a harrowing account of his capture at Shoemaker's Tavern, Arnold's courts-martial, and then his own

escape. Yes, yes! Arnold had two thousand soldiers. Maybe more. They were going to pay the British back for what had happened at Oriskany. Old Honikol was dead, and the two thousand soldiers were coming up the river now!

Fear spread among the Indians like smallpox. When the Oneida arrived and confirmed what Han Yost had said, that was all that was needed. St. Leger and Sir John cajoled and pleaded, but the Indians were listening downwind for Arnold's men.

When other Oneida braves, prompted by the first one, began arriving among the frightened Senecas with hints of terrible things revealed to them by an oracular bird, fear turned into panic, and St. Leger's Indians took to the woods.

The panic quickly spread to the troops. Knapsacks and arms were thrown into the underbrush. Blankets and kettles were left by the fires. Panic turned into a rout when the troops heard firing in the rear, and voices yelling, "They are coming! They are coming!"

They didn't know it at first, but their own Indians were having their little joke. One by one the British stragglers were picked off, bayoneted with their own guns they had just thrown away. Tory scalps, the Indians knew, would bring just as much in Canada as any other kind. St. Leger was now retreating as fast from his own allies as he was from the ghost army Han Yost had conjured up.

The bright deception had worked, and Han Yost Schuyler's task was over. The men of Fort Stanwix, on Friday, August 22, must have looked across their parapets in amazement. Where was the enemy? At noon they took in a deserter who told them three thousand men were on their way up to raise the siege, and furthermore, that Burgoyne's army above Albany was in retreat.

It was a great day at the carrying place. In the fort "the

woman who was wounded with a shell last night was brought to bed in our southwest bombproof of a daughter." All the fort's cannon were now brought to bear on the enemy's works, and fired several times; but there was no one in St. Leger's camp to return the shots.

Han Yost struggled up to the fort's gate that night, clutching one end of a heavy chest he and a terrified British soldier had just pilfered from the deserted camp. Once inside, there was no problem in getting Han Yost to talk. The whole weird story tumbled out of him, including the little plan to frighten the Indians. He was pleased with the attention he got, and would the gentlemen like to see the holes in his coat?

Beyond the walls of the fort one could hear the forgotten, friendly night sounds again: frogs in Oriskany swamp, leaves shaking in the wind.

Saturday morning the men took "the free air agin," and helped to clean up for General Arnold's arrival. The baby girl born on Friday was doing well. Major Cochran made a sweep of the area and brought back three prisoners, four cowhorn mortars, and wagonloads of British baggage. There was plenty of loot everywhere, a wonderful confusion which included even St. Leger's private papers. Around noon a sad-looking German was brought in, one of the Hessians. He had been cowering in the woods, hoping the Indians would miss him. He told the garrison he had seen fleeing Tories butchered right and left as they fled toward Wood Creek. Han Yost was around, showing off his ventilated coattails.

Five miles east of Fort Stanwix Arnold's men skirted the fields of Oriskany and Bloody Creek, their stomachs knotting as the stench closed around them like a putrid fog. There was no avoiding the Tryon County dead. Some say the men stopped to bury them; others swear no man could have stopped among those corpses, two weeks gone under the August sun and the ceremonial of the blowflies.

By late afternoon the relief column, drums beating, moved out of the forest and into the open fields of the Trow-Plat. There, beyond the great bend of the Mohawk, they saw Fort Stanwix, the ramparts crowded with Colonel Gansevoort's men, shouting wildly. Someone organized the uproar into three hearty cheers. As the column moved ahead there was a crash of all thirteen cannon, half of which had been St. Leger's.

Some of the more curious, as they marched through the gate, were wondering what kind of flag that was waving over the northeast corner of the fort. They had no trouble recognizing the five captured British flags underneath it, but the one on top was something new: red stripes, white stripes, circle of stars on a blue square. They heard later it was the one the Congress had approved. The officers of the fort had made it up during the siege out of an old shirt, a British officer's blue field coat, and a woman's red skirt. It looked nice up there, as it caught the wind. It was the first time the American flag had ever been flown in combat.

17

Whipping Boy

Beneath the pew in which you sit
They say that Walter Butler's buried.
In such a fix, across the Styx
I wonder who his soul has ferried?

. And so the ages yet unborn
Shall sing your fame in song and story
How ages gone you sat upon
A Revolutionary Tory. . . .
> From *Alexandria, and Other Poems,* by
> Dr. Rogers Tayler, former rector of St.
> George's Church, Schenectady, N.Y.

Is the body under the right aisle, third pew from the front?
Who would have dared to bring it, bloody, newly scalped,
down the back trails from West Canada Creek to the Mohawk, and then to a midnight burial under the pavement of
St. George's Episcopal Church, Schenectady? Who would
have dared!

They say that on a night in early November, 1781, when
runners brought the news that Walter Butler had been killed,
every Whig house in town was illuminated to celebrate the

event, and that the Whigs marched around to the houses of known Tory sympathizers and made them fill their windows with candles, like it or not.

"Archfiend . . . rapist . . . baby killer . . ." the whole valley went on an orgy of metaphor making until you would have thought Walter Butler had walked along the river on cloven hoofs. If he is buried under the third pew of the right aisle of starched and godly St. George's, it would be simple justice to cut into the stone over his shattered skull: "Here Lies the Whipping-Boy of the American Revolution."

Terror, anger, hunger for revenge were the emotions men lived by, Tories and Whigs alike, for the war in the Mohawk Valley had been all violence, a vast feud between neighbors and brothers. Hate hung like a mephitic mist over the summer river, and like an ice-fog over the bloody winter snow.

This was a climate for myths and legends. Here, in the half-lights, Walter Butler the Tory walked back and forth over the disemboweled bodies of his victims, as real a devil here as Satan was to Cotton Mather. Like Satan, Walter Butler was everywhere, and, like Satan, he was incarnate Evil. "Butler's burned Wyoming!" "Butler's south of Cobleskill!" "Butler's murderers are on the Flats!" Butler—Butler—Butler . . . The name finally had a ring to it like the cracked bell of the Black Mass.

The Butler legend began to take shape after the Battle of Oriskany, as the valley waited for St. Leger to sweep down it, when Walter Butler stood in the court-martial room at Fort Dayton and told his judges he recognized only King's Law. He implied they were a pack of Whig criminals without power to try him. He was twenty-five then, arrogant enough to think he could recruit Tories in the heart of enemy country.

People remembered he had run with Sir John Johnson in the days when Sir John and his mistress Clara Putnam and

Sir John's two bastards were living at Fort Johnson. That's what people said, anyway. Walter was handsome as the Devil, but he had a bad eye. That's what people said. They remembered him as a young law student in Albany. Very gay, he was, at the patroon's parties, very gay with the girls. People remembered these things when, after he had escaped the noose or a firing squad at Fort Dayton, he had been taken down to the Tory jail at Albany. Lucky Walter Butler! Handsome devil, but a bad eye.

He escaped from Albany of an April night in 1778. No one had seen him go, but for a man like Walter Butler it must have been done in high style: "It is said . . ." so rumor has things, that he got his sentinel drunk, that there was a horse waiting for him outside the private house where he had been jailed, that he fled north, or west, or south. There must have been dark plotting to let such a Tory prize escape in a dark-o'-the-moon jail break. There's magic in the man! Walter Butler was now well on the way to becoming a Folk Figure.

March of 1778 began the bloodletting in the valley. The Fairfield settlements, north of Little Falls, got the first of the year's hit-and-run raids. The pattern was typical! Tories and Indians down from Canada, back among their old homes, this time on snowshoes, burning out farmers, smashing skulls, taking prisoners. John Mabee, age fifteen, cutting potatoes for cattle, tomahawked and scalped. The Klocks, Forbushes, Shafers, no females this time, carried into captivity. No Tories burned out; their houses were left for their owners to move back into, come the day when the last rebel was chased into the hills.

Then Ephrata was attacked late in April. Along Garoga Creek was a huddle of log cabins and grainfields owned by some twenty German families. Some of the men were in the sugar bush when the Indians and Tories sifted among them. A young girl ran to where the settlement's small militia company was drilling and screamed she'd just seen her father tomahawked. That stopped the soldiering. The men became fathers and brothers as the company broke up and rushed pell-mell to their own cabins. The rest was a matter of selective murder. One settler was found the next day propped up against his oven, a bayonet through his heart. The scalped body of his four-year-old son was found in a nearby creek, a spoon clutched in his hand. A girl was shot as she was driving cows home. Those who escaped crowded into Fort Paris, just north of Stone Arabia. The rest were herded up the Canada trails into captivity.

The German farmer on Garoga Creek, a militiaman at Fort Dayton, bateauxmen ferrying supplies from Schenectady up the Mohawk to the forts, these saw the war in wholly personal terms: a father murdered in his barn among the cattle, a sister killed and scalped as she drove her cattle in from pasture, a baby smashed against a cabin wall. They saw the Revolution in terms of their burning barns, the summer crop lost, and the cattle slaughtered or driven off. For them the war was what Tom did, was Dick turned Tory and gone to Canada, was Harry killed. It was doorstep war, and any moment the doorstep might be your own.

The survivors of the raids and their friends, of course, were not privy to British grand strategy. Ruin the grain that feeds Washington's army. Push back the frontier east as far as you can: cut off Fort Stanwix and the frontier falls back to the middle Mohawk and the grain will rot on the stalk in the German Flats. Keep hitting the valley, and perhaps the frontier will shrink east again until it runs north and south from Schenectady. If that happens, the Continental Army may starve to death, and your rebels are licked. Such thinking, to the Butlers, made sense.

And so there was the first of the Butler "massacres." Before the Mohawk Valley, Pennsylvania, and Jersey were laid open for final destruction, it would be good strategy for the raiders to protect Unadilla, their advanced base of operations. South of Unadilla was the Wyoming Valley, with its three American forts. North and east of it was Cherry Valley and Fort Alden. The Cherry Valley streams flow into the Susquehanna, but its people looked north toward the Mohawk Valley for help, and did most of their trading there along its banks.

The Wyoming raid preceded the Cherry Valley horror. By the time Major Butler had dismissed his Indians and had got his Tories back to Fort Niagara he was being damned for a murderer as blackhearted as Genghis Khan. No one stopped to think that he hadn't invented Indian warfare, or knew that it was Major John Butler who had resisted as long as he could the pressure from above to use Indians in the frontier fighting. The patriots had a border villain now. The Wyoming stories were quickly improved by introducing Walter Butler as villain-assistant to his father on that occasion, though the young Ranger captain was actually in Canada.

Unadilla was safe from the south, however. The elimination of Wyoming had been a sound tactical move. The arc of attack logically swung north now, where the Mohawk Valley waited, its borders defended only by Fort Stanwix, thirty miles west of the still-occupied river settlements, and Fort Alden, at Cherry Valley, named for the incompetent New England colonel who commanded it.

That September the Mohawk Valley proper found out what an Indian raid, well organized, could really do. Under

Joseph Brant, Sir William Johnson's protégé, one hundred fifty savages and three hundred Tories moved on the German Flats, coming up from the base at Unadilla. That was the September day the scout Adam Helmar ran twenty-six miles, enemy Indians at times within rods of his heels, to bring the news to Fort Herkimer that Brant was coming.

When that raid was over, ten miles of the valley, from Little Falls west to Frankfort, was a smoking ruin. The summer harvest was gone. Gristmills, sawmills, better than sixty houses and as many outbuildings had been destroyed. A thousand horses, and cattle and sheep were killed or driven off by the invaders. Adam Helmar had saved his neighbors from the hatchet, but Brant had left them ten miles of dead land.

Smash the Indians! Smash the Indian castles around Unadilla and you pay back Bloody Butler and Brant. Tit for tat, and a thoroughgoing tat it was. The Albany command sent out a detachment with specific instructions to destroy everything it could along the Unadilla River. It did. Walter Butler said later that his Indians really went out of control at Cherry Valley because of the destruction the Americans wreaked on the Unadilla people and villages.

Everyone in command positions knew Cherry Valley would be next. No one thought the attack would come when it did, but then Walter Butler had always surprised people. November was no time for Indians to fight; that was their hunting season. The British wouldn't be fools enough to move that far away from comfortable Fort Niagara with snow weather closing the trails.

Walter Butler, on November 10, 1778, however, came into Cherry Valley with fifty British regulars, about a hundred fifty Tories, and six hundred Indians led by Joseph Brant. If Butler had been asked how he would like things arranged at Cherry

Valley in order to make his conquest easy, he probably would have been satisfied to leave things as he found them the next day. All except the weather. They spent that night about a mile southwest of the fort, cursing a cold rain which turned to snow before morning.

The Walter Butler of legend, whose death Schenectady celebrated with a general illumination, was born that next morning in the mists that hid Colonel Alden's fort and the forty houses of the town. When the attack came at eleven o'clock the colonel and his chief officers and the headquarters company were enjoying the heat from Mr. Wells' fireplaces, in a comfortable house about a quarter of a mile from the fort. Colonel Alden had been so sure there would be no attack that he had told the townspeople to stay away from the fort, that their houses were quite safe enough.

And so the colonel had his head smashed in and his scalp taken as he ran from the safe house to his fort, whose gates were closed as the enemy rushed the stockade. The rest of Mr. Wells' military guests were either killed or taken prisoner before they knew what had happened. Butler and the Tories kept the fort under heavy fire. The Indians, who never liked siege tactics, apparently filtered back through the village and into the houses, where they ran amuck. There was no order from Walter Butler to do this. The Senecas and the Mohawks with Brant, however, were remembering Oriskany and the recent wrecking of the Unadilla villages. Thirteen members of Mr. Wells' own household were killed. Eighteen or nineteen other villagers were killed at the same time in an orgy of scalping and burning.

What did Walter Butler do? As soon as he heard what was going on behind his back he sent out a detachment to round up the village families in order to give them protection.

But Walter Butler and his Rangers were in the minority, and the Indians in an ugly mood. In spite of them, he gave the stricken men, women, and children protection through the grim hours that followed.

The fort held out against the next day's attack. The order was given, finally, to break off, and begin the dismal journey back to Niagara. Of all the civilian prisoners he could have taken back with him Butler took only nine, hostages, he wrote later, for his own mother and aunt who were held in custody in Albany. These prisoners, he said, he would exchange for his own family at the first opportunity.

The Cherry Valley Massacre was no tortured invention of a revengeful, murdering Walter Butler, the mythmakers to the contrary. British grand strategy required the destruction of Fort Alden as part of the plan to starve Washington and push the frontier as far east as possible. At Wyoming and Cherry valleys the Butlers learned again the old lesson that Indians will not be bound by army orders: Walter Butler, sick of the whole business, swore after he got back to Niagara that he would never again take out a force in which savages were in the majority.

From the time of Cherry Valley until today, however, Walter Butler has stalked in massive horror back and forth along the frontier, ankle deep in blood. His reported genius for evil was exceeded only by his ability to be in two places at once. There are still those in the Mohawk Valley who like to lay a lash across the back of this whipping boy.

One writer says that Cherry Valley so horrified the governor of Canada that he refused to see young Butler. The truth, which is so often printed in history's smallest type, is that Governor Haldimand was delighted with his Ranger captain's success.

"Bloody and barbarous deeds . . . one of the greatest scourges . . . deeds of rapine, of murder, of hellish hue," Walter Butler's conduct "was stamped with the deepest, the darkest, most damning guilt . . ." so writer after writer testified, one happily copying the prejudices of his predecessor, or improving on them.

A new high in verbal hysteria was hit almost a hundred fifty years after the massacre, when a local historian delivered himself of this blast on the Butlers: "Barbarous, treacherous, revengeful, ferocious, merciless, brutal, diabolically wicked and cruel, with the spirit of fiends, they committed cruelties worthy of the dungeons of the Inquisition." Move over, Satan!

A few historians have troubled themselves to look at the record. Briefly, all the official contemporary accounts, Whig and Tory alike, diaries, letters, reports, agree that where there were Indians there were barbarities, and where there were Indians in numbers there were massacres. In none of these records, however, were the Butlers ever charged with the crimes heaped on them by the mythmakers. British and American policy sanctioned the use of Indians, and the Butlers were British officers waging war according to orders. They had an ugly assignment, and there is good reason to believe they hated it.

Walter Butler the Whipping Boy was more interesting, more exciting, however, than Walter Butler the British officer. From 1901 through 1921 novelist Robert Chambers drove Walter Butler from one blood-wet tale to another. *Cardigan, The Maid at Arms, The Reckoning, The Hidden Children,* and *Little Red Foot* are strong meat-and-drink stories of the days of Sir William Johnson and the Revolution. Walter Scott's music is in all of them; an antiphonal choir of heroes and villains sings, not under Scott's Gothic roofs but as romantically, nevertheless, at Johnson Hall, along the raid trails from

Canada, "through the dusk of primeval woods," at Oriskany and Cherry Valley.

Here, from *The Reckoning*, is what the tuned soul may expect from a visit to the Butler house, above Fonda: ". . . ghosts of the victims of old John Butler, wraiths dripping red from Cherry Valley—children with throats cut; women with bleeding heads and butchered bodies, stabbed through and through—and perhaps the awful specter of Lieutenant Boyd with eyes and nails plucked out, and tongue cut off, bound to the stake and slowly roasting to death, while Walter Butler watched the agony curiously, interested and surprised to see a disemboweled man live so long!" Nice? A small detail, but John Butler was not at Cherry Valley, and Walter Butler was elsewhere when Lieutenant Boyd was made a living sacrifice by the Indians in part payment for General Sullivan's fire-and-sword tour through the Seneca country.

The Hidden Children tells how the Indians were paid back for Cherry Valley in the Sullivan-Clinton campaign of extermination in 1779. Here is the brutalized Ranger captain of all those frustrated, poorly protected valley people who needed a whipping boy to help drain off their rage: ". . . young Walter Butler damned his soul for all eternity while men, women and children, old and young, died horribly amid the dripping knives and bayonets of his painted fiends, or fell under the butchering hatchets of his Senecas." That was Cherry Valley again, of course.

Walter Edmonds, in his fine, honestly focused *Drums Along the Mohawk*, puts Butler's part in that massacre straight, though in doing it he played a dirty trick on our mythmakers. Fort Alden, which was what Butler wanted, was under attack. Behind him in the town he heard the "shrill screeching of the Seneca war cry . . . Captain Butler raised up one arm to look back. His face was bitter and hopeless.

He said distinctly, 'Oh, my God. Brant's taken all the Indians into the town!' " And then: "The weary Rangers were mustered and sent to protect the burning houses, but it was too late. . . . All through the settlement were signs of the Indian work."

In 1781, the year the Tryon County people killed off their villain, a tour of the valley would have shown why they were full of bitterness and hatred for everything British: the militia had begun the war with a muster of twenty-five hundred men; there were now eight hundred men left capable of doing duty. Seven hundred buildings had been destroyed. Twelve thousand farms in the Mohawk River watershed were fading out into wilderness, and Washington's armies had lost 150,000 bushels of grain. Among the people who stayed in the ruin, almost four hundred of the women were widows and two thousand of the children were orphans. Fort Stanwix had capitulated to unexpected enemies when floods and an incendiary's fire drove the garrison back to Forts Dayton and Herkimer. What life there was left in Tryon County revolved around the twenty-four blockhouses and forts higher authority had been able to establish. Brant's Indians and Sir John Johnson and the Greens had made the preceding two years a monotony of horror.

So Walter Butler, on his third trip to the valley during the Revolution, made a part payment on the enormous bill his old neighbors had ready for England. Oriskany, and Cherry Valley, and at last for him the end of bright danger on the bank of West Canada Creek.

On his last raid he was second in command to a Major Ross. There were six hundred thirty Greens and Rangers and perhaps one hundred thirty Indians. They left their bateaux at Oneida Lake. Through the rain and mud of late October 1781, they tramped toward Cherry Valley, and then north to the Mohawk, where they came out on the south side of the river in Warrensbush. By the 25th, Schenectady was only a dozen miles east of them. Ross wrote later: "Near one hundred farms, three mills and a large granary for publick service were reduced to ashes." It was the old story. Although Cornwallis had been defeated at Yorktown, the Canadians were far from ready to admit that the war was over. Their stakes in the Mohawk Valley were too big.

Ross moved fast and cautiously, for the neighborhood forts were islands of danger around him. With seven miles of the valley in flames, and no question but that Colonel Willett's regulars and militia were after him, Ross beat a retreat across the Mohawk below Amsterdam, and then circled back toward Johnstown.

In the woods back of Johnson Hall, in the rain, with night almost on them, Colonel Willett's men and the Ross-Butler raiders fought out the last real battle of the Revolution in the Mohawk Valley. If Willett hadn't divided his forces, he might have won a quicker victory. As it was, he sent half his men around the raiders' flank; until they were in position, he took a terrible beating. His men lost a cannon, and broke once, and fled into Johnstown. By the time Willett had rallied them, his strategy proved itself, for he found the raiders wildly trying to turn the attack which rushed in on them from the rear.

Night ended the Battle of Johnstown. Ross and Butler and their men, desperately weary, began their hounded retreat. For the next two days they were dogged by Willett's scouts as they struggled west and north, toward the Canada trails, all hope of backtracking to Oneida Lake abandoned.

On the 29th, Colonel Willett, after having received supplies at Fort Dayton, was camped a few miles south of Ross, on the royal grant, once the center of Sir William Johnson's huge barony. Ahead of him the raiders were still floundering in the new snow, trying to find their trail, getting what strength they could out of a ration of a half pound of horse meat per man.

The chase was getting hot. The next morning, as Willett's men approached West Canada Creek, they found the woods around them strewn with the enemy's packs, his horses turned loose. The scouts knew Ross and Butler were in full flight, their men dogtrotting north as fast as they could go.

Between two and three that afternoon Walter Butler settled all his scores. First, there was his death, according to Olendorf. Daniel Olendorf, of Mindon, one of Willett's militiamen, said he was there at the kill. He said he saw Butler on the west side of Canada Creek try to rally Ross's rear guard, just as he and Anthony, one of Willett's Indians, broke into the clearing on the east side of the fording place. Walter Butler, Olendorf said, then came down to the creek with a tin cup, and filled it. As he started to drink, Anthony and Olendorf each took a bead on him and fired. As Butler fell back, the Indian splashed across the ford, brandishing his tomahawk. Butler, writhing in agony, called out to Anthony, "Spare me . . . give me quarter!" "Me give you Sherry Valley quarter!" With that curtain-line retort Anthony is supposed to have brained his victim.

Olendorf remembered that just as the captain expired Colonel Willett forded Canada Creek as Anthony was in the act of slitting off Butler's scalp. Anthony, apparently thinking of his manners, asked permission of an Oneida Indian officer who was with the colonel to go on with the scalping. The finale was in the grand manner. Willett was reported to have said to the Oneida, "He is of your party, Colonel Lewis." The Oneida gave the nod to Anthony, who then completed his job of woodland surgery.

The Mohawk Valley reveled in that scene for years.

Another report of the death of Walter Butler has the low-comedy note that must have lent itself to tavern narrative: A Major Thornton of Schenectady claimed to have the facts. First, there was a heavy fog, hiding most of the action. Americans and Britishers blazed away at each other across West Canada Creek, unable to see their targets. When the enemy decamped, Thornton was one of the first to ford the stream, where he found the inevitable Indian gazing at the lifeless body of Walter Butler. Thornton pulled off Butler's hat with the gold band around it, and saw that a bullet had passed through his skull. Then, having performed these coroner's rites, he had the Indian pull off Butler's pants, and there, behind the draperies of the fog, made a pantaloon exchange with the dead man.

On one point only were the eyewitnesses in agreement: Walter Butler was dead.

Robert Chambers, who was certainly not there, performed a literary requiem over the body when he had Renault, the spy of *The Reckoning*, come on the bloody scene at West Canada Creek and deliver himself of the following soliloquy: "As I gazed down at him the roar of the fusillade died away in my ears. I remembered him as I had seen him there in New York in our house, his slim fingers wandering over the strings of the guitar, his dark eyes drowned in melancholy. I remembered his voice, and the song he sang, haunting us all with its lingering sadness—the hopeless words, the sad air, redolent of dead flowers—doom, death, decay."

One can be sure that some of the girls of Albany missed him. For Schenectady, his death called for candles in the windows. Perhaps, after the candles had guttered out that night, Tories did bring down the naked body and lay it under the third pew of the right aisle of St. George's Church. No matter. Walter Butler, the Whipping Boy, is easily resurrected. We like to condemn him without a trial. The sound and fury of our own curses frighten us wonderfully.

PART TWO

The New Breed

*T*HE *Furies pursued Walter Butler to the bank of West Canada Creek. He was stopped there, killed, stripped, and scalped. His face went slack. Americans in the Mohawk Valley would have been glad, that day, to see wolves maul his naked body, lying by the ford and the black water.*

Eighteen months later the Revolution was over. Captain Alexander Thompson, citizen of the United States, traveled from Fort Plain on the Mohawk River to British-held Oswego, where he presented letters from General George Washington's headquarters proclaiming a general truce and the impending peace.

When the captain arrived at Oswego he found the valley's old enemy, Major Ross, in charge. He was courteously received, but, before he left, he and a Captain Crawford of Johnson's Greens had a significant exchange of views on the war that was now over. Captain Thompson wrote later that Captain Crawford "had the wickedness to observe that he had made more money in the British service than he would have made in the American service in 100 years."

"American officers, sir," replied the Flag, "fought for principle, not money."

". . . principle, not money." Captain Thompson, remember, was an artilleryman, not a headquarters' general, nor a politician, and certainly not a philosopher. But there in the wilderness of western New York an American told an uncomprehending Tory that he and his fellow officers had fought for principle.

Captain Thompson and men like him were a new breed. They were as new to the world as Christians had once been.

209

The comparison ends there, for, though these men wanted to plan a new heaven, it must be done with their own surveying instruments. They wanted to lace their heaven with wagon roads running to towns like Utica, with canals linking rivers like the Mohawk to lakes west of the mountains, lakes as big as oceans. Heaven was here and now.

What mutation had taken place? Captain Crawford, a Johnson Green, and Captain Thompson, of Lieutenant Colonel Marinus Willett's Mohawk Valley command, had shared a common colonial experience: What fire had changed the temper of one of them? What had men like Thompson taken from the soil and the air? Why had Thomas Paine's talk about democracy become a religion with some men and made the word "principle" a justification for revolution?

Certainly it is not enough to interpret their revolution solely in terms of economics or politics. Economics, for the Tryon County farmers who fought at Oriskany, was a matter of cleared fields, getting the grain down to the Mohawk for shipment to Schenectady, buying a gun, or cattle, or cloth for a wife's dress. Politics and Democracy for the poor hardly existed, for nine out of ten men had no voice in national affairs.

The captain's word was "principle." But for all those who lived without books, his word was three words: "Liberty," "Equality," and "Independence," words as variable as "Heaven." But the heaven-dream once moved Christians to go on crusades, ugly marches to ugly lands beyond which the visionaries could see Jerusalem the Golden.

The mutation was complete. The men who had now become Americans, who cried "Principle!" "Liberty!" "Equality!" and "Independence!" had taken over the land. Some, even then, were wondering whether their victory was real, or whether, like the victory of the visionaries, it must degenerate into ritual, incense, and obeisance.

18

"Whitestone Country"

I SPEND August on an upland farm, a "summer resident" farm, in New Hampshire. It was a going farm once, with hay in the big barn (which blew apart in the hurricane of 1938) and corn following the line of gray stone fences that disappear deep into the woods among the rock maples and the windfall. One hundred fifty years ago my woodlot was an open field and my neighbor's sugar bush was a side-hill clover meadow.

I hope you'll hold that picture of stone fences settled into the mulch of deep woods, great, awkward stones sprawled in a broken line which, a hundred fifty years ago, was a mended fence dividing open fields. It will help you to understand one reason why New Englanders streamed across the Connecticut River, across Vermont, across the Hudson River, to move like a spring tide up the Mohawk Valley, filling the empty lands they found there, flooding on toward the valleys of the Unadilla, the Chemung, and the Genesee, moving on west to the Great Lakes, on and on, to the Ohio and the Mississippi. New Englanders were not moved by the musical names of these western rivers. Rather were they sick of the stones, and soil sometimes as thin as a carpet, ragged and worn through by the granite hills.

Many a veteran of the Revoluution who had cut a farm out of the New Hampshire hillsides took his wife and boy, the pine chests, his bedding, and the clock and his tools, loaded them into an ox cart and trundled west to Albany, where he bought a farm section of flat land in the "Oneida Woods" at the western end of the Mohawk Valley. But he left memorials to himself in the corner of each of the old hill fields: vast piles of rock, monuments to backbreak and thin living against which he and many of his neighbors finally rebelled.

I have signed one veteran's letters "Eliphalet Stark." His name, however, is missing from the county histories.

Oneida Woods
July 25, 1787

Dear Father and Mother and Brothers,
Sally and the baby arrived three weeks ago from Albany, where I left them in June with the Campbells. They came up the Mohawk River in Eben Campbell's bateau as far as Old Fort Schuyler where they staid with the Widow Damuth until I could borrow Mr. White's cart and fetch them here. I was favored when Sally married me. She's a brave girl to leave Middletown and her father's fine house for this Indian country. We're living with Mr. Hugh White above the Old Fort on the road to the Carrying Place for the Lakes until Sunday next when he and his boys and Mr. Wetmore, who lives near by, are going to help me raise our cabin. Sally's to be with Mrs. White all the time learning what she can. I wonder at her, pounding out corn in Mrs. White's samp mortar. Yesterday she made her first bread in a bake-kettle, hung over the fired logs we're clearing from Mr. White's pasture. Mrs. White said she'll teach Sally to use our gun. She said a woman could do the teaching better than I could, and if there were bears in our tract Sally had better know how to shoot. Nobody

has said very much about the Indians yet, but Mr. White goes to a lot of trouble to feed them and sleep them when they come here, which is almost every day.

I've been here in the Oneida Woods now almost two months. If it hadn't been for father's letter to Mr. White and then all he and his boys did for me I would have gone back down river and home to New Hampshire in time for harvest. I just can't tell you what this country's like. You remember the stories Captain Hardy told about it, when the Massachusetts levies went with General Clinton in the war for Independence up the Mohawk and then through the Seneca villages, almost to Fort Niagara? He said it seemed like walking forever through an empty, dark world of trees where the sun stopped in the upper branches, where the lakes were cold as Nantuckett water and as big as a Massachusetts county. He said if they ever got roads beyond the frontier at the carrying place at Fort Stanwix all of New England would be over to settle. He was right about the country, but it will be a hundred years before they can get roads to the Lakes through these forests. Mr. White's place and the other settlements on the Mohawk at Old Fort Schuyler and Dean's Patent, just beyond Fort Stanwix, are about as far west as anyone in his right mind would dream of going for years. Once we get our land along the Mohawk cleared it will be fine, though, for we've got rich land, near Mr. White's place on Sauquoit Creek which is just about the best mill site I ever saw. He says he thinks the location here may in time become the biggest mill center in the Mohawk Valley, and that Old Fort Schuyler below us will be our "port," for the Mohawk River above it is too shallow most of the summer for heavy boating. Anyway, we're almost all New Englanders in this new country, and the land is pretty nearly flat. There's no piling stones in the corner of every field you clear, for which I praise the Lord. Mr. White thinks about 200 Yankees have come into the Oneida Woods west of the Germans on the middle Mohawk since he got here four years ago. If he keeps writing letters back to Connecticut and sending his neighbors samples of his potatoes and wheat and oats he'll double the population in the next five years. He has the green thumb.

If it hadn't been for Mr. White I'd have bought some of General George Washington's land. I don't say it isn't good land, but it's away south of the river, five or ten miles back from it on the Indian path that goes toward the Oneida village. They say that the General and Governor Clinton got it amazingly cheap from Colonel Willett who was in command at Fort Stanwix toward the last of the war, but they want up to two pounds, six shillings, York currency an acre for it, and the only way you could get to one of the lots would be on a blaze trail. It will be some time before the General and Governor Clinton sell off all of their 6000 acres, Mr. White says. Mrs. Herkimer, widow of the famous General Herkimer who was killed at the fight on Oriskany Creek close by us, says General Washington and the Governor tried to buy the curative springs at Saratoga, and the carrying place beyond us at Fort Stanwix. I don't think the springs would have amounted to much, but they could have done well at the carry, for the trade through there for the Lakes country and Canada will get heavy in time. The generals seem to have got most of this upper Mohawk River land. General Schuyler and three of his friends own most of the flats around Old Fort Schuyler. Colonel Willett and Governor Clinton and General Washington have land, and they say General Steuben is to have 16,000 acres for his services in the war. None of the New York soldiers can take up any of their military grants west of Fort Stanwix because the Indians claim the land, though in time the Indians will be pushed out, Mr. White says.

For a long time, I guess, we're going to have to lean on these fumigating "Vans" down the river from us. I never saw people more set in their ways. They're poor farmers, though their bottom lands along the Mohawk River are so rich they can't help but get a crop. Most of them who were driven out by the Tory raids during the war are back now on their farms, though they've got very few cattle yet, and meat just can't be bought.

They don't seem to like Yankees. I rode from here forty

miles down to the grist mill at German Flats and they wouldn't even say "good afternoon." When I asked the miller's boy to hold the reins of Mr. White's horse until I could get the sack down he just looked at me and said, "Who was your servant last year?" The mill Mr. White, Mr. Wetmore and Beardsly are building is almost finished, and I'll be glad when it's done, for there will be one less reason for trying to get on with these Germans.

The whole river from Schenectady to Herkimer's and the Flats is Dutch and German. They've been on the river for better than a hundred years and they've done little more than carve out farms along the flats. They've got a cart road up both sides of the river from Schenectady, though the one on the north shore is far better until you get to Walrath's Ferry, east of Fort Dayton, where you have to ford the river and then go up the south side around Little Falls. Of course there are no bridges over the Mohawk, and until there are, most of the freight will have to be boated up and down stream. The river's too shallow and the rifts are so bad you can't ferry any more than a two-ton load at a time. Sally was ten days getting herself and the baby and the furniture from Albany to Old Fort Schuyler, and Eben Campbell said at that they made good time because the rains had given them seventeen inches of water at the rift narrows. It took six yoke of oxen to get their bateau around the carry at Little Falls. Mr. White says if they ever get a canal around Little Falls and one across the carrying place at Fort Stanwix, these Mohawk Dutch will begin to see things happen along the river that will make their eyes pop. Canals and bridges will bring in Yankee families and we'll be glad to see them here. Sally says the seven log cabins in Mr. White's neighborhood hardly make a town.

Mother would never like Mr. Van Horne's store down at German Flats. He sells more grog and rum than anything else. His prices are high, but he sells everything from peace warrants to check handkerchiefs. One Dutchman drank up four nips of rum and cider while I was waiting to get Mrs. White's order filled, and paid two shillings sixpence for it.

What a waste. A whole quart of spirits costs the same, and I took one back for Mr. White, against sickness. I got him a pound of pigtail tobacco for a shilling, and turned in three certificates for wolves he killed, for which I got three pounds. I bought four ells of corduroy for twenty-four shillings, which Sally says is high, one ell of blue shalloon, three shillings sixpence, enough leather for one pair of shoes, seven shillings. Father will yell when he sees that price, but you can hardly find a hide west of Fort Hunter. You can buy Indian shoes for three shillings twopence, but they are no good in the stump fields. Mr. Van Horne told me he'd pay good prices for all the ginseng I brought in. He said he didn't hold with it himself, but the heathen Chinese thought it was a cure for the plague. He said if I didn't have cash he'd take his pay in spinning, or carpentry, or playing the fiddle for dancing. You can see why mother would never take to these Dutchmen.

Sally is worried because we have no church up here, but I tell her churches and schools have to wait on housebuilding and clearing the fields. The Methodists send a circuit rider through to Dean's Patent sometimes and our Congregationalists are talking about organizing. We have a religious society of sorts now. We'll have churches and preaching soon, and enough to show the Dutchmen God's way.

We can't wait to get in our own cabin. It will be hovel style, and one room, but it will do until I can get crops and flax in, and money ahead for the house we want. I've got four acres cleared now and Sally says I should stop work long enough to let her sew up the tears in my tow breeches and wash the smell of log burning out of my hair. While it's daylight I'll be in the woods and when Sally doesn't hear my axe it will be time for her to come complaining.

Mr. White sends his regards to all of you with this and wants father to know he's never been sorry he left Middletown. I've written more than I meant to, but your letter said James was talking about coming out to the Oneida Woods. We will all be glad to have him come, but he should know it is hardly thrifty country for a schoolmaster. If he means to

turn farmer, good. Those of us who talked liberty and then
fought for it in the war live it here. The trees are the only
things that hem us in, and we've got our axes.

> Sally sends love,
>> as does your son and brother,
>>> Eliphalet Stark

Thousands of Eliphalet Starks, following the war, gave
up their harvests of stone for the better crops they knew they
could raise in the Mohawk Valley and the lands west of it.
New England levies had been stationed at Fort Stanwix and
Fort Dayton. They had fought in most of the bloody actions
from Saratoga to the dismal business at Cherry Valley and
the pursuit on West Canada Creek, when Walter Butler was
killed. They had gone with General Clinton south and then
west from Canajoharie when he and General Sullivan cleared
the Senecas out of the richest, sweetest land the New Englanders had ever seen. No granite hills there. Well-watered
lands, meadows, flats, forests of beech and maple and pine,
clear, cold lakes and streams crowding with salmon. When the
generals finished their work these lands were vacant lands,
the Seneca apple orchards standing by burned-out Indian villages, the corn acres trampled, and the storehouses smoking
ruins.

The Yankee levies that saw the far west of the Oneida
Woods and the Genesee country went home to spread stories
about a land fit for the New Jerusalem; or even a second New
England, one without the stones. They talked so convincingly
that they started the Great Migration, one of the greatest land
rushes in history. The frontier which ran through Fort Stanwix, on the old carry from the Mohawk River to the west-
running streams, was picked up by the New England immigrants and pushed to the shores of the Great Lakes within

twenty years of the time Hugh White made the first settlement west of German Flats.

Men like Eliphalet Stark and his brothers came up the Mohawk River, the east-west path to the lakes country which was never really challenged. Turnpikes were pushed over the Pennsylvania mountains. In New York the Catskill Road, the Appian Way, the Cherry Valley Turnpike took their tolls, but the flood tide of immigration followed the old Iroquois trail through the empty Long House, the valley along which the empire builders had always moved.

What is unique in the story of the Mohawk River stands out in startling relief during these years of the Great Migration. Along other rivers men bargained for furs, carved farms out of the forest, fought invaders, built their cities, put up their liberty poles, and slowly integrated their region with the life of the new nation. It was the peculiar function of the Mohawk River, however, to carve out the easiest passage through the Appalachian plateau along which men could move to other regions. The men of the Great Migration found the river important because it carried them beyond its own valley to other valleys. In that service, for generations, the Mohawk River had been perhaps, the most important river on the continent. Its story from the Revolution into our time is the story of a vital region, but the great chapters are those which tell of men moving along it, east and west, on its waters and along its banks, on the greater business of building America.

Eliphalet Stark arrived in the "Whitestown Country" with cabin builders. His neighbors who could not sink roots into the clearings they hacked out of the forests of the upper Mohawk were swept on farther west as the New England tide rolled up the river toward the lakes. Eliphalet Stark stayed, however, and built a gambrel-roof house, and saw the blazed trails turn into roads. He saw the beginning of the Erie Canal and heard talk of railroads, and missed his guess at last that Whitestown would become the great city of the new west.

Whitestown, Herkimer County
June 15, 1797

Dear Brother Ephraim,

Yours came by the mail-stage today. I'm glad you've sold the home place, now that father and mother have gone. I'm happier still that you and Elizabeth have decided at last to leave New Hampshire and try our western country. You both must come here to Whitestown directly from Alworth, and plan to stay with us until you decide what you want to do . . . we have room here in the new house, and Sally will not take "No" in this matter.

Your route to Albany is best by way of Springfield, Massachusetts. From there to Schenectady you'll take either Mr. Beal's or Mr. Hudson's stage, though I recommend Mr. Beal's, and a stop overnight at his fine tavern in Schenectady, which, by the way, the driver will probably call "Snacady," and a dirtier place on God's footstool you never saw. There's a new college there, Union College, under the celebrated Jonathan Edwards, the Younger, who organized our Congregational churches here in Whitestown. Call on the Doctor and tell him you are interested in finding a Parish among our New England people.

Mr. Beal's stage will bring you on to Canajoharie. I trust you stop on the way at Pride's for breakfast; he keeps tavern in what was one of the great Tory houses, Guy Johnson's "Park." There's no finer stop on the river. The Whitestown coach may be a day or two late leaving Canajoharie, but Shepherd runs a good house there. If you have a long delay betwen stages, hire a wagon and go on to Little Falls, that is, if you and Elizabeth can abide more sight-seeing.

I want you to walk along the towpath of the Inland

Lock Company's canal there for two reasons. First, because
you'll see God's handiwork as you never saw it before. What
river and what giant waterfall cut through those rocks and
left those vast pot-holes high above the canal and the Mohawk
that flows there today? I've heard the natives say in Little
Falls that the Mohawk disproves the story of Creation, for no
river, they swear, could have cut through those rocks in 5,000
years. You'll hear much of such doubting of the Bible in this
new country, Ephraim, where there's a tavern and grog to be
had for every mile of road.

And I want you to see the Inland Lock and Navigation
Company's canal. Twenty-five hundred feet of it were cut
through solid rock. That's the canal that's doubled the value
of my land and every acre of land from here to Lake Erie.
You'll see the new Durham boats locked around the falls
where in the old days we dragged the bateaux around them
with oxen. The Durham boats, Ephraim, carry up to 20 tons
of goods! You'll know what that means when you get here,
and see John Post's store at Old Fort Schuyler outfitting the
wagons for the Genesee country. Durham boats can go right
on now into Wood Creek through the new canal at Fort
Stanwix and on into the Seneca rivers. Look at the canal a
long time, Ephraim. It's like a vein pouring fresh blood into
this young land. Some people are predicting a canal that will
connect the lakes with the Atlantic Ocean, but I doubt that.

You remember when I came here and bought land from
Mr. Hugh White, who knew father in Middletown? And I
thought General Washington's land was too far back from
the Mohawk River for settling? Ephraim, it's God's miracle
worked before our eyes and you're coming just in time to par-
take of it! The General's lands are better than half settled
with New England families. Instead of the Oneida Woods we
have Yankee towns west, south and north of us by the dozens.
They button onto the Genesee Road that now runs from Old
Fort Schuyler through the Military Grants and into the heart
of the richest farm country in the world, I'd guess, where
Mr. Phelps and Mr. Gorham bought millions of acres from
Massachusetts. New England families are going west from

here better than a thousand a year. Someone told me that in three days last winter 1200 sleds were dragged up State Street hill in Albany, headed for new towns in Herkimer County, and on west of us, too. The year I came here, Ephraim, and began cutting my farm out of the woods, Mr. White was honored by having all the land west of Old Fort Schuyler called "Whitestown." Our twenty-one cabins then stretched from the Old Fort to Dean's Patent, on Wood's Creek. We kept our children close to the cabins because we were afraid of bears and wolves, and we never knew what the Indians would do when they got drunk. Then Governor Clinton bought up most of the Indian lands west of Fort Stanwix for the State, and now we see Oneidas and Brother-town Indians often enough, but they're little trouble, and a feeble shadow of the people who were here when the Dutch and the British first came to the Mohawk Valley. Mr. Kirkland, who has been a preacher to the Oneida Indians since before the war, tells me the Mohawk Indians were the terrible ones, but they've been gone since the first year of the war, and are going to stay in Canada on lands the British have given them for the murdering they did along the Mohawk. The Yankees have taken care of the wolves, bears and Indians, Ephraim, and we'll build the Lord's Temple yet, build it out of these great trees. We've got iron in the hills of some of our towns, enough for the Temple gates, and we'll soon be weaving our own cloth along our mill streams for the banners, and making our own plow-shares. But we need more men of God, like yourself, Ephraim.

I despair of these Dutchmen and Germans in the old towns down the river. They resent Yankees more and more. In spite of their petition against us, Judge White and the rest of our New England families were able to cut Herkimer County out of their Montgomery County about six years ago. They still take their spite out against us at Militia Musters, but we're begining to out-vote them, and soon we'll have our own companies, and officers who speak an English you can understand.

There's no bustle or enterprise among them, though I

must except a Dutchman like General Schuyler who heads the Inland Lock Company, and some of the Durham boat builders in Schenectady. The German Flats farmers are already beginning to find out that their part of the valley is having a harder and harder time competing with our New Englanders when it comes to working the land. If there ever is a canal from the Hudson River straight across the state to the Great Lakes, the Mohawk Valley Dutch will have to find something else to raise besides grain, for the Genesee country will become the breadbasket for New York.

I'm enclosing a copy of our "Western Centinal" which Judge White suggested I send. There's Yankee push and go for you. Whitestown had this newspaper before any of the Dutch towns thought of starting one. If there is any thought in your mind that the Oneida Woods is still the far west, disabuse it by reading the "Centinal's" advertising. The farms for sale along the new Genesee Road here have framed houses on them. Log Cabin country is now out on the Military Grants and in the Genesee Valley. We've got sawmills and grist mills, oil mills for flax seed, fulling mills, a chair factory, tailoring establishments, and stores as well stocked as any down the Mohawk. Parker's mail-stage advertizement means more to me than the rest, for I used to walk the forty miles from here to German Flats nine years ago. But we've got things here, Ephraim, which I hope men like you will come prepared to fight. Every store and tavern sells rum, and the boatmen on the river grow worse each season. And there's a dancing school at New Hartford. Some of the new women powder their hair, and the cursing at the docks and taverns is worse than it was among the troops.

Come as soon as you can, Ephraim, and add a new congregation to this western country. We've begun a New Jerusalem. Come, and help us to finish it.

Sally sends love, and know your young nephew would if he were here, but we keep him boarded out at the Hamilton-Oneida Academy in Clinton which Mr. Kirkland started some four years back. There's strong discipline there.

Your brother,
Eliphalet Stark

They found iron, all right, in the new Mohawk Valley towns like Clinton and Salisbury, but not enough to give the valley a Pittsburgh. Mills were naturals for swift-running streams like the Sauquoit. On Moyer's Creek, just east of modern Utica, the valley's first woolen mill began operation in 1807. As this mill and the cotton mills that sprang up at Whitestown, or Whitesboro now, in the next year, and as new enterprises up and down the valley and all over the new country gained headway our economic bondage to England slackened. The America of looms and anvils and Yankee inventors and speculators boomed, and with the change a dozen unknowns were intruded into the shifting equation of American life.

Eliphalet Stark, before he died in 1817, saw his beloved Whitestown shatter into a hundred towns that stretched from Utica, where the great Seneca Turnpike had taken over the older Genesee Road, to Buffalo at its western end. Tryon had become Montgomery County, and Montgomery County in its turn had been broken into numerous new counties whose names memorialized those Iroquois tribes whose fame and dignity was to grow as their numbers shrank, and their hunting grounds were laid out in town plots and farmsites. The middle and western Mohawk Valley was divided between Herkimer County on the east and Oneida on the west, and Utica became the boom city. Utica, which had been Old Fort Schuyler, by 1817 was a brash village of almost four hundred houses, a place of cotton mills and docks for the roaring river traffic, and the chief point of departure for the far west of the Morris Reserve and the Holland Land Company's fabulous counties.

The "miracle" of new life in the upper Mohawk and in western New York about which the young Stark had written

to his brother Ephraim could be measured now in those numbers which Americans were coming to love. When Eliphalet arrived by three-handed bateau in the Oneida Woods in 1788 there were some fifteen thousand people in all of Montgomery County, and that meant in the whole shadowed wilderness that spread west from Schenectady to the Great Lakes, including the thin line of Dutchmen and Germans whose farms and towns and abandoned blockhouses stretched up the Mohawk to Herkimer and German Flats. By 1810 the Great Migration had brought almost three hundred thousand settlers into the once-quiet forests. No one could say, however, not even the hopeful Eliphalet, that the trees they cut down were being used to build a temple in a New Jerusalem.

Dr. Todd, in Salisbury, was building a distillery in order to utilize the grain his patients paid him in lieu of hard cash. Rome had four distilleries. There was a new market for liquor, for a man needed refreshment after a day of stagecoaching on the roads of the turnpike companies.

The new industries were making a most secular music as their wheels ground out the plows and pottery and cow bells and the dozens of other articles needed now along the old highroad of empire builders. The cloth mills of Utica and New Hartford and a dozen other Mohawk Valley towns paid as much as $200 a year in wages to a worker and gave their owners as little as 20 per cent on their investment. Tweeds and flannel, "satinets," cotton goods and broadcloths, the latter at $10 and $12 a yard, made the embargoes against England a joy and the War of 1812 a temporary embarrassment as far as the millowners were concerned. During that conflict the Mohawk Valley was again the line of march for the watch on the lakes, and the scene of wild enthusiasm as Commodore Perry came home from Lake Erie, a triumphant hero who bound Germans and Yankees together in a common celebration.

The opening of the Great Lakes country meant the end of the old pattern of life along the Mohawk River. Where could dynasts like the Johnsons fit into the turbulent life created here by a transplanted New England? Little Falls, which should have boomed with towns to the west, stagnated because its river front and millsites were for rent, not for sale. The Ellices, absentee landlords of most of the village property, thought to continue the baronial system into new times and among a breed of men who had no use for landlords and quitrents.

Eliphalet Stark's brother, Ephraim, came west to Whitestown by stagecoach, fare $2, and the road was execrable. By 1800 the Mohawk Turnpike Company had begun to widen the north shore road and cover it with crushed stone, the improvements to be paid for by the tolls collected at the twelve gates set up between Schenectady and Utica.

Within the fifteen years after Sally Stark began her musket lessons with Mrs. White, the Mohawk was bridged at Utica, Little Falls, and Canajoharie. Theodore Burr, distant cousin to the infamous Aaron Burr, threw a 330-foot wooden span in a single arch across the Mohawk at Canajoharie that was the wonder of the times.

In 1806 it took a three-day celebration to quiet the natives in the neighborhood of the new Montgomery, or "Oothout's," bridge at Fort Plain. Two years later Theodore Burr again amazed bridge builders with his 1,000-foot masterpiece across the Mohawk at Schenectady, perhaps America's first suspension bridge.

"Uncle Stoeffel," who collected its tolls, was beloved of the Union College boys of Schenectady for his special hangover medicine, which he would administer at the tollhouse. Farm wagons were waved by for 6½ cents, and the rich man's spring coach cost its driver 25 cents. If you were bound for church you could walk across for the price of a "good morning" to Uncle Stoeffel.

The old patterns changed indeed. Schenectady was jolted out of its Dutch conservatism by the war and by the hordes of Yankees who crossed the pine plains from Albany to take the Durham boats or the stages west. These New Englanders sneered at the pig wallows, and looked with disapproval at the Dutch faces of the older houses. The town was booming and not quite sure it liked it. In 1811 there were four stages east and four west daily along the whole length of the energy-charged turnpike, and Beale and Hudson's taverns in the old Dorp echoed louder to the Yankee twang than they did to the gutturals of the descendants of those who first settled the Groote Vlachte. But boatbuilding and freighthandling along the Binnie Kill and the Mohawk docks were making fortunes for the ancient town's more enterprising citizens. They alone of all the Mohawk Valley people were dreading the "Grand Canal" which had been taking shape in surveys and legislative reports for several years past. They knew that if it was ever dredged across the state it would end forever Schenectady's monopoly of the Mohawk-River-to-the-Hudson freight and passenger transfers.

In the meantime, John Post's river packets *Accommodation* and *Dilligence* would ferry those passengers upriver to Utica who could afford the time to buck the rifts and wait their turn at the Little Falls locks.

Utica was the river Mecca. Hugh White and Eliphalet Stark thought it would become Whitestown's "port," but how wrong they were! Without water power, this site of the "Old

Fort" seemed doomed to crossroads stagnation. But it was the crossroads themselves that began its rise and final domination of the western Mohawk country. Here began the Seneca Turnpike through to the Great Lakes. A road south joined the Cherry Valley Turnpike and a road north ran into the Black River region and joined the new roads fanning west from Johnstown and the stump towns north of the Mohawk that were tapping the lumber and mineral resources of the Adirondack highlands. Traffic, swelling like the April Mohawk, gave Utica growing pains.

"Utica," wrote Timothy Bigelow in 1805, on his way to Niagara Falls, "is now a little city, and contains several elegant dwelling houses, some of which are of brick, [and] a great number of stores and manufactures of different kinds." Trowbridge's Hotel impressed Timothy, the New Englander, always on the lookout for those niceties of progress and Hubculture. "The house is of brick," he wrote, "large, commodious, and well attended. We found good fare here; in particular, excellent wine."

Progress! That was the word which now made the catchwords of the Revolution seem almost dated. Progress was being made on a hundred levels, from the movement of a Yankee wagon from A to B along the Mohawk Turnpike, to the surveys for the Grand Canal and that last, sweet evidence of progress, that "excellent wine" Timothy Bigelow noted as proof of Utica's sophistication.

If the men of the Great Migration had bothered, in the years of their hegira, to define the word, the definition would have rallied such synonyms as speculation, turnpikes, canals, mills and more mills, and Yankee.

Later, the unreflective pioneers were to see, dimly, in the Mohawk Valley, and all over America, that "progress," like "liberty," was not pronounced as a benediction, for with the new life they so eagerly created came unplanned-for problems. The men of these first years of the new dispensation could put most of the problems by for the work in hand. But the new cities, the expanding mills, the hordes from Europe who would soon follow on the heels of the New Englanders, these bred problems which the children and the grandchildren of the cabinbuilders and town fathers were to receive with protest and violence.

Eliphalet Stark died at Rome, New York, on July 4, 1817, on a day when progress hit a new high in America. He suffered a heart attack during the ground-breaking ceremonies for the Erie Canal, that awe-inspiring waterway which was at last to connect the Great Lakes and the Atlantic Ocean. "Nature," Canal Commissioner Young was saying as the old settler was removed to a nearby tent, "has kindly afforded every facility; we have all the moral and physical means within our reach and control. Let us then proceed to the work, animated by the prospect of its speedy accomplishment, and cheered with the anticipated benedictions of a grateful posterity."

The brief eulogy for Mr. Stark that appeared in several local papers a week later was said to have been written by the deceased's brother, Mr. Ephraim Stark, pastor of a church in the Military Grants:

ANOTHER REVOLUTIONARY SOLDIER GONE:—Died, on the 4th of July, 1817, at Rome, N.Y., Eliphalet Stark in his 59th year. Mr. Stark, at an early age enlisted from Alworth, N.H., into the American Army, and was a soldier under General Gates at the surrender of Burgoyne. He removed to Whitestown from New Hampshire while it was a wilderness and was one of the pioneers in its settlement. He had the wisdom to be content with his first choice, and remained upon it to the day of his death.

A great concourse of people testified their regard by attending his funeral solemnities, on the Sabbath succeeding his demise.

His was a belief in the Kingdom of God. He loved his neighbor as himself. For such as he there will be the resurrection and the New Jerusalem.

19

The Wedding of the Waters

DANIEL TOMPKINS, vice-president of the United States, unintentionally saved the Erie Canal. "England," he warned New York State's Council of Revision, "will never forgive us for our victories on the land and on the ocean and on the lakes; and, my word for it, we shall have another war with her in two years!" Don't waste the state's money, he continued, on anything so chimerical as this vast Grand Canal. Build arsenals with the money, arm the militia, erect forts, prepare for war!

The vice-president had dropped in, uninvited, on the council's final consideration of the Canal Bill, which had just been sent up to it by the Assembly for approval or veto. These Supreme Court justices were elder statesmen, and the Canal Bill was radical, unsettling. The majority of the council were for scuttling it that April day, in 1817, when the vice-president came into their chamber. The decision would have ended De Witt Clinton's dream of the "Big Ditch" for that session of the legislature, and quite likely for good, for the opposition was growing stronger every day.

Tompkins's warmongering tactics, however, were too

much for Chancellor Kent. The author of *Kent's Comment-
aries* preferred orderly thinking and an orderly growth of society. "If we must have war," he said to the council's uninvited guest, "or have a canal, I am in favour of the canal, and
I vote for the bill!" The chancellor carried a majority of the
elder statesmen with him, and the Canal Bill became law.
The chancellor's choice was perhaps the greatest one he ever
made, for when Clinton and his radicals finished their canal
they had given the United States the kind of strength not
even England would dare to challenge.

If you'll look at a map of canal country you'll see what
De Witt Clinton and the amateur engineers had been battling
a gorgon-headed opposition to win: nothing less than a Grand
Canal, as they called it, a man-made cut running west from
the Hudson River through the Mohawk Valley, west to the
Genesee Valley, to join at last the waters of Lake Erie with
the waters of the Atlantic Ocean. The legislators from New
York City called the canal a "gutter," and, to a man, voted
down every measure to make it possible.

The key to the canal, as it had been to every thrust
toward the Great Lakes country for generations, was the Mohawk Valley. Canoes, scows, bateaux, Durham boats, none of
these could carry the freight that was now piling up along
the northwestern ridges of the Alleghenies. The river improvements of the old Western Inland Lock Navigation Company
served only to make men realize what a golden harvest would
flow down a real waterway, independent of the droughts and
spring floods and rifts that cursed navigation on the Mohawk
and the crooked streams west of it.

Thomas Jefferson and George Washington had looked
sidewise at the Mohawk River, and hoped the honor of linking the new West and the rich East would be Virginia's.
". . . a canal," wrote Jefferson to the squire of Mount Ver-

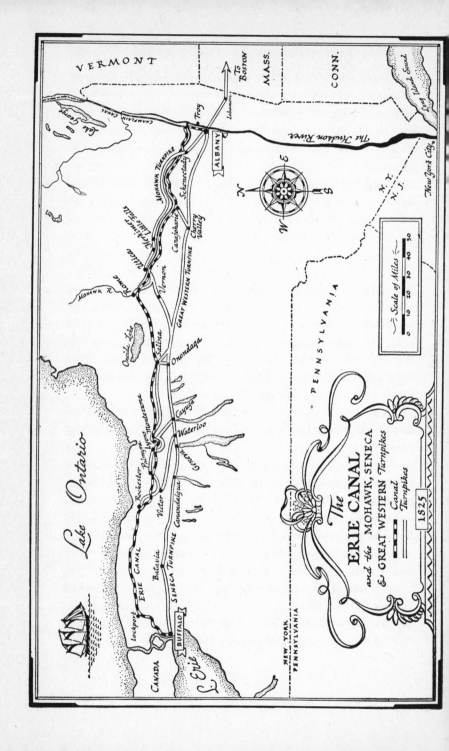

The
ERIE CANAL
and the MOHAWK, SENECA
& GREAT WESTERN Turnpikes

—·—·— Canal
————— Turnpikes

1825

non, "will infallibly turn through the Potomac all the commerce of Lake Erie, and the country west of that, except what
may pass down the Mississippi; and it is important that it be
done soon, lest the commerce should, in the meantime, get
established in another channel." Men of vision, those Vir-
ginians, for that letter was written in 1788, twenty years before anybody got around to urging New York to take advantage of that other channel of the state's God-given Mohawk
Valley route to the Great Lakes.

Virginia, Maryland, and Pennsylvania rested their chins
on the rock wall that ran down their western boundaries,
watched the feast being laid out in the Northwest Territory
that would soon break up into grain and ore-rich states, and
schemed to sit in on it. But none of them had a valley like
the Mohawk. They probed every mountain pass for a way to
Lake Erie and had to be content at last with their turnpikes.
Pennsylvania courted bankruptcy with a canal whose boats
were hoisted over the Allegheny peaks by inclined railroad,
and saw the project collapse.

New York fumbled with the Lakes-to-the-Atlantic canal
idea for decades, and good men got themselves laughed at
for proposing such a fantastic scheme. Jesse Hawley's essays
in 1807 urging surveys for a canal were barred finally from
continuation in a western New York newspaper because the
publisher feared his readers would laugh his newssheet out
of existence.

The next year, however, New York decided to risk $600
on a survey of the route, generously concluding that "it could
do no harm, and might do some good." Judge Platt, from
Oneida County, and some of the other western legislators
were telling stories of what was going on in New York's
Whitestown country that gave the canal scheme a real urg-
ency. There were dim notions of rainbow gold in the lands

west of New York. Where would it go, once the earth gave it up? Canada? That was a haunting thought, for canals from Lake Erie to Lake Ontario and around Niagara would turn the St. Lawrence into a British highway. Down the Mississippi? Then the United States would be anything but united. There might even rise up a trans-Allegheny nation, oriented north and south, giving little more than courtesy allegiance to the East.

Full of such frightening thoughts, and equipped with maps and land profiles of three possible routes from the Hudson to Lake Ontario or Lake Erie, a New York legislator called on President Jefferson, who had been talking about using surplus federal funds for some big national project: turnpikes, or canals, wherever they would stimulate the commerce of the country. New York got a robust "No!" from the White House, however, to its canal plans. Jefferson, perhaps remembering Virginia, said the whole scheme was wild-eyed, impossible for a hundred years at least.

What the canal planners needed was a smart politician, and they got one in 1810 when they persuaded De Witt Clinton to fight along with them. From then on no one mentioned the Western Inland Lock Navigation Company. Philip Schuyler had been a good general but he had proved himself a poor engineer; his failing company had made a mess of its building program and its finances. And there was Gouverneur Morris, a fine man, member of the canal committee, but a trifle impractical. It was a mistake to include Morris's moonbeam idea for an artificial river in the survey report of the next year. It frightened sensible men. Morris wanted an inclined plane all the way from Lake Erie to the Hudson, a fantastic river to be carried on aqueducts across valleys and channeled through inconvenient mountains. By the time it was brought down to the middle Mohawk Valley it would have been coursing happily along its aqueduct 150 feet above the heads of the natives.

The War of 1812 quieted talk about canals, but as soon as the Commodore Perry celebrations were over, De Witt Clinton and the canallers returned to their old arguments, and the new ones the war had given them. The Mohawk Valley had groaned with the burden of war supplies jacked through its rifts and old locks, and carted along the Mohawk Turnpike. Surely the federal government could now see how important the canal was to the nation's safety?

President Madison saw it that way, but not Congress. There were members in Congress from Virginia, Maryland, and Pennsylvania. Philadelphia, then the premier port, looked askance at New York City, which was then in a slump, losing population. With a canal, though, the city might become a threat. The federal government was having no part of New York State's Grand Canal.

But the canal idea was now public property. Robert Fulton had been added to the commission. Morris's wonderful river-in-the-clouds plan had been dropped, and De Witt Clinton, in 1815 mayor of New York City, was urging New York State to dig its own canal. As enthusiasm mounted, so too did the noise of the opposition. The whole scheme, some were saying, was a ruse of the Clintonians to capture the state. Vicious, tax-burdening plan. Impossible to dig canals four hundred or more miles long!

But how the men of the new West wanted it! The Holland Land Company offered the state better than one hundred thousand acres of its lands in the hope of action. And the canal could be built! Geddes and Wright and the others who had run the surveys weren't engineers—there weren't any engineers in the country—but these men had Yankee confidence, and they persuaded the commission that they could pull off the greatest engineering feat since the ancient world brought Alpine water to Rome.

Their plan was ready. Dig the Erie Canal in three sections. Begin at the old carrying place on the Mohawk, at Rome, and dig east to Utica, and west to the Seneca River. That was the smartest part of their plan, for the digging would be easiest in the middle, and people, once they saw canalboats in motion, would demand the rest of the project. Then dig the Mohawk River section. Once that was done, the pressure to push west of Seneca Lake to Lake Erie would be irresistible.

Mass meetings, memorials, oratory in the grand manner climaxed in April, 1817, in a narrow victory for the bill in the State Assembly and Senate, a bill calling for the construction of the Erie and Champlain canals. There was heart-burning as it went up to the Council of Revision, most of whose members were known to be hostile to "Clinton's ditch" and its backers, dangerous fellows full of democratic notions. If Daniel Tompkins had not been so enthusiastic about war and Chancellor Kent had not been touched with the larger vision on the day the bill was considered, there might not have been an Erie Canal. But the miracle happened. And so they began to dig.

"Let us proceed with the work," Commissioner Young had said at Rome on Independence Day that year, as the first shovel load of dirt was turned out of what the amateur engineers called the "prism," the bed of the Erie. There was a lot of digging to be done. A "V'd" ditch 4 feet deep, 40 feet wide at the surface inched east and west, through a wilderness of virgin timber, through rock, through the Montezuma swamps where the fever knocked diggers out by the thousand, up and down the mountain wall on water-stairs, locks of tailored stone you can still see if you know where to look.

How did these untrained engineers, these lawyer-survey-ors, do it? The first Civil Engineering Department in America was set up at Union College in Schenectady, but that was almost thirty years later. They were Yankee experimenters, most of them, the kind of men for whom the hum of wheels was the voice of God. Take the way they got rid of trees, for instance. There were thousands along their right-of-way. They fixed things so that one man could pull a forest down. They threw a rope around a treetop, hooked the ground end on a wheel turned by an endless screw, and let a pair of horses do the rest.

Their stump puller had the loafers lined up along the fences to watch it work. They swung an axle 20 inches in diameter, 30 feet long, between a pair of wheels 16 feet in diameter. In the middle of the axle was another wheel, smaller, a mere 14 feet in diameter. When the contraption was in position, Paddy, the crew leader, would brace the outer wheels, wind one end of his chain about the axle, and lash the other end around his stump. Then the oxen went to work, dragging on a rope wound around the center wheel. Stumps came out of the ground like corks out of the grog crock. Paddy and his crew of six could pull thirty or forty stumps a day and cart each one off the canal track by simply un-blocking the stump hauler's wheels and driving off to a dump.

A freak accident gave the canal's stonemasons America's first hydraulic cement. Common quicklime was the binder they expected to use, and it was quicklime contractors Harris and Livingston thought they were delivering to the masons working on the middle section west of Rome. When the masons were ready for their lime, however, they discovered it wouldn't slake. The lime that wouldn't slake became the talk of the section. Canvass White, then an assistant engineer, heard about it, took some of this ill-behaved lime "to Dr.

Barto, a scientific gentleman from Herkimer County," who "burned a parcel, pulverized it in a mortar, and in Elisha Carey's barroom . . . mixed it with sand, rolled a ball of it, and placed it in a bucket of water for the night. In the morning it had set, was solid enough to roll across the floor, and by Dr. Barto pronounced cement." Canvass White continued experimenting, and finally took out a patent to cover his mixture, a cement equal to anything then used in Europe.

If the Erie Canal was a great school for engineers it was also a vast workhouse. The first few years there weren't many foreigners employed, because there weren't many foreigners around. Less than 1 per cent of New York's population were aliens in 1817, although the canal and the new prosperity that came with it would change that. All kinds of Americans, farmers, lawyers, small businessmen, turned themselves into contractors, and bid on sections of the work that passed through their own neighborhoods. Canal work paid laborers more than the mills, and the mills were paying a good $200 to $300 a year to an honest man.

When the Irish began to pick up the pickaxes and shovels most of the Americans were glad to put down, the singing started. Before the towpath songs there were the diggers' songs, full of nostalgia for an Ireland few of the singers ever saw again. Paddy's song came early, a Paddy who arrived in Philadelphia but couldn't stand the place and moved on to New York:

When I came to this wonderful empire, it filled me with the
    greatest surprise
To see such a great undertaking, on the like I ne'er opened my
    eyes.
To see a full thousand brave fellows at work among mountains
    so tall,
To dig through the valleys so level, through rocks for to cut a
    canal.

So fare you well, father and mother,
Likewise to old Ireland, too,
So fare you well, sister and brother,
So kindly I'll bid you adieu.

I being an entire stranger, be sure I had not much to say.
The Boss came around in a hurry, says, boys, it is grog time today.
We all marched up in good order, he was father now unto us all.
Sure I wished myself from that moment to be working upon the
canal.[1]

Paddy and his fellow diggers, and the amateur engineers,
finished the middle section from the Seneca River to Utica
by October, 1819, and could hardly wait to let the first waters
roll down their ditch. A "gentleman from Utica" caught the
spirit of that occasion:

"On Friday afternoon [he wrote] I walked to the head
of the Grand Canal . . . and from one of the slight and airy
bridges which crossed it, I had a sight that could not but
exhilarate and elevate the mind. The waters were rushing in
from the westward and coming down their untried channel
toward the sea. . . . You might see people running across the
fields, climbing on trees and fences and crowding the banks
of the canal to gaze upon the welcome sight. A boat had
been prepared at Rome, and as the waters came down the
canal, you might mark their progress by that of this new
Argo, which floated triumphantly along the Hellespont of the
west, accompanied by the shouts of the peasantry, and having on her deck a military band."

That boat was the *Chief Engineer*, named for Benjamin
Wright—Rome to Utica, and the first trip on the Erie was
over. The "gentleman" reporter was the key to the times,
with his condescending "shouts of the peasantry," most of

[1] From *Body, Boots and Britches*. Copyright, 1939, by Harold W.
Thompson. Published by J. B. Lippincott Co.

them Whitestown country New Englanders, and his classical "Hellespont" and "Argo" tags for the "ditch" and its Yankee engineer's canal boat. Town names like "Rome" and "Utica" were a comfort to Republicans and Federalists alike, for in those early canal days the commoner and the imperialist could each find his ideal America in the patterns of the ancient world.

Hellespont or ditch, the Erie Canal had sold itself to New York. Work was now pushed east. The Mohawk Valley section produced the worst of the engineering headaches. The old "Western" locks at Little Falls were simply abandoned, for the canal ran along the south bank of the river now. In order to appease Little Falls, an aqueduct was eventually built across the river, feeding into a basin where boats could pick up or deliver goods for the north shore.

East of Little Falls the river became the builders' worst enemy. They ran survey after survey, hoping to by-pass the whole lower valley on their way to the Hudson, but the Mohawk, which had given them their gateway to the west, had also given them the only possible route to tidewater. Stone embankments were laid up against the spring floods. At Schenectady, where the whole canal idea was anathema, the engineers ran head-on into civic controversy. Mr. Givens, the big hotelkeeper, wanted the canal routed through the center of the city, as close to his establishment as possible. Mr. Yates, then governor of the state and a Schenectadian, wanted the canal to keep to the line of the river. Feeling ran high until the engineers made the decision: the canal would go through the center of Schenectady, all right, not because Mr. Givens wanted it that way but because the canal would be safer from the Mohawk floods. Governor Yates, meeting Mr. Givens a little later, vented his annoyance by calling the hotel keeper "an uneasy Yankee (who) cannot be kept still!"

From Schenectady to Cohoes the Mohawk River had made things really difficult. The glacial Iromohawk, draining the Great Lakes, had cut itself a deep gorge about four miles beyond Schenectady and then had gone on to carve out a wide waterfall a mile or so above its junction with the Hudson. Canvass White, engineer for this section, had no choice but to shape his canal to suit the will of the ancient river. At Alexander's Mills, as the gorge area was then called, he ran an aqueduct over to the north shore, and from there pushed his canal on east until he came to Fonda's Ferry, a point some four miles above the river mouth. There he built another aqueduct, which carried the Erie back again to the south shore. After by-passing the Cohoes Falls, the canal was dropped down to the Hudson through a series of locks, and a terminal was built opposite Troy, and another at Albany.

Four years after those opening ceremonies at Rome there were 220 miles of the canal streaming with traffic. "Low bridge, everybody down!" could be heard along the towpath of the whole middle section and most of the Mohawk Valley section of the Erie. "Canawl" was the familiar word now, not "canal." Bumpers' hotels were growing up in the neighborhood of the locks and basins, chatty places where

> It's one cent for coffee
> Two cents for bread,
> Three for mince pie
> And five for a bed.[1]

Four miles an hour was the speed limit, and not even "Dandy, my leader" or "Charlie the buster" could exceed it.

[1] From *Body, Boots and Britches*. Copyright, 1939, by Harold W. Thompson. Published by J. B. Lippincott Co.

Attend, all ye drivers, I sing of my team;
They're the fleetest and strongest that ever was seen.
There is none will toll with such speed down the crick
Or start at the word of a driver so quick.[2]

The canal of romance was taking shape, along with the canal of the surveyors and tolltakers.

In November of 1823 the *Hector* arrived in Albany from the head of Seneca Lake, piloted by two "western" farmers who had made the boat themselves out of Seneca trees, had had the sails woven on their home place and the boat packed with things they and their crew had grown themselves. Virginia, Maryland, and Pennsylvania had cause to worry, and those New York City legislators who had voted against the canal should have begun to wonder.

It took the next two years to finish off the western section of the Erie, to decide between Black Rock, on the Niagara River, and Buffalo as the western terminus, and to build the great series of locks at Lockport. But when the job was done in the fall of 1825, New York married her waters in a celebration suited to the Olympian occasion everyone agreed it was.

De Witt Clinton was the center of the cheering. He was governor now, his office the people's reward for risking his career on what President Jefferson had called a mad scheme. The stage-setters had everything arranged by October 26, when the wedding of Lake Erie and the Atlantic Ocean was to begin. Cannons were in place. When the first one at Buffalo roared its salute to the first barge to enter the canal from the lake, its sound was to be the signal for the next one east of it to be fired, and so on down the Mohawk Valley, and down the Hudson until the artillery blessing reached New York City.

[2] *Ibid.*

At nine o'clock that morning the *Seneca Chief* with the governor and the chief engineers and distinguished guests on board started east, two kegs of Lake Erie water on its deck. It was followed by the *Chief* and the *Superior*, the *Commodore Perry* and the *Buffalo*. *Noah's Ark* carried "products of the west," including two eagles, a bear, two fawns, a couple of fish, and a pair of Seneca Indian boys. The roar of the cannons rushed ahead of them, proclaiming to the waiting thousands along the canal that the great work was done. The rumbling of the artillery reached New York City in an hour and twenty minutes.

The jilted town of Black Rock swallowed its pride, and sent the *Niagara*, which, with the *Young Lion of the West*, joined the flotilla at Lockport.

Governor Clinton and his party had to be stout men to survive the toasts and trenchermen feasts that had been prepared for them at almost every stop. When they arrived at Rome, however, the epithalamium to which they had been listening changed to a funeral dirge. The citizens, to the sound of muffled drums, solemnly marched down to the canal landing with a black barrel, the contents of which they poured into the water, a mark of their annoyance that the canal had been built a half mile south of the town. That gesture over, however, everybody marched back to Starr's Hotel, "where they put aside their ill-humor, and joined with heart and hand in celebrating the event."

Little Falls, as the boats pulled in at night, must have been an awesome sight. Great bonfires roared out of tar barrels lined along the edge of the cliffs above the locks. Here, of course, there were the inevitable speeches and a banquet.

Fort Plain outdid herself. The day the canal opened, Wagner's Hotel spread "a sumptuous dinner" the whole length of its ballroom. During the course of the meal there were

thirteen "regular" toasts and nineteen "good volunteer" toasts.
The local schoolmaster finished that part of the celebration
by leaping onto the loaded table, which promptly collapsed,
to the huge enjoyment of the befuddled guests.

The night the *Seneca Chief* arrived at Fort Plain Governor Clinton was startled out of his wits by two huge mush-
rooms of light that seemed to float in the air above the banks
of the canal. To his "My God, what is that?" the soberest
members of the crowd answered that the local boys were
merely burning pitch barrels they had hoisted on poles erected
on top of Prospect Hill. John Taylor, another schoolteacher,
suddenly found himself pushed onto the deck of the *Seneca
Chief* and standing in front of the governor. He was complete
master of the situation. With a mild hiccup, he said, "Governor Clinton, this is my friend John Warner's store," bowed
low, and fell into the canal.

At Schenectady there was real gloom. The old dorp was
no longer the port of entry for goods and passengers going
west. The Durham boatbuilders could turn to canalboats, but
the big warehouses along the Binne Kill were strangely quiet.
The Union College cadets marched down to the canal in full
uniform, and fired a welcoming salute, and that's about all
that saved the day. The town's newspapers had suggested a
funeral procession, and no one had made plans for any kind
of official reception. A commentator said later, "The distinguished guests were received respectfully, but without enthusiasm, and conducted to a hotel where dinner was eaten in
a sober manner." There were no volunteer toasts in the dorp,
and probably no regular ones.

Albany, next to New York City, turned on the most elaborate reception of the trip. There was a procession of state
officials, army and navy units, and societies of every kind,
which ended at the Capitol, where the canal backers had so

long battled for their "ditch." After that there was a parade
back to a dinner, served on tables set up for six hundred on
the gaily decorated Columbia Street Bridge.

The final benediction on the wedding of the waters, of
course, could be pronounced only in New York harbor. The
canalboat flotilla arrived on the morning of November 4.
When at last the naval pageant was ready, exceeding "in
beauty and magnificence any fete which the world had ever
witnessed," a ringing pre-Grover Whalen outburst declared,
the solemn nuptials took place. And De Witt Clinton, as high
priest, rose to the occasion.

"This solemnity at this place," he said, pouring his Lake
Erie water into the Atlantic, "on the first arrival of vessels
from Lake Erie, is intended to indicate and commemorate the
navigable communication, which has been accomplished between our Mediterranean Seas and the Atlantic Ocean. . . ."
There was more about the public spirit of the people of New
York, and a request "that the God of the Heavens and Earth
smile most propitiously on this work."

In the meantime a procession some five miles long had
been marching down Broadway to the Battery to welcome the
returning ships. Public buildings were illuminated that night,
and there was a great ball, where, during supper, the guests
found "floating in its proper element (the waters of the Erie)
a miniature canal-boat, made entirely of maple sugar."

New York City, which hadn't wanted the canal at all,
oh'd and ah'd before its City Hall, ablaze with 2,300 candles
and lamps. The New York City that went to sleep that night,
as the magnificence guttered out, was a transformed city, as
was the state and the nation. Virginia, Maryland, and Penn-
sylvnia, resting their chins on the wall of the Appalachians,
could watch the procession of boats move west along the
Erie Canal to the promised land, and return east again to the

city at the mouth of the Hudson, heavy with all the new land had to offer. They could watch, but that was about all, for none of them had been given a river like the Mohawk, with its gateway to the West.

20

The Towpath Miracle

Schenectady, Schenectady
Is halfway up to Uticy . . .

THE old dorp took very little pleasure in listening to the
canal drivers along the towpath sing about their mules or call
out their "Low bridge!" warning to their passengers on the
cabin roofs of the packet boats. Right through the heart of
town the bumpers would go, singing:

> I've got a mule and her name is Sal,
> Fifteen years on the Erie Canal,
> She's a good old worker and a good old pal,
> Fifteen years on the Erie Canal . . .

Fifteen years after the canal began operations, however,
Schenectady was still trying to recover her early prosperity.
The great fire that burned out most of the lower town in 1819,
and then Clinton's Ditch, slowed down life in the dorp considerably.

The new canalboats, passenger packets of thirty-one tons,
"line boats," lake boats, and the big "bull heads" of seventy-
two tons with their deckhouses that just scraped under some
of those low bridges, floated serenely through the old Dutch

town and on to Troy and Albany and New York City. No
bateaux and Durham boats unloading at the Binne Kill any
more and transferring their goods to the wagons for the haul
over the pine plains to Albany.

Troy, though, grew by leaps and bounds. Fifteen years
after the gala "Wedding of the Waters," Troy, helped by
traffic on the Champlain Canal, had jumped from a village of
4,800 people to a bustling transfer point for New England
goods, a city of 17,000.

And Philadelphia mourned with the dorp Schenectady,
for what the canal took away from one community it gave to
its rivals in double and triple measure. New York City—no,
they hadn't wanted the canal—tripled its population during
the first twenty years of towpath life and became the greatest
port on the Atlantic seaboard. Sing, you drivers, and bring
on the riches of the West!

> Haul in yer bowlines,
> Stand by the saddle mule;
> Low bridge, boys, dodge yer head,
> Don't stand up a-like a fool,
> For the Erie is a-risin'
> And the whiskey's gittin' low;
> I hardly think we'll git a drink
> Till we git to Buffalo.

Buffalo! Where the West begins! In 1816 the Buffalo
fathers were offering $5 for every wolf killed in the village
limits. The 1,000 people there four years later were increased
by 8,000 more five years after the *Seneca Chief* and her bridal
party of canalboats began the long nuptial trip east. Five
years after that there were another 10,000 people in Buffalo,
and the Lord knows what had become of the wolves.

The new towns of the Whitestown country blossomed

and fruited without regard to season. The sweetest music in their ears was Erie Water music:

> Three days out from Albany
> A pirate we did spy;
> The black flag with the skull and bones
> Was a-wavin' up on high;
> We signaled to the driver
> To h'ist the flag o' truce,
> When we found it was the *Mary Jane*
> Just out o' Syracuse . . .[1]

The *Mary Jane* was probably heavy in the water with Star Brand salt from the great salt mines of Salina township. Salt was the beginning of Syracuse's meteoric rise. In 1820 one traveler said Syracuse was "so desolate it would make an owl weep to fly over it." By 1840 ten thousand people had swelled this wilderness town into city size.

That was what the wild-eyed scheme New York had taken to President Jefferson was doing to the lucky towns. By 1840 any place worthy of being called a city in New York State was flexing its statistics on the banks of the Grand Canal. The state itself doubled its population by that year— and its productivity. Paddy and his Irish cousins had helped dig the ditch. They quickly spread the pie-in-the-sky news of the wonderful, rich land, and the rush was on, from Ireland, from Germany, out of the Old World into the New. By 1835 New York's foreign population was increased by 450 per cent, until there was one alien for every twenty-four Yorkers, and one for every ten citizens in the new Queen of Ports.

The puzzled questions of the farmers along the Mohawk River who saw their old grain monopoly pass west with the

---

[1] John A. and Allan Lomax, *American Ballads and Folk Songs*. The Macmillan Company, 1934.

westbound settlers was answered in part by such pioneer
songs as this:

> Then there's the state of New York, where some are very rich,
> Themselves and a few others have dug a mighty ditch,
> To render it more easy for us to find the way,
> And sail upon the waters to Mich-i-gan-i-a—
> Yea, yea, yea, to Mich-i-gan-i-a!

The "far West" of Michigan, Wisconsin, Indiana, and
Minnesota grew on the new life that poured in through the
Mohawk Gateway to the Lakes. The tide rolled fast. In 1820
a mere 120 boats arrived at and departed from Buffalo. Five
years later 359 of them loaded cargo and passengers there.
Two years after that the number jumped to 972!

> . . . yea, yea, yea, to Mich-i-gan-i-a!

Detroit, in 1830, struggled to start some 15,000 pioneers
on their way to the western settlements. A Mississippian wrote
that "perhaps more than half the northern immigrants arrive
at present by way of the New York Canal and Lake Erie."
Between 1830 and 1840 Indiana added almost 350,000 people
to her population and Illinois did almost as well, the majority
of the pioneers crowding in along the 363-mile "Big Ditch,"
old folks and children, doubting mothers and anxious fathers
jammed into packet-boat cabins like "two mice in a mitten,"
as one traveler wrote.

"We left Schenectady," he said, "about five, with a full
cabin of passengers, of whom a good part were ladies . . . in
fact we were as thick as two mice in a mitten: there were
not seats enough for us to sit in . . . the drivers were halloing
and swearing, the boat was bumping and thumping against
others . . . [that night] when we came to stow twenty-four
of us into a little room 10 x 15, 2 or 3 deep, my hope of sleep

was but small. The air was hot as an oven. Some were groaning and scolding. Some were snoring like a steamboat. . . . I attempted to thrust my legs out the window, but the noise of a passing boat made me glad to draw them in."

The inconveniences of canalboat travel were not stopping anybody. The Schenectady boys who today use the abandoned lock a mile or so west of the city for a swimming hole might be startled by the thought of twenty thousand canalboats shoving into their summer tank in one season, one every seventeen minutes, night and day.

Although New York State and the rest of the nation were reborn in the traffic that "locked" through the Erie like motes in a sunbeam, the great valley that made it all possible made the least profit out of the early canal years and was forced to change many of its ancient ways.

Johnstown, nerve center of the forgotten Iroquois world, the Tory roost during the Revolution and the raids of the "blue-eyed Indians," once the seat of a Tryon County that stretched to Lake Erie itself, the shire town of Sir William Johnson's barony, lost its old dignity as the Erie Canal diverted the town's traffic to Fonda. A group of Fonda land speculators threw Johnstown into mourning when they persuaded the legislature to make Fonda the seat of Montgomery County. Some amends were made in 1838, when Johnstown was made the seat of new Fulton County, named in honor of the steamboat's inventor.

"Stumptown," now Gloversville, a few miles north of Johnstown, grew as the canal carried east and west the fine buckskin moccasins and gloves its leatherworkers were turning out.

But it was chiefly along the towpath that the sound of the mills grew louder and louder. Amsterdam, by 1840, with its new rug factory, was well on the way to becoming the carpet capital of America. Here also were a scythe factory, two furnaces, and two gristmills, crowding along Chuctanunda Creek. The valley's water power was turning new wheels, and the canal was carrying off the mounds of knit goods, and scythes, and pottery, and cowbells, and the rest of it to customers deep in the woods of new frontiers.

Fultonville was practically a child of the canal. Here was a dry-dock where the boats damaged by the "raging canawl" could put up for repairs, and there were places for the crews to take on liquid courage for the storms west of them.

> The captain came on deck, with spyglass in his hand,
> But the fog it was so 'tarnal thick he couldn't spy the land;
> He put his trumpet to his mouth, as loud as he could bawl,
> He hailed for assistance from the ragin can-all.
>
> The sky was rent asunder, the lightning it did flash.
> The thunder rattled above, just like eternal smash;
> The clouds were all upsot, and the rigging it did fall,
> And we scudded under bare poles, on the raging can-all.
>
> A mighty sea rolled on astern, and then it swept our deck,
> And soon our gallant little craft was but a floating wreck;
> All hands sprung forward, after the mainsheet for to haul,
> And slap dash! went the chicken coop into the ragin can-all.[1]

The bumpers had to dream up some excitement to compensate for an "ocean" only 4 feet deep and 40 feet wide from shore to shore.

There was the new canal village of Canajoharie on the south shore of the Mohawk, which drew its life from the Erie, and paid for its prosperity with "suds" from its own brewery and the whisky of its two distilleries. On West Hill, behind the town, was a quarry from which much of the fine

---

[1] John A. and Allan Lomax, *American Ballads and Folk Songs.*

stone was taken for the Erie locks and retaining walls. In later years the quarry became known as "Brooklyn Bridge Pond" because it furnished the stone for the abutments of that grandfather of Manhattan's bridges.

The turning wheels of the expanding Mohawk Valley factories meshed perfectly with the endless chain of canal-boats. Little Falls gave up being picturesque, although a Gazetteer of 1840 said the town was "situated on both sides of the Mohawk River in a most romantic situation . . ." but how busy its mills were with quite unromantic activity! The Gazetteer goes on to note that there were "a woolen factory, 3 paper mills, 3 flour mills, 2 plaster factories, 1 trip hammer, 4 furnaces, 1 machine shop, 1 distillery, 1 brewery, 1 fulling mill, 1 sash factory." It was a new kind of life the Erie Canal brought to the Mohawk Valley towns; the Gazetteer's picture is a good measure of the change that had swept over the land of the Long House. The Iroquois Trail had been wide enough for a man with a pack on his back. Wagon roads, turnpikes, a river only good enough for bateaux and Durham boats, and now the Grand Canal; hundreds of thousands of tons of goods moved easily east and west now where a hundred years earlier oxen had sweated to haul scow loads of beaver skin around the Little Falls rapids.

> Schenectady, Schenectady
> Is halfway up to Uticy.

"Arrived in the 'Dorp Von Schagnactada!'" wrote a Yankee student at Union College in the early canal years. "The good Dutch city preserves well its ancient character for want of change, and were it not for a few enterprising New England souls would be ten times more insupportably dull than the sleepy energies of the fumigating 'Vans' have already rendered it. Five years past has brightened the face of things

more than the preceding fifty." The "fumigating Vans" may
have protested the changes these Yankees were working, but
it was too late; the quiet Dutch world of the Groote Vlachte
was gone. Arendt Van Curler's "most beautiful land" was being planted to broom corn, and the canal had by 1840 restored
most of the prosperity it had taken away at first.

"Uticy," at the other end of the valley, however, was a
hive of bobbins and looms, a city now of almost thirteen thousand. The Erie ran through the center of the business section,
and was crossed by a series of "elevated and elegant bridges."
Shades of Hugh White and Eliphalet Stark of the "Oneida
Woods"! Old Fort Schuyler, or Utica, they had said, was to
be Whitestown's "port." But Whitestown, or Whitesboro now,
was a modest mill village of 1,800 Yorkers and New Englanders, an appendage to booming Utica, the sophisticated city of
18 churches, 188 stores, 10 academies, a public library, and
six weekly newspapers, its streets dignified with imposing
Greek Revival houses.

It was the farmers along the Mohawk River and in the
uplands who had to change their old ways after the Paddy
boys finished digging the Big Ditch. Mohawk Valley wheat,
which had fed Washington's armies, was no longer able to
compete with Genesee wheat, floating into the New York market now at prices too low for the Mohawk farmers to try to
meet. When the first settlers moved into the Whitestown
country it cost $100 to move a ton of goods west from New
York City. After General Schuyler finished his locks at Little
Falls and Rome in 1796, the haulage charge from Seneca Lake
fell to $32, and the Erie Canal completed the price revolu-
tion by bringing the freight rate down to $12 a ton from Buf-
falo to New York City, a transportation miracle, if there ever
was one.

So the valley farmers turned to broom corn and vegetable

crops and cows. Many of the old grainfields were turned to pasture, and cheese and butter regained for the descendants of the Palatines along the river and the New Englanders and Scotchmen who had cleared the upland acres much of the wealth that had long come from their land. "Herkimer County cheese" went east and west along the canal in huge shipments until Wisconsin captured the cheese market and borrowed the name "Herkimer" for her own cheese.

The canal was the great catalyst. Not only did it cause the Mohawk River farmers to shift from grain to cows and orchards, to broom corn and vegetables. Towpath life had its attractions, and many a young man preferred the $12 a month "and found" which he got as a driver of boats like the *Mary Jane* to standing in front of a frame in one of the cotton mills. Men got $12, and boys about $10, and the life wasn't soft.

> . . . it's tramp, tramp, tramp,
> And tighten up your lines,
> And watch the playful horseflies
> As o'er the mules they climb.
> Gidap, gidap, whoa!
> Forget it I never shall
> When I drove a pair of spavined mules
> On the Erie Canal.

Towpath life was rough, and not only for the boatmen. The locktenders were a breed all their own. They had to be smart politicians, for, unless they guessed right on election day, they were out of a job. The tenders were generally appointed for seven months, and held their jobs as long as their politics were in good order. Salary: $32 to $40 a month in the latter years of the canal; and the duties were simple enough: lean your back against the gate when you see a boat coming, and shove. Keep your 10 by 10 shanty meticulously clean and the poker stove polished against an unscheduled visit of an inspector.

Lodging was usually provided for a locktender and his family in a lockhouse in full view of the incoming boats. Here the local arguments were thrashed out, and frequently rescue parties organized to rush down to a nearby "horse hole," gouged in the bank of the canal, in order to pull out some hapless "Sal" that had got tangled in the lines and then tumbled into the water.

The canal store alongside the locks carried chiefly hay and oats, and usually a stock of groceries and dry goods for a canaller's "missus." If a canal store had a good supply of fresh drinking water always on hand, the proprietor could be sure of steady business.

Death on a canalboat was one of the gruesome aspects of towpath life. A boat would tie up at a lock, its cargo of potatoes forgotten while a dour-faced steersman and his crying wife took off a child who had succumbed to the airless, cramped sleeping quarters, the stink of the cattle, and the swarming flies. Burial over, the parents would return, "lock" their boat through, and the singing and the noise would quiet down among the bumpers until the boat was well on its way.

One group of canallers, sick of quarreling with the poormaster of the towns where they had had to leave the body of some unfortunate crew member, established a little cemetery of their own between Vischer's Ferry and the great aqueduct at Rexford, or Alexander's Mill then, near Schenectady. It's an unkempt, weedy spot today, near a canal jog still known as "Fundy's Basin."

Towpath life was rough, but it was always changing. Towns seemed to grow almost as you looked at them. A farmhouse on what had been the edge of Schenectady found itself

included in the town, and then "improved" by the addition
of a Greek portico and four "carpenter's Doric" columns. The
new courthouse at Fonda would have made a satisfactory
backdrop for Brutus's oration over the body of Caesar; there
wasn't a valley town that wasn't touched by the Greek and
Roman Revival in architecture. The millowner could now re-
tire at night to his new house, a classical pseudo-Greek
temple, and his "hands" to the row-houses of the mill village.
And each of them could hear, morning and night:

> Low bridge, everybody down!
> Low bridge, we're comin' to a town!

Deckhands got $8 a month. When the boats laid up at
night, a man could bunk on board, or take his chances in a
bumpers' hotel where:

> There's eighty-three boarders
> All packed at my door
> And they paid their five cents
> For to sleep on the floor.
>
> The breeze from the gutter
> Is the salt-water smell
> On the European plan
> At the bumpers' hotel.[1]

The songs Erie Water generated were rough and full of
sound and smell, wild exaggeration and tear-jerking senti-
mentality. They were full of wonderful characters like "Sal":

The cook we had on board the deck stood six feet in her socks,
Her hand was like an elephant's ear and her breath would open
    the locks.

[1] From *Body, Boots and Britches*. Copyright, 1939, by Harold W.
Thompson. Published by J. B. Lippincott Co.

A maid of fifty summers was she, the most of her body was on
    the floor,
And when at night she went to bed, oh, sufferin', how she'd snore!

Or dumb beasts like Sal, the mule:

> I don't have to call when I want my Sal,
> Fifteen years on the Erie Canal;
> She trots from the stall like a good old girl,
> Fifteen years on the Erie Canal.
> I eat my meals with Sal each day,
> I eat beef and she eats hay;
> She ain't so slow, if you want to know,
> She put the "Buff" in the Buffalo.

The Grand Canal changed life in America enormously.
It spawned the new states in the Ohio Valley and the Northwest Territory, and forced Philadelphia to yield to New York
City as the first port in the nation. But, most important, it
bound the West to the East, and gave the states on both sides
of the Appalachian barrier common interests. It's ironic, in a
way, to think back to Jefferson's "No!" to New York's plea for
federal funds to help in the building of the Erie. It was New
York's canal, more than any other agent, that strengthened the
hand of the Washington government in the early days of the
Republic, and strengthened the impulses toward federal control.

"Haul up at either end, and git what you can!" was the
towpath rule when the ice locked in the boats at the end of a
season. The rule expressed a growing American philosophy,
nowhere more clearly than in the cutthroat competition of the
railroads, which had never entered into De Witt Clinton's
thinking when he was carrying on his fight for the Big Ditch.

The fight began, and grew hot in the Mohawk Valley,
as the railroad dynasts drove the iron horse through the same

gateway where Erie Water rolled. From canoe to oxcart, and oxcart to stagecoach, and then to the canal's *Mary Jane* and the railroad's iron horse the story was the same: an unhappy Philadelphia merchant summed it up when he wrote, after a discouraging visit to booming New York City, "Transportation is king!"

21
The Great Abstraction

IT WOULD BE easy to write a Sunday Supplement account of the coming of the railroad. I could call the chapter "The Iron Horse" and tell you how that skittish creature was coaxed into the Mohawk Valley. I could key the tale to Mr. Brown's silhouette of the first train that rolled up to the edge of the valley, headed by the *De Witt Clinton*, New York's first locomotive. Mr. Brown said the cars were filled with excited excursionists that day. The impetuous "forward movement" of the monstrous three and a half-ton engine knocked off stovepipe hats, while ladies' parasols went up in smoke as the cinders from the "chimney" ignited the bright silk. Wayside gapers fell out of the carriages they had driven up to the railroad's right-of-way, Mr. Brown said, as their horses shied at the hissing horror that scorched by them at fifteen miles an hour, headed west from Albany toward Schenectady.

The story of New York's first railroad, however, is two stories, a story within a story.

The story behind the coming of the iron horse of course isn't quaint. It's a story of a raid, of many raids. It's a story of very honorable men—at least, most of them beyond reproach, family men, who muscled in—how they would have gagged at that phrase—on the people of New York State.

If I called the chapter "The Iron Horse" I would tell you how poor Henry Meigs lost his reputation in 1817, and the respect of his friends in the New York legislature, because he flatly affirmed that steam locomotives would work. I'd bring in Colonel John Stevens of Hoboken, New Jersey, who as early as 1812 proposed connecting Lake Erie and the Hudson River with a railroad on which cars were to be drawn by a steam engine. The colonel, who said a hundred miles an hour would be possible, must have got tired of big men like Chancellor Livingston and Gouverneur Morris, who thought he was crazy.

The raid story has certain comic overtones. It begins with an Englishman, wealthy, an Oxonian, who married a Duane and set up a gentleman's estate at Duanesburg, southwest of Schenectady, on the edge of the Mohawk watershed. His name was George Featherstonhaugh. The valley people pronounce the name just as it's spelled, though it was rumored foreigners came by asking for "Mr. Feastonhay."

George Featherstonhaugh, too, believed in railroads. By 1825 he had a hardheaded plan laid out for a railroad between Albany and Schenectady, a double-track affair over which some fifty horses were to cart the cream of the Erie Canal traffic. He planned "60 hired men and boys at $150 a year" apiece, who would be busy hauling 200,000 tons of freight between the Mohawk and the Hudson. He noted the Erie Canal figures for 1824, some 157,000 tons, and then proceeded to "abstract" 100,000 of those tons for his horsecars and another 100,000 tons which would be available as soon as the canal froze up for the season. He figured the canal freight and toll charges on 200,000 tons would amount to $217,000. The same number of tons carried by his railroad "at 3 cents per ton per mile," would be

	$ 96,000	
	$121,000	gain to the Publick
Deduct Annual Charge	$23,000	
Profit	$73,000	

The bigger of the two stories is not concerned chiefly with the coming of the railroad. That was as inevitable as the fact that pushed wheels roll. The story I'm going to tell begins with Mr. Featherstonhaugh's word "abstracted." It begins with his plan to abstract freight from the Erie Canal, taking for his railroad 100,000 tons of its trade, and the tolls which it paid to the state of New York. "Profit: $73,000," George Featherstonhaugh wrote on his estimate sheet, as he put his other hand into the treasury of the state and counted out a large part of that "profit" in public money.

With George Featherstonhaugh begin the raids on the "People's Highway," the Grand Canal, dug with public money through the Mohawk Valley, through the Whitestown country, to Lake Erie. The men who followed him knew that transportation was, indeed, king of a golden empire, and they thought they had found a way to usurp the throne and turn the reign into a dictatorship.

And they had.

First, though, before I tell you how they did it, let me point out a few things about the Erie Canal, this golden ditch, that you may not know. It was the great hope of its backers that it would not only pay for itself out of its tolls, but that it would forever abolish taxation on real and personal property in New York State. The success of the canal gave them every reason to believe that the state could forgo taxgathering indefinitely.

"On the canal every man can be the carrier of his own property," wrote one discerning railroad man. The Grand Canal was, in truth, Everyman's Highway, built by the state, the great gamble that won. The winnings belonged to the citizens of New York. The "take," direct and indirect, however, proved so enormous that it enriched the whole nation. If the state could have held off the raiders in those early days, Everyman's Highway could have gone on for generations doubling and trebling its golden traffic. The state's first plan, indeed, was to make the railroads public property. There was room for them, many said, not only physically, along the side of the towpath, through the Mohawk's gateway to the Lakes, but within the transportation kingdom that in New York had just become a democracy.

"Profit: $73,000." George Featherstonhaugh figured there was that much return a year possible on an investment of about $150,000 in building his little horsecar railroad across the pine plains between the Hudson River and the Mohawk. The fact that much of that profit would have to be "abstracted" from the traffic on the state's Erie Canal was not a matter for discussion.

No, the other story that must be joined to the tale of the coming of the iron horse into New York is in a way the story of the coming of a horse bent on claiming the public pastures for itself. As Featherstonhaugh's horsecar idea grew into the Mohawk and Hudson Railroad, and Schenectady was linked to Utica, and then Utica to Syracuse, link on link until the rails ended in Buffalo, the process of abstracting passengers and freight from the People's Highway was turned into an art. With its perfecting was born the New York Central Railroad in the middle of the century, and so died the great dream of transportation democracy, in which canals and railroads were to be joined for the benefit of only one master: the citizens of New York State.

Don't misunderstand me. Men who could break down any frontier set up against them, the fragile boundaries east of the Iroquois hunting grounds, the paper boundaries of the colonial land grants, the political and social boundaries of George III's England, would hardly pause before the shadow boundary the state of New York tried, in the early days of the Grand Canal, to establish along the margins of the People's Highway. Jefferson had told De Witt Clinton that his canal plan was one hundred years too early. So visionary New Yorkers dug their canal only to discover that the truth of Jefferson's statement lay in the inability of their neighbors to follow democracy out of their convention halls, to see it alive as heart's blood in the great ditch they had dug for themselves and the nation.

So the abstracting began. In 1826 neither side was sure of how much of a war had been declared, or could have guessed at the dark powers they were releasing. When that first railroad charter was granted there wasn't a steam locomotive in America. It wasn't until three years later that Horatio Allen, the son of a Union College professor, ran the *Stourbridge Lion* for its only trip down the tracks of the Honesdale Coal Company in Pennsylvania. Peter Cooper's *Tom Thumb* made its initial run out of Baltimore in August, 1830, and it was five months after that, in South Carolina, that a steam locomotive pulled the first passenger coaches in anything approximating regular service.

There's a touch of mystery about Mr. Featherstonhaugh and New York's first railroad. The whole scheme was his. It was he who filed the charter application, and published it in the Schenectady *Cabinet* in December, 1825. The doubting

editor of that sheet offered to return the $1.56 the notice cost
if the legislature turned the application down, and fully expected to have to make good.

The state granted the charter all right, but the turnpike
company operating out of Albany smelled competition and
protested vigorously. The result was an unworkable charter:
the railroad company's directors and stockholders were made
personally liable for any debts their road contracted, and the
charter killed off any hope of financing the business by a
proviso that the state could take over the company at the end
of five years.

So there were few takers for the stock of the Mohawk
and Hudson. George Featherstonhaugh and the company's
chief engineer now went off to England in order to study
John Bull's railroads. Steam locomotives had won the day
there, though some doctors were predicting that the wild 15-
mile-an-hour speeds would addle the passengers' heads.

After two years of observing England's steam triumphs,
Featherstonhaugh returned to New York, determined to get
rid of the hobbling charter clauses. The Mohawk and Hudson Railroad Company, tabled during his absence, came to
life with a rush. But the new charter was at least workable.
Big names filled out the new board of nine directors, among
them John Jacob Astor, James Duane, and the patroon,
Stephen Van Rensselaer.

Board meetings were held at Astor's house in New York
City. Orders went out to buy timber, buy up the right-of-
way into the Mohawk Valley, at Schenectady. And then, in
March, 1829, the whole fury of activity stopped. Orders were
sent out to stop buying. James Duane disappeared from the
board roster after April 1, and George Featherstonhaugh no
longer attended the meetings. On July 31 the author of the
whole project resigned, sold his stock to the company, and

disappeared from the pages of railroad history. Why? Personal tragedy, the loss of two of his children, then his wife, and on his return from England, the burning of his Duanesburg estate were enough to sour any project for a man, though Featherstonhaugh went off to find a full life as a notable geologist and author, and the Mohawk and Hudson Railroad Company, stimulated by its high-powered directors, was turned into track, and construction gangs, into the West Point Associates' third locomotive, the *De Witt Clinton*. By March, 1831, the New York Exchange listed Mohawk and Hudson par stock at 196¾. One wonders a little about those early board meetings, and Mr. Astor, and if, perhaps, Mr. Featherstonhaugh may not himself have been abstracted from the affairs of the company.

The battle of the People's Highway opened as though it were Race Day at the county fair. The *De Witt Clinton*, its firebox roaring, stood at the western edge of Albany, its five stagecoaches remodeled so that they could run on the twelve miles of strap-iron and wood rails laid across the pine plains to Schenectady. The "Exhibition Run" had sold out at 50 cents a head. Mr. John Clark, New York's first conductor, collected his tickets from the apprehensive passengers, climbed into his buggy seat behind the tender, and "gave the signal with a tin horn."

There was a violent jerk. Beaver hats collapsed against the coach roofs and a shower of smoke and sparks surged back among the passengers. Everyone was delighted, and frightened to death, and the train moved. The cheers of the sightseers were answered by the screeching of the iron-rimmed wooden engine wheels. At the water stop the coaches banged into each other, so Conductor Clark invented a rough coupling on the spot by borrowing rails from a nearby fence, which he wedged between his carriages.

The *De Witt Clinton* came to a halt at the railhead, alongside an inclined plane which the company had had to build to get their coaches from the high ground above Schenectady down to the canal basin; it was similar to the plane at the Hudson River end of the line.

Mr. Brown, the silhouette artist, reported that the passengers were welcomed by cheering thousands. Following ample refreshments at Mr. Givens's Hotel, Mr. Clark herded his excursionists back to the coaches, and "without any accident or delay" got them back again to Albany. That was August 9, 1831, the day the nine directors and their stockholders began abstracting the life of the Grand Canal. It was a little like a day in the life of Mrs. Kinfort, a lady in a shocking poem. Mrs. Kinfort ate her husband, a little of him at each meal, and he never knew it until she reached the edge of his mind one day. Then it was too late, for he had lost the will to resist.

Ten days after the Exhibition Trip the Albany *Argus* indicated what an appetite the Mohawk and Hudson was developing:

> Travel amounts to 3 and 4 hundred persons a day and is yet only commenced. The income of this company from present appearances will be about $140,000 a year for passengers only and the stock instead of being worth 70 per cent advance is worth 6 or 7 hundred per cent.

The *Argus* exaggerated, but in a little more than four months the new road banked almost $9,000 profit.

The "beautiful, light race horse-looking machine" was ready now to run for the stakes, and they were obviously going to be enormous. In the next ten years New York State granted 106 railroad charters, and in doing so, unwittingly invited 106 Mrs. Kinforts to feed on its lifeblood.

The nibbling was easy to take, at first. No one seemed to care, for instance, that the Mohawk and Hudson broke its agreement with the state as soon as it began its freight-carrying career. The charter had put no ban on freight; there was just the matter of charges and tolls: don't exceed the canal rates, the company was told, for 1826. In fact, a good many canallers hoped passengers would quit the boats for the newfangled railroad, and maybe take some of their light-weight goods along with them, and leave the heavy work to Erie Water.

So the Mohawk and Hudson did some figuring. For 45¼ cents per ton they thought they could pay costs on any kind of freight between Schenectady and Albany. Imme-diately the road bought some thirty "freight wagons" and two locomotives, the *Mohawk* and the *Hudson*, to do the hauling. Charges to customers were modest: $1.25 a ton, plus transfer charges of 50 cents and 75 cents a ton at the Schenectady and Albany ends of the line. The canal was charging only 60 cents a ton on eastbound freight. Nobody complained.

Railroading was new in 1833, and there was much to learn about costs. The Mohawk and Hudson's figuring was all wrong, but it took the depression of 1837 and a growing awareness of what competition with the People's Highway really meant to revise the directors' early dreams of huge freight profits. By 1840 the revised dream was producing bet-ter results, however. The rates were a tiny bit discriminatory: if you could lure freight from a canalboat, you charged only 62½ cents a ton; a Schenectady citizen paid $1 a ton on his freight; but to anybody transferring goods from the new Saratoga and Schenectady Railroad, well, a $1.25 charge seemed fair. Seven years later the road was carrying freight only as an "accommodation," and privately cursing the canal for spoiling a good thing.

For the Yankee and the Dutchman who rode in those early "Gothic" coaches, modeled after the cast-iron stoves invented by Union College's president, Eliphalet Nott, the railroad was the greatest thing that had ever happened. One of Dr. Nott's students really let himself go, when he wrote in his diary, after returning from a jaunt to Albany in 1837:

> It is a majestic sight to see a train of carriages with a locomotive at their head move off at the rate of 30 miles an hour and bidding defiance to every obstruction—scouring the country with the quickness of light and annihilating space.

Railroads were thrilling. Speed, and the sound of whistles and bells, and escaping steam were enough to crowd out any philosophizing on the place of this wonderful iron horse in New York's economy.

Mrs. Kinfort liked to walk with her beloved husband in their garden before she continued her carnivorous activities. Railroad directors enjoyed walking down the legislature's hallways, filling them with good talk about charters. Erastus Corning, director of the Mohawk and Hudson, had no trouble in seeing the railroad paralleling the towpath from Schenectady west to Utica. The wide green valley of the Mohawk, narrowing to its gateway through the rock pass at Little Falls, widening again into the old Whitestown country, there was the most valuable railroad right-of-way in America: the water-level route to the Lakes.

The thirteen directors of the Utica and Schenectady Railroad Company were elected at a stockholders' meeting at Congress Hall, in Albany, on August 17, 1833. Mr. Corning was made president. Their charter was a little different from the Mohawk and Hudson's. No freight carrying for the Utica and Schenectady Railroad. The canal commissioners, unlike

Mrs. Kinfort's husband, were beginning to set up defenses
against the traffic appetite of these railroad men.

Obviously, the passengers who for years had been jolted
over the north-shore road of the Mohawk Turnpike Company
would turn now to the new annihilator of space. Before the
Utica and Schenectady could enjoy the stagecoach business it
was compelled to buy out the turnpike company, for which it
got the tollhouses and the out-of-repair road. It was worth it,
for the Mohawk Valley was crowded with an ever-growing
throng of travelers, emigrants, settlers of all kinds, sightseers,
heading for Genesee country and the Lakes.

By the fall of 1835 a Mr. Fink of Manheim, a post town
just east of Herkimer, could, if he protested enough, collect
$500 from the Utica and Schenectady Railroad for blast dam-
age to his tavern; the arbitrators were told to pay less, if
possible. Six locomotives had been ordered from the Baldwin
Company of Philadelphia. There was trouble in getting the
red cedar from Canada needed for roadbed. Wages were
high: as much as $18 a month "for a common laboring man."

But the wooden rails, with their strap-iron facing, were
laid on their sleepers, and the company's agents debated
where to locate the stables and the watering places. There was
still some reluctance to depend wholly on iron horses. Hoffman's Ferry, between Scotia and Amsterdam, was decided
upon, and then Spracker's Tavern in the town of Palatine, provided, of course, these sites were turned over to the company as gifts. Ground was taken over for barns and stables
in Little Falls and Herkimer, and, after a good deal of
wrangling, a station site was chosen for the western terminal,
on the square at the foot of Genesee Street in Utica.

The directors got seventy-eight miles of railroad for
about a million and a half dollars. They had great plans. Once
the road was open, they would double-track the route. There

would be two kinds of passengers, those who rode in the "50 pleasure cars" and the second-class passengers, those who would fill up the "50 wagons for the accommodation of emigrants."

Mrs. Kinfort would have enjoyed that garden ride up the Mohawk Valley on August 1, 1836, with the directors of the Utica and Schenectady Railroad Company. It was the first run, and a gala day in every town along the route. It took two trains of ten cars each to haul the directors and their invited guests to Utica, where the town turned out and cheered as loudly for the arrival of these iron horses as it had when the canalboat *Chief Engineer* had drifted into town on the first Erie Water, almost seventeen years earlier.

The trip back was the one that counted. Special fares were collected that day. It took from 8:00 A.M. until 2:30 P.M. to get to Schenectady, but there were no complaints. Some of the passengers were hazarding the guess that soon the 12-mile-an-hour rate might be raised to twenty miles an hour. Even at $3 a trip this was better than packet-boat traveling at three miles an hour, and a lot better than jouncing along the turnpike. The tavernkeepers, of course, didn't like this new dispensation, seeing their best grog passengers steaming by from Mr. Givens's hotel in Schenectady to Mr. Bagg's elegant hostelry in Utica, with nothing more for their old turnpike haunts than a wave of the hand.

Remember, the Utica and Schenectady could carry no freight. The packet-boat owners groaned to see their trade go over to the railroad, but the canal commissioners were satisfied to cut down Erie passenger travel; the packets ruined the canal's banks with the wake they threw up, and the owners demanded precedence at the locks. The railroad ruined the packets quick enough. By the end of 1840 the Utica and Schenectady had made almost a million dollars profit on passengers; fifteen years later there were no packet boats left.

Get rid of the canal! Railroads are the thing! The legislature was told that it should drain the Erie Canal and turn the prism into a right-of-way for the iron horse. Yet in the first year the Utica and Schenectady Railroad Company operated, the canal collected in tolls alone $4,440,000, almost a half million more than its backers had estimated. Boat operators made millions on top of that, and warehousemen and transfer companies more millions. The indirect profit to the cities and towns of the nation would be beyond estimation.

Never mind. Get rid of the canal. Dividends on railroad stock were 8 per cent, and if some way could be found to break the canal's monopoly on freight—the possibilities were astronomical.

The siren voices of the railroad men were quieted for a time when New York's Canal Investigating Commission, in 1835, turned up with some simple truths. The canal, they said, is everyman's highway. Profits go back into everyman's pocket. It costs four times as much to carry goods on a railroad as it does on the Erie. The commission recommended, rather, a bigger canal, more locks; let Erie Water, they said, be forever the great regulator of commerce.

Railroad men fought such a doctrine with all the bitterness De Witt Clinton's old enemies had used against the "ditch." They needn't have, for the legislature, foolishly counting uncollected canal tolls, took the state into heavy debt, laid out massive canal improvements, and made no plans at all for orderly payment of the debt. Canal contractors made a field day out of mulcting the state; auctions were held among them for the better contracts, in one of Albany's hotels. No railroad could have survived the mismanagement that more and more became the lot of the People's Highway. Yet in spite of the Mrs. Kinforts who now fed along its course, the canal tolls mounted, and the railroad directors had first to look at the canal's charge sheets before they could make up their own.

The dark struggle to control the flow of men and goods through the Mohawk Valley grew in magnitude as railroad men turned their novelty engines into real work horses, and slowly strong-armed their way through the ranks of canal defenders.

The first great railroad objective was to close the gaps in the rails between Albany and the Lakes. By 1839 the Mohawk Valley was joined to Auburn on the west, by the Utica and Syracuse Railroad as far as Syracuse, and then to Auburn, by the Auburn and Syracuse. The first trip from Utica to Syracuse was recorded in the rhapsodic vein the "annihilator of space" seemed always to bring forth:

> Syracuse is now within nine hours of Albany and within nineteen hours of New York. W..... was at Syracuse at half-past eight o'clock yesterday morning, remained until four o'clock and was at home this morning, breakfasting on a salmon taken from Lake Ontario night before last, having traveled 300 miles, passing a night at Utica, nearly a whole day at Syracuse, and being absent only forty-two hours.

Speed, and 8 per cent dividends, and the hope of "abstracting," at last, the control of the east-west flow of traffic through New York State closed that final gap, in 1842, between the little town of Attica and the port of Buffalo. Eight little railroad companies were soon sucking comfortably on the great vein that was the Erie Canal, devouring its passengers chiefly, but more and more absorbing its freight traffic.

New York State, aware too late of its eight Mrs. Kinforts, struggled weakly to keep them in their place. The Mo-

hawk Valley was the canal's heartland; the railroad that ran
through it was told flatly not to handle freight. The Syracuse
and Utica could carry freight if it paid the canal tolls on what
it carried during the season of open water. The last road in
the link between Albany and the Lakes had no restrictions
placed on it at all.

Kill the canal! Drain the prism and make it a bed for
railroads!

The eight little railroads quickly learned to live together
and to work to a common purpose. They learned how to
schedule through traffic, how to avoid some of the canal-toll
payments on the freight they could carry. By 1844 the Utica
and Syracuse was given the legislature's permission to carry
freight "during the suspension of canal traffic only," and, of
course, enjoined to pay tolls.

Business between Albany and Buffalo was, generally, fine.
Every dollar of operating cost brought back $3; sometimes
more; only occasionally a bit less. The wooden rails, iron-
strapped on top, were the worst troublemakers. Sometimes a
strap would come loose and curl up like an ugly, monstrous
snake, tearing through a car floor and disemboweling a passenger. The state ordered the roads to re-lay their tracks with
iron rails. They had the money to do it, or could borrow it
from an enthusiastic public easily enough. Safety devices and
improved engines came along fast. Schenectady got itself
the first Union Station in the country: a Greek-temple sort of
affair which served the Mohawk and Hudson and the Utica
and Schenectady companies.

If I were to end this chapter in the Sunday Supplement
manner, I'd tell you about the wonderful inventor's triumphs
that brought Mr. Featherstonhaugh's railroad plan to fine
maturity. The locomotive's "bogie," for instance, came into
existence on the Mohawk and Hudson; it was that swiveling

platform under the front of the engine that followed the track curves so easily. George Westinghouse, who was advised at Union College to "give up his studies rather than his inventive habit," began his work in Schenectady on the air brake, as important now to a railroad as its locomotive.

The bigger story, however, ends ineffectually, or, to borrow a line from "The Hollow Men," "not with a bang, but a whimper." The railroads won, and the people of New York, without knowing it, lost their hold on the greatest transportation route in America.

The story concludes quite painlessly, in the best Mrs. Kinfort manner: In 1851 the railroad lobby forced the legislature to lift the restrictive tolls that the roads bordering the canal had been carrying and, under pressure, paying into the state's treasury. In that year the lobby had become so strong that it was able to tell the state that the program of canal enlargement would not continue unless the state removed the railroad tolls. It was as blunt as that.

A noted canal historian, Noble Whitford, writing in a state publication, has said of that act: "By it the Legislature gave to the railways redoubled power as competitor for the traffic of the canals—the people's own highway. . . . In after years, the railroads, in the full tide of their opulence, gratefully repaid this generous gift of the people by cutting summer and raising winter rates to a point which has more than once driven the boatmen—partners of the State—from the canals, by combinations, trunk-line pools, and 'differentials' . . . it has also been claimed that every dollar of the subsequent canal debt and of the millions which have been raised by taxation upon the people for its payment—principal and interest—were the result of this act."

> I've got a gal, and her name is Sal,
> Fifteen years on the Erie Canal.

In 1851 "it still remained a fact that the golden stream of (canal) revenues, coming largely from the increasing traffic with the East and from beyond the borders of the state, was enriching its people beyond all other sources, building up the state, paying not only the costs of the canals and their improvements, but the general expenses of the state government, rendering direct taxation for this latter purpose in previous years the exception rather than the rule."

Then there's the state of New York, where some are very rich;
Themselves and a few others have dug a mighty ditch,
To render it more easy for us to find the way,
And sail upon the waters of Mich-i-gan-i-a,
Yea, yea, yea, to Mich-i-gan-i-a!

The coming of the iron horse is a real Hollywood story, full of glamour and civic parades, regular toasts and special toasts, and good, solid human achievement. There was great public rejoicing when the eight little railroads running across the pine plains to Schenectady, and west through the Mohawk Valley and on to the Lakes, became one big railroad, and called itself the New York Central, two years after the passing of that "act to abolish tolls on railroads."

The story within the story, the story of the Great Abstraction, however, ends as sad tales should end, in a farce scene. You may not believe the scene could ever have taken place, but it did.

Five years after Mr. Corning became the first president of the New York Central the legislature of New York received a petition. The petitioners earnestly begged the legislature to ask the voters to call a state convention for the purpose of revising the state's constitution. What were the revisions the petitioners wanted? First, they wanted the executive and legislative branches of the state government abolished. Then they wanted the governor's and the legislators' powers and duties transferred to the president, the vice-president, and the Board of Directors of the New York Central Railroad Company.

Wait. The legislature solemnly agreed to submit the proposition to the voters, who, at the next general election, turned it down by a margin of 6,360 votes!

Mr. Kinfort, it was said, shivered a little, as his good wife made her first meal on the edge of his mind. He may even have been humming something as gay as:

> I eat my meals with Sal each day;
> I eat beef and she eats hay.
> She ain't so slow, if you want to know:
> She put the "Buff" in Buffalo.

BONNY ELOISE [1]

Oh, sweet is the vale where the Mohawk gently glides
On its clear winding way to the sea,
And dearer than all storied streams on the earth besides
Is the bright rolling river to me.

(Chorus)

But sweeter, dearer, yes dearer far than these,
Who charms where others all fail,
Is blue-eyed, bonny, bonny Eloise,
The belle of the Mohawk vale.

Oh sweet are the scenes of my boyhood's sunny years,
That bespangle the gay valley o'er.

[1] In 1860 G. W. Elliott lived in Fort Plain, New York, where he was editor of the *Mohawk Valley Register*. He is remembered now as the author of one of the most popular sentimental ballads of the Civil War days, "Bonny Eloise," who it is said was Mary Bowen of Fort Plain. The song bears the copyright of 1858. J. R. Thomas was the composer of the music.

And dear are the friends seen through memory's fond tears
That have lived in the blest days of yore.

Oh, sweet are the moments when dreaming I roam
Thro' my loved haunts now mossy and grey,
And dearer than all is my childhood's hallowed home,
That is crumbling now slowly away.

22

Union Street

THE ghosts of the ancient builders—Greeks, Romans, Italians, the artisans of Notre-Dame, London's Christopher Wren, the fakers of romanticism's false ruins, the arts-and-crafts Victorians—you meet them all on Schenectady's Union Street. They were the guides of the master builders of the whole Mohawk Valley. They were the invisible ones who moved west on the oxcart roads, in the chattering stagecoaches, whose shadows are seen on the houses that grew up beside the Grand Canal, and, distorted almost beyond recognition, on the Victorian horrors, built in what has been called the "Mohawk Valley Style."

Greece and Rome left their imprints everywhere. Down Union Street, for instance, an Athenian of Socrates's day could walk and find a hundred reminders of the glory of his Greece. Cinna, poet of Republican Rome, might see through the elms that border Union Street and the south edge of the Union College campus a hint of a forgotten forum.

Patron-popes and city-states—their Renaissance Italy has cast its shadows, too, on Union Street. Here, between the river and College Hill, is a recapitulation of five thousand years of

283

man's hope, a restatement in wood, brick, stone, and con-
crete of the journey we've made from long-forgotten homes.
Here we can measure our inheritance in the shape of a roof,
in a pediment over a doorway, in the columns and capitals
that support it. Here, too, we can measure in broad outlines
the changing patterns of life along the river by the character
of the houses men built on this one street.

Union Street and Church Street form the only crossroads in America, as far as I know, from which you can see
an honest Gothic house, not a Revival house, but a real pro-
jection of feudal Europe, and then, in another direction, a
building that would have been acceptable to Dr. Johnson's
London, and then a pseudo-Greek temple, and then, below it,
a house touched by Louis Philippe's France and Victoria's
England.

The first house beyond the site of the Dutch Reformed
church, the small white building with the high pitched roof:
there, by some miracle, still stands a house built by a brick-
layer-carpenter whose background was as feudal as a suit
of armor. There is the Abraham Yates house, built about 1720,
a Dutch-Gothic town house on whose "stoep" an Amsterdam
member of a goldbeater's build or a burgher out of Rem-
brandt's "Night Watch" would have been at home. That house
is a survival of the same Europe which bred the Hudson
River patroons, their "Courts Leete and Baron," and a peasantry bound to the soil by a system of land tenure which survived here into the middle of the nineteenth century, when
the treasurer of Union College still collected ground rents
from what had been patroon's property in the city of Troy.

No New England Puritan built the Yates house, for he
would never have tolerated that butterfly brickwork along the
sides of the high rake above the "Holland brick" gable that

faces the street, or those handsome iron beam anchors. There on lower Union Street, its windows rattling to the rhythm of trucks and cars, stands a monument to guilds and morality plays, community pastures and woodlots, to the Holland of Vermeer and Breughel.

Feudal Europe extended its Gothic architecture into the Mohawk Valley, to the edge of the Groote Vlachte, on the south shore of the Mohawk River, where the Mabie house is still standing, its walls fortress thick, built up of the local limestone and shale. Although farmer Mabie bought none of the Holland brick being made by Dutchmen along the Hudson, he roofed his house in the ancient manner, narrow and high, the sort of roof one sees in the background of Cuyp's landscapes of green meadows, fat cows, and windmills.

These Mohawk Valley Dutch-Gothic houses are not architects' houses. Their sheds and additions, which trail off beside them and behind them, grew along with the families that lived in them. The broken roof lines and the shadows that fill the corners of ells make a beauty of their own. Here is a simplicity that belongs to a time before the valley's craftsmen separated themselves from their fellow craftsmen to become architects, builders who were soon working from the European stylebooks that flooded America in the years just before the Revolution.

There is no "style" in those low stone farmhouses the Palatines built for themselves in the Schoharie and mid-Mohawk valleys. There you see old Europe's peasant houses, strong, heavy walled, the roof lines low and broken by a huddle of sheds, uneven lines that seem to be a part of the dark hills behind them. These Dutch and German farmhouses were functional houses, built only to serve the daily lives of their owners. These houses could be forts when the "wilden" were on the warpath, and yet their barnyards and orchards came close to the doorsteps, as though the river's society could be one fabric of men and beasts and harvest.

A few steps along Union Street, and time shifts as easily as stage-setting. If you look west from the Abraham Yates house to the northwest corner of Union and Church streets, you'll see a building in which every line is disciplined. Orderly, balanced, groomed, the three-story gray stone building of the Mohawk Club is Renaissance Europe, the architect's Europe, filtered and refiltered by the stylebook compilers.

Men along the Mohawk in the opening years of the nineteenth century, as well as in the rest of the United States, were experimenting with all kinds of disciplines, social, political, and economic. Their buildings reflected their new order. Buildings were tailored now, as men tailored their clothes, according to prescription. Style in houses, like style in coats, was organized to please the eye, though they often bore little relation to the life of the owner.

I don't know who the master builder was who drew up the plans for this Georgian building, now the best-known city club of modern Schenectady. It was designed, however, to house the old dorp's first bank, about 1817. Its builder has written all over it his debt to the England of Christopher Wren and Inigo Jones, and, more directly, to the Boston of the prosperous sea captains. He belonged to the Era of the Five Orders. His building was a late bloom of its kind in our valley, for fifty years before the Mohawk Bank moved into its Graeco-Roman-Anglican-cum-New England counting-house a colonial soldier and fortifications expert brought what we call the "colonial style" to Schenectady.

Samuel Fuller, of New England, his mind full of Boston

and Salem architectural elegance, came to this Dutchmen's village to help patch up the moldering fort, in the last days of the French and Indian Wars. He stayed after the fighting to become the valley's first architect.

He built, first, an English stylebook house for a Daniel Campbell, a Tory merchant who became a reluctant patriot in 1776. This merchant's house on lower State Street, and the Mohawk Bank building, though fifty years separated their construction, were fashioned out of the same elements: disciplined lines, the domesticated Greek pedimented doorway framed by classical columns, and, though gone now from the Mohawk Club, a Roman balustrade to hide the juncture of the roof and the street wall. These two buildings might have been town houses for London traders of the eighteenth century, although the American frontier was hardly more than a day's journey west.

Look closely at the Mohawk Club's old building. Nothing feudal about its architecture. No gay butterfly brickwork, no decorative anchoring of beam' ends, no weather vane to mark the instability of the seasons. Here, and in Samuel Fuller's earlier Johnson Hall at Johnstown, and in his Guy Johnson "Park," at Amsterdam, are written the valley's increasing interest in the life of the ancient world. The essence of that world—the dignity of man, the philosophic mind, oneness-in-nature—was understood by the Iroquois elders whose councils were often held in the grove in front of Sir William's classic "Hall." For most of Sir William's white guests, however, the Hall was simply "in the best style," and the Iroquois were a damned nuisance.

Schenectady and the banks of the Mohawk east and west are crowded with good and bad Georgian houses, or "colonial" houses, as you like. We sentimentalize about them easily.

They were a godsend, certainly, to the nameless local builders who had only to turn to Asher Benjamin's *American Builder's Companion* for the plans for a house or a church which would fit a client's purse and his site. The cornices and pediments, the classic columns and the pilasters, the balustrades, the quoins, and the flower moldings were all in the stylebooks, waiting for the builder to organize them into a would-be English gentleman's home or an elegant church, for the owners of Durham boats, and the season's lucky men in the fur trade.

It took Eliphalet Nott, the awesome Yankee president of Union College, to show the Mohawk Valley the ancient world that really lay behind the stylebooks. He and his family of students outgrew their Georgian, three-story "Stone College" on Union Street a few years after it had been completed by Philip Hooker, the master builder-architect of New York's first capital building.

Stone College was a handsome schoolhouse, a dignified rectangle, complete with all the classical decorative elements Samuel Fuller had brought into the valley before the Revolution, rearranged, in 1804, according to Mr. Hooker's taste. Eliphalet Nott, however, when he began to think of new buildings, was not sure he wanted any more of Mr. Hooker's schoolhouses, borrowed, as they were, from a defeated enemy.

And then the planets conjoined, in the winter of 1812-1813. Eliphalet Nott, the Republican, and Joseph Jacques Ramée, a self-exiled French architect, met and planned a new campus, the like of which had never been seen in America. Ramée was well prepared for his work, for he had already built a palatial Bourse for the city of Hamburg and great country houses for his Danish patrons. It was in Hamburg that he met David Parish—you may have met that amazing char-

acter in the pages of Hervey Allen's *Anthony Adverse*. David
Parish invited the young architect to come back to America
with him, to the wilderness of northern New York where he
had bought a village and one hundred thousand acres of land,
a site for another barony on the Sir William Johnson plan.

The Frenchman followed his patron to Ogdensburg.
There, instead of manor houses, he busied himself with fortifications to ward off British attacks from across the St. Lawrence, and the building of Russian stoves to temper the winter of 1812-1813.

Schenectady was always a welcome way station for David
Parish and his architect on their winter trips out of the wilderness, and, for Eliphalet Nott—what was more natural than
that they should all meet at dinner in the ancient Dutch
town?

Dr. Nott drove his guests down Front Street, the frozen
Mohawk visible occasionally at the end of the alleys that divided the dorp's Dutch and Georgian buildings. In the late
afternoon light the high-roofed Holland houses must have
startled Jacques Ramée. He'd seen them before, in the Low
Countries. Strange, to find them here in the New World, by a
river flowing out of the wilderness.

After an inspection of Mr. Hooker's schoolhouse, there
was the ride up Union Street, beyond the edge of the town,
up to the hill where Eliphalet Nott wanted to erect his new
college, well beyond the contaminating influence of the
Schenectady taverns.

On that cold hillside, facing west toward the Mohawk
and Arendt Van Curler's "most beautiful land," toward which,
it is said, John Jay had hoped New York would face its capital building, Jacques Ramée caught a vision of "a great court
of honor, reminiscent of Versailles . . . a monument to learn-

ing for royal occupancy." Eliphalet Nott was delighted. He
was a Republican, a Yankee-Roman at heart, whose dreams
for his college came earlier than and were as vast as those
of that other college planner, Thomas Jefferson of Virginia.
Let the Federalist Anglophiles build their cautious Georgian
houses. For Union College, however, the first college to be
chartered under the Constitution of the United States, a
"union" in truth of men of Dutch, English, and German
stock, of many faiths, there would be no facing toward the
meetinghouse primness of the Harvard Yard, or the closed
monastic quadrangles of Oxford and Cambridge. Dr. Nott
needed little persuasion from the Frenchman to accept his
scheme for the great Roman forum he saw flanking the empty
east hill above the Mohawk River, the domed Pantheon and
the framing dormitories connected with a great "U" shaped
cloister. It would all open to the west, "flung wide," as someone has said, "in a gesture extending educational opportunity
to all."

The Frenchman collected the then staggering sum of
$1,500 for his plans, lingered a few years in an America newly
disturbed by imperial planners, and then returned to France.
Eliphalet Nott's "Literature Lottery" paid for the two buildings that are still called North and South College, the dormitories Ramée had projected as the frame for his campus
and its Pantheon. The War of 1812, however, and then New
York State's Roman enterprise of canal building dampened the
legislature's ardor for the direct support of education.
Ramée's plans fell into the hands of lesser men a half century
later. What they built at Union College pleased their own
generations, though their buildings bore little relation to the
Frenchman's "great court of honor." Thomas Jefferson's University of Virginia, started ten years after Eliphalet Nott began

building in Schenectady, copied Ramée's Roman scheme a little more modestly. In our own time, however, Columbia University, the Massachusetts Institute of Technology, and the University of Rochester have built the forum-campuses you see detailed on those beautiful water-colored plans of Ramée's "pour le collège en Schenectady."

Union Street, after the completion of the Erie Canal, really turned away from the English Renaissance. Its residents thought, as did all of Jefferson's America, that the new Republic was the direct heir of Republican Rome and ancient Athens. Union College's seal spoke out the sentiment of the times: "Nous devenons tous les frères, sur les lois de Minerve." In the shadows of both North and South College were shortly born the first of those Greek-letter societies in which the Mysteries of the Ionian Brotherhoods were restated in terms of American campus democracy.

New York State's Chancellor Kent had finally put England in her place when he voted for the building of the Erie Canal rather than for a program of waiting for a new war. The canal, no sooner completed, had made war seem ridiculous. Everywhere, after the canal opening, the Honey of Hymettus mingled with Erie Water. The master builders of the Mohawk Valley now put by their Georgian stylebooks for the *Antiquities of Athens*. Soon the whole length of the Grand Canal was bordered with little Parthenons, a series of rustic shrines to celebrate our economic, cultural, and political liberty.

On Union Street, opposite, and just east of the Abraham Yates house, Schenectady built an Attic temple designed to house local justice. There was nothing like it, certainly, in England, and nothing like it in Greece. The county's solons, however, went through its portals quite as happily as though its Doric columns and pediment (in the center of which was the Yankee touch, a window for ventilation) and its Roman porch and side walls were part of Lord Elgin's shipment of the Acropolis marbles.

At the foot of College Hill a farmhouse was masked with a carpenter's pediment and four square pillars, as though its owner had decided to convert his house into a shrine to his household gods. The pediment cut off all light from his front rooms but, never mind, the house was in the new mode.

The Mohawk and Hudson Railroad Company and the Utica and Schenectady Railroad Company now combined forces with the Greeks to build in Schenectady America's first Union Station. "It was evidently designed," wrote a nine-teenth-century local historian, "by somebody familiar with the remains of the Forum at Rome, and the Pantheon at Athens (*sic*)." That first wedding of the Mechanic Age and the dimly remembered age that built the Parthenon must have had cosmic reverberations, for fire, either from Olympus or from the bowels of a Mohawk Valley locomotive, destroyed the station in 1843.

At the western end of the Mohawk Valley the spirit of the Athenian builders came alive in the monumental portico of the Utica State Hospital. Six great Doric columns here rose forty-eight feet to a huge, undecorated pediment which covered a porch vast enough for the whole cast of a Greek tragedy. The doorways to this porch and the great wings that flanked it opened on tragedy, for this was New York's first planned hospital for the insane.

It was in the smaller river towns like Fonda and St. Johnsville and Little Falls that the houses reflected the val-ley's sympathy for a Greece in revolt, Lord Byron's Greece which was fighting off Turkish bondage in the early canal years. Along their Main Streets you can still see these temple-houses, the best of them touched with dignity and grace that was soon to be smothered in mill smoke. Their wooden peri-styles were no barricades against the spreading crowds of millworkers, for the authors of the *Antiquities of Athens* had included no defense plans in their sourcebook for the owners of the Greek Revival houses. For a few decades, however, the egg-and-dart moldings, the tight volutes that capped the Ionic columns, and the precise pediments above the deep porches were like strange, lovely accents in the changing speech of the valley.

In those days of the Greek Revival, most of the valley's men voted a Democratic ticket. It was then that Elizabeth Cady Stanton, daughter of a Johnstown judge, caught the vision of a golden age for women, and began her long cam-paign for woman suffrage. In 1850 Susan B. Anthony left her pupils in the academy at Canajoharie to join Mrs. Stanton in what was to become a nation-wide crusade for women's rights.

A short walk south of Union Street will show you what happened to those Revival dreams as they were tempered by the hard realities of the Industrial Age. Liberty Street east of the old canal crossing runs to the brow of College Hill. Here were erected the "mechanics houses," as one of Dr. Nott's in-structors referred to them, most of them walls, roof, doors, and windows as expressionless as unlabeled boxes. Here lived the families who helped the Ellises build locomotives, after 1845, and George Westinghouse, Sr., operate his thresher-machine factory. The Five Orders, the balustrades, and the porticoes are gone. The houses of Liberty Street are almost gardenless. Here art and utility drew farther apart as its residents multi-plied, along with the machines that could live without sun and soil.

The new mills themselves, the carpet mills along the Chuctanunda Creek in Amsterdam, the paper mills in Herkimer, the gun and machinery factories of the Remingtons in Ilion, and the wool and cotton mills of Utica and Whitesboro were simply larger boxes in which men and machines had to be packed as efficiently as possible. The millowners, to escape the ugliness, could retreat to their little Parthenons. The growing throngs of mill hands, however, were crowded into the mill villages and the row-houses close to the factory walls where the choice of the height of a Doric column or of the proportions of a living room was irrelevant.

Here, near the mills, lived the Irishmen who had dug the canals, and, later, the Italians who were the "worka Johns" of the expanding railroads. All these foreigners were a part of the swelling pool of cheap labor that began to overflow into the elm-shaded streets of the river towns. Soon there was a Liberty Street wherever there was a stream full and swift enough to turn the wheels of a mill.

On Union Street there were new kinds of buildings, too. Pinnacles, towers, battlements, casements designed to open "on faery lands forlorn," pointed arches and Gothic traceries: here the builders now began to speak a romantic language which would help Union Street shut out the immigrant slums and the overwhelming problems of an industrial age. "English cottages" began to appear next to the weathering Georgian houses, stucco and wood affairs, heavy with jigsaw traceries and elaborately bracketed eaves, their rooms dim with perpetual afternoon behind their latticed windows. Between the canal and the river one Union Street resident built himself a miniature Tudor manorhouse, a dark Gothic brownstone, complete with Sir Walter Scott battlements and monastery casements.

On College Hill, at the end of Library Lane, Edward Tuckerman Potter, Dr. Nott's grandson, undertook to erect the Pantheon Joseph Jacques Ramée had drawn on his plans "pour le collège en Schenectady." Instead of the classic, low-domed building designed to fit the monumental scheme of 1813, Potter built, sixty years later, an iron-framed "free interpretation" of the Gothic baptistery at Pisa.

From the Civil War on, Union Street and the valley west became a builders' record in mass production brick, cast iron, jigsaw scrollwork, sheet glass, and molding by the roll and yard. Where the master builders of Asher Benjamin's day had at least to contribute their personal skill to copying the classical details from the *American Builder's Companion*, the men who now fabricated the new Victorian horrors could order their Greek and Roman moldings and columns by number. Schenectady and the other valley towns are full of buildings which prove their tireless ingenuity. So prolific were the builders that the form they gave these houses has come to be known, to our sorrow, as the "Mohawk Valley Style."

You can still see these square, squat monsters from the railroad, their frames draped and crowded with any architectural patch the builder chose to tear from the pages of classic architecture. Their caste mark was the functionless cupola from which the owner could look, usually, only at a neighbor's roof. Union Street has its share of these catchalls of architecture. Soon the owners of some of Union Street's Georgian houses were "improving" them by adding bay windows, mansard roofs, and "captains' walks," blurring their earlier elegance past recognition.

In the dye-stained Mohawk you could see, after the Civil War, the bellies of river fish white in the sun. There were growing refuse heaps beside the mills and the mill villages, and there were confused and sometimes worried men in the Victorian houses, houses which themselves were patterns of confusion. The valley had lost its Georgian graces and its hopes of an American revival of the golden age of the ancient republics. Nor had it learned how to live with its machines and the men who must tend them.

There was no dead center, however, for either machines or men at the end of the nineteenth century. By 1892 the Mohawk Valley's industries were represented at the huge Columbian Exposition, at Chicago, where they helped America proclaim dominion over the new frontiers her Edisons were now invading in force. Thomas A. Edison himself and his pioneers had already moved their shops to the banks of the Mohawk, at Schenectady, where the Erie Canal and the railroads were ready to carry their dynamos to customers anywhere.

There was also a new kind of house on Union Street. Here the Ellis and De Forest families put up their "mansions" of massive granite blocks, Roman arches, and stone pillars, their capitals carved into vines and leaves after the manner of the Romanesque basilicas, with carriage entrances as big as cottages. They reflected not Jacques Ramée's restrained and imaginative Forum borrowed from Republican Rome but rather the imperial manner brought back to America by such Beaux-Arts architects as H. H. Richardson, Richard Hunt, and their imitators.

There was not room on the old street, below College Hill, for many of these great houses. Too massive for their sites, they belonged rather to the style of the Chicago Fair, and to the New York State Capitol Building whose acre of massed styles, royal stairways, and elaborate carving proclaimed America's wealth and ambition, and, somewhat sadly, our dependence on Europe's amphitheaters, basilicas, doges' palaces, and Loire chateaux for our models of magnificence.

Have you noticed yet? There isn't an American house on

Union Street. I mean an *American* house. There's the Abraham Yates house, born in feudalism; there's the Mohawk Club's graceful building, blocked and decorated in the manner of George III's England; there's Eliphalet Nott's Union College campus that is both Rome and Renaissance Italy. There are a dozen buildings that reach back pathetically to a Greece of unheard melodies, brick and wooden mirages that still quicken the imagination. There are houses that mark our retreat deep into Gothic romanticism, strangely out of key with the bursting life of the Grand Canal and the new railroads of the 1850's. There are the Victorian houses, ostentatious clutters of every traditional architectural device, and there are the big and little houses in "Richardson Romanesque." East of College Hill you'll still find the arts-and-crafts villas of the 1900's, and Norman cottages with their shingled towers, and California bungalows. Today there are the country club subdivisions where the houses are Georgian, or Spanish Baroque, French Peasant, or Brick Bastard, according to the owner's taste, the zoning laws, the availability of contractors and unionized labor.

But there are no *American* houses.

Most of the valley lives behind borrowed façades. Schenectady was given a railroad station that looks like a toy version of the Baths of Caracalla, complete with coffered ceiling, marble veneers, and a huge clerestory to light an interior almost impossible to heat in a Schenectady winter. In Utica, a variation on a doge's palace was built by the railroad for the use of her citizens and the landless thousands who moved along the New York Central's right-of-way from job to job.

Marble came into the valley from Vermont, and limestone from Indiana; but the fine quarries behind Canajoharie were not much used by the stonecutters, for the local materials that had gone into the Erie Canal locks and "cuts" and the truly imperial aqueducts were now out of favor.

The valley's State Streets and Main Streets have been lined with banks and libraries in the Caesar tradition; but no one put up an American building along the Mohawk River until 1938. By then the beginnings of an American synthesis were felt in the valley; it was that strange coagulation of Portland cement, steel fabrication, elevators, central heating, the magic of electricity, plastics, and an unnamed ingredient Americans call "industrial know-how." Skyscraper architecture was part of that coagulation, though it had no place on the great flats of the Mohawk.

A new generation put up this American building. Here, in Schenectady, on the edge of the Groote Vlachte, the General Electric Company erected a building which has this in common with the farmhouse a seventeenth-century Dutchman had built near it: both of them were designed to serve the daily needs of their tenants. Radio Station WGY's studio is brick and chromium and glass walls and soundproofed interior: it is wholly a radio studio, shaped and decorated to the one end that its broadcasters may be served as effectively as the Dutch-Gothic Mabie house served the husbandman of the Woestina.

We may be coming full circle along the Mohawk River, approaching a time when our machines will be as well controlled as the cattle and wheat farmer Mabie once raised just west of our radio studio. The American Synthesis, of which this WGY building is a small part, may yet result in a society designed to serve men, a society which the Medieval Synthesis foreshadowed.

Perhaps the leaders of the General Electric Company, the vast half-corporation, half-guild that has its headquarters in

Schenectady, which has given the valley its first *American* building, will be among those to find American answers to the hard, unanswered questions that have long been asked along our Liberty Streets.

23

"Mohawk Valley Formula"

Helen was not involved. The factory towers of Ilion were guarded by Pearl Bergoff's strikebreakers and the lady in question was a "Madam X." On June 10, 1936, Ilion, New York, had much in common with Homer's Troy. It was under siege Madam X was partly to blame for the strife, and there was a Trojan horse of sorts which had long since disgorged its mayors and councilmen, its ministers and storekeepers, and imported rumor spreaders and armed deputies, to do what they could to deliver up the town. There was an ominous quiet that day, along the roped-off streets, as the enemy prepared to march through the open gates.

The strike at Remington Rand was fourteen days old. The two thousand men and women who worked in the Ilion plants of the big typewriter and business-machine company had, with great care, been robbed during the preceding two weeks of their dignity and rights as citizens of Ilion and members of the American Federation of Labor. They were beginning to behave as do the citizens of all towns under protracted siege: rumor and fear had eaten out the heart of their defense. Five hundred of them had already sold out their rights to the besieger, who planned that day to take the town.

To understand the siege of Ilion you must know something about the forces that had raised its factory walls, and which finally drove Mayor Whitney to declare martial law on the night of June 10, 1936. First, warfare had been Ilion's diet for more than a hundred years. In 1843 a local postmaster's love of Homer had fastened "Ilion" on what had been, simply enough, Steele's Creek, or sometimes Morgan's Corners, and then, in the 1830's, Remington's Corners. Near this country crossroads, in 1816, young Eliphalet Remington had made himself a gun, and his neighbors had liked it, and so he began to make guns for them. Industrial America began that way. The Ilion of June 10, 1936, was born in the heat of the Remington forge, and grew as the consignments of guns grew.

By 1846 the Remingtons' arms shipments were too big to drop through the hole in the old Steele's Creek canal bridge and so onto the deck of a passing line boat, as young Eliphalet Remington had done with the rifles addressed to his first customers. Ilion was making two thousand carbines in that year for our war with Mexico. Next came the Harpers Ferry muskets. It was said that the strain of keeping up with Civil War contracts killed Eliphalet Remington in 1861. Pistols, breechloaders for army buyers here and abroad, and then guns for the Franco-Prussian War: the succeeding Remingtons made guns by the tens of thousands, and spread out their red-brick mills and brought in hundreds of skilled mechanics.

Philo Remington hoped to make Ilion depressionproof by becoming the Universal Fabricator. The Remington Works saw inventors come and go. Agricultural machinery, sewing machines, flat key locks, bicycles, fire engines, printing presses, engines of all kinds, and always guns, and then, for the Remingtons, failure. But not before Philo Remington had bought the rights to a writing machine which became, in 1874, the "Model 1 Remington type-writer," a "curiosity breeding little joker," according to Mark Twain, who seems to have been one of the earliest purchasers.

The typewriter soon bore the same relation to the Remingtons' guns that the pen bore to the sword, but too late to save the sprawling factories for Philo and his brothers. Overexpansion, the post-Civil War depression, and a tortured system of manufacturing forced a series of plant auctions in the 1880's which divided the huge family enterprise into separate companies. Although the name "Remington" still straddles gun barrels and lies in gold-leaf elegance across the faces of typewriters, others have ridden the waves of empire building and nationalism to enormous profits, and still others have built that "curiosity breeding little joker" without which the world of business would be mute and helpless.

The name "Remington" had undergone a mutation by 1936, and was currently "RemRand" to those who worked for James H. Rand, Jr. Ilion was the heart of RemRand, an industrial state which was then turning out its goods in six American towns. Odd, though it should be in Ilion, a hundred twenty years after young Eliphalet Remington had made his first gun, that the Rand organization should forge a new weapon, one which James H. Rand, Jr., was to call the "Mohawk Valley Formula." It was an invisible destroyer, more deadly than anything the Remingtons had been able to assemble.

The old Remington carbines, muskets, breechloaders were fine weapons for their day. New times, new enemies, however, require new weapons, and so, by 1936, the Mohawk Valley Formula was ready; it was noiseless, smokeless, effective at any range, and particularly useful against women.

RemRand's enemies were very much a part of the new times. Twenty men had helped the Remingtons forge gun barrels in 1832, and probably called each other by their first names. Distribution was made to customers through the hole in the local Erie Canal bridge and the problems of an industrial America were hardly anticipated. Sixty years later there were six hundred men in Ilion making typewriters, because the new times needed the "curiosity breeding little joker." They missed mortgage payments and starved when typewriter sales fell off. They had become not personalities but payroll numbers.

No one was to blame that "Tom" and "Dick" and "Harry" in Ilion, in Utica, in Schenectady, all over America had become, through the years of the Industrial Revolution, No. 1, column 1, No. 2, column 2, No. 3, column 3 on the mill ledgers. No one was to blame for the box houses on the Liberty Streets, and the mill villages, and the dead fish in our river. Things just happened that way. The rains came, Topsy grew. Suddenly there was a flood and a Negro Problem, or, for the mill owner, a Labor Problem.

No one, in the Mohawk Valley or any other place, was to blame for the transmutation of many human beings over that hundred years into ciphers, by the Circe-magic of the machines they are called upon to serve. No one is to blame that these things happened, but, having happened, no one can stand aside, untouched, when the flood must be contained, Topsy heard, when the men and women who serve in the mills organize to regain some measure of their humanity.

Ilion's June day call for martial law was the reaction of

puzzled and frightened men in the face of a new problem and a new responsibility for which they had no preparation. They were like the panicked baggage train in General Herkimer's militia at Oriskany. They'd have liked to fight, but the enemy had rushed them, and so they ran, leaving the field and the dirty battle to braver men than they.

I keep thinking of Old Honikol, General Herkimer of the mangled speech, and his motley crowd of Palatine farmers, American revolutionists who gathered at Fort Dayton across the river and a little east of what was to become Ilion. Their problem was not unlike the problem that faced Mr. Rand's workers a century and a half later. The Palatines owned farms and cattle and their summer grain was ready for cutting, and west of them, coming down on the valley, were Britishers and Johnson's Tory Greens and a grunting, angry swarm of Long House Indians. The Palatines' problem was to save their houses and the cattle and the grain. They had organized themselves into a militia so that they could be as effective as possible if it came to a fight; and that's what it came to in August, 1777.

Plant No. 1 and Plant No. 2, of the Remington Rand Company, in 1936 were houses and cattle and grain fields to Ilion's aligners and polishers, and the boys in the shipping room and the factory girls. Old Honikol's farmers could blame themselves or the weather when their crops were poor or their cattle died. If they had the courage and the strength, they could do something about these things. They could clear new fields, breed better stock, call in their neighbors to help raise a new barn. In 1777 a workman had that kind of control over his own fate.

Old Honikol beat the Tories finally, and they put up a monument to him a hundred years after the fight was over.

The Revolution somehow got won and the Mohawk Valley of farms and cattle became a channel for the Erie Canal and a bed for railroads and a long east-west millsite, stretching from the falls at Cohoes to the great bend of the river at Rome. Here, one hundred fifty-nine years after the battle at Oriskany, factory people who worked with their hands could no longer blame the weather or poor seed or sick cattle for their griefs. Instead of the south cornfield, Tom Fisher tended two machines in Plant 1. Instead of milking at dawn, Dick carried a lunch pail to the foundry, and Tom sharpened tools, not in his barn, but at a RemRand bench. They married, bought houses, and began families, in 1936, on the money they were paid for building typewriters.

Old Honikol's Palatines could lay their hands in the corn rows of their own acres and know why it was they were marching west to the nettle fields to fight. A man couldn't see his RemRand job; he couldn't measure it, or weigh it; but it was as real as a corn row, and out of it he got his wage, and that, in 1936, was all a factory worker had to defend. In 1777 the Mohawk Valley farmers organized a militia to guard their river flats and their houses when possession of them was challenged. It was the fight to possess what Greeks thought to be theirs, raised to the level of high romance, that had charmed the postmaster of Remington Corners and led him to give the name "Ilion" to his Mohawk Valley mill town.

New times, new weapons, new enemies.

Consider Harold Beers, for instance: polisher at the Ilion plant. Wages, $32 a week. Shop committeeman of the Joint Protective Board. He and its members were officers of the American Federation of Labor, a union which, by democratic processes, had been chosen by a majority of the men and women of all the Rand plants to speak for them when there was job trouble.

Harold Beers was product of the new times. He and his fellow members of the Joint Protective Board were, in a way, pioneers working in strange country. Their country was the territory of the American Federation of Labor, but within it there were levels of pride and privilege and dignity which had come down with the old craft union. Years earlier these unions had organized their separate bands of skilled workers. Ilion's aligners and polishers, however, had, during the depression years, joined with the newer all-embracing federal union of Rand workers to make the A.F.L. Joint Protective Board their voice in labor disputes. Yet many of the older men had loyalty only for their private guilds. Harold Beers and James Rand knew that these divisions within the union defense made it easier for the opposition to divide it for quick defeat. Harold Beers knew he could never count on the guild men; they were like the Tory farmers during the Revolution, who never quite dared to skip off to Canada and were just as afraid to sign Congress's Articles of Confederation.

Throughout May Harold Beers and the members of the union's Joint Protective Board had been facing shadows who pretended to speak for Remington Rand's president. The questions were always simple enough, but the answers seemed to be ventriloquist's answers from off-stage, blurred and garbled.

"Will you discuss, Mr. Rand, the provisions of our contract with you, and the matter of our rates of pay?"

No answer to that question, but a letter from the wings: "The matters referred to . . . will have to be taken up with Vice-President R. E. Benner, who is away at present on an extended absence."

"What about 'Madam X,' Mr. Rand? Do you own a factory in Elmira, and will your new typewriter, 'Madam X,' be made there?"

Voice, not Mr. Rand's: "I doubt that I will be able to give you a satisfactory answer . . . I do not know."

"The reason the people say the plant is owned by Remington Rand is because Mr. Benner said so."

Voice, not Mr. Rand's: "The plant may belong to Remington Rand."

The Voice said that Mr. Rand would not appear to speak to Harold Beers and the men who were hoping to take answers back to six thousand waiting factory workers.

Harold Beers has said, loudly enough for anybody to hear, "Mr. Benner, Mr. Rand and practically all of them have freely admitted that the wages were not as they should be and gave us assurance that they would pay more money when they were in better financial condition. They have never come through with any of it."

The Voice replied, ". . . there can be no general increase in wages."

"Our contract with you says . . ." It said, beyond misunderstanding, that the American Federation of Labor was the bargaining agent for Mr. Rand's employees. It said that work which could be performed in the company's plants was not to be sent somewhere else. And it said unequivocally that "grievances, if not settled satisfactorily, might be taken up directly with the Works Manager, or higher executive of the company." Before negotiations broke down, the Joint Board heard voices, but never saw a "higher executive." No one ever came on-stage who could say, finally, "Yes" or "No."

A strike vote was inevitable as rain in June. The ballot stated that Mr. Rand had refused to meet with the Joint Protective Board, that a Mr. Anderson, who had been sent to talk with it, had refused to discuss higher wages or to admit he knew anything about Rand activities in Elmira. It authorized the Joint Board to call a strike, "when and if in their opinion, all other means have failed to bring about a satisfactory conclusion." Ninety per cent of the organized employees, said the Joint Protective Board, voted to strike if necessary.

May in Ilion was ugly with promise of serious trouble. On May 21 the Remington Rand Company, without warning, passed out a company ballot to all its employees. Harold Beers and the other union officials who protested were fired for interfering with the balloting. Mr. Rand said his contract with the union allowed him to by-pass its officials, and cited a clause against discrimination and intimidation which the A.F.L. Joint Protective Board had always understood simply meant that after a strike "we were not to bother or harm the few scabs and they were to keep their shirts clean. . . ."

Rand's ballot was like stage money. The union, it said, had not made its demands known to the company; and its members did not represent the majority of the company's workers. The workers were then told to vote "Yes" or "No" to the questions: "Are you dissatisfied with present working conditions?" and "Are you in favor of a strike?" which is a little different from asking a man if he will strike as a last resort.

New times, new enemies, new weapons. Rand's plants closed, and in Ilion, on May 26, the picket lines were posted.

Behind the ropes and the police on the afternoon of June 10 crowds of strikers backed up against the mill walls. High above them, in the windows, were Captain Foster's strikebreakers, strong-arm technicians hired to keep the peace according to Captain Foster's formula. Tear-gas guns were pointed in the direction of the roped-off crowds. Three hundred armed deputies were there, many of them store-keepers and bank clerks, and salesmen from Frankfort, Mohawk, and Herkimer, who showed, by their badges, how the lines of sympathy had been drawn.

"For Sale" was lettered across a huge sign hung on the face of one of the Remington Rand buildings.

It took skill and deadly purpose to set up that scene, which, in point of time, was the curtain scene of Act Two of this drama. All the props, visible and invisible, were in place: Greek-porticoed houses, romantic, carpenters' Gothic cottages, Victorian uglies in the "Mohawk Valley Style"; up and down the river, symbols of old and persistent states of mind, they were in place. Mingling with Sheriff Malsan's deputies that day were the ghosts of Sir John Johnson's Greens, still aching for revenge against their neighbors in the valley who had given their loyalty to a new flag. Standing alongside of James Rand, who was waiting in the wings for his cue, was the ghost of Britain's colonial Governor Hunter whose Palatine workers had broken his hold on them and had made, at last, a granary out of the Mohawk and Schoharie valleys. Behind the ropes that June afternoon there were other ghosts, Palatine men like John Conrad Weiser and Old Honikol's militia-men, invisible fighters in the ancient struggle.

"Scab! Look at them scabs! Get out of that yard! Get over here where you belong!"

Somebody in the crowd of strikers behind the ropes said something, and voices got loud, and the crowd surged around the pair who were sounding off. Deputies and police leaned against the bulge in the human wall and flattened it out. After that, tear-gas bombs were tossed into the crowd. Someone threw a tear-gas bomb out of an upper-story mill window. Before one of the strikers could heave it back it burst in his hand, cutting it badly, spraying the crowd around him with gas.

Across the street, in the mill yard, the new weapon, the Mohawk Valley Formula, was being tried out. There, under the protection of all the police and deputies the intimidated local mayors could organize, some five hundred workers were gathering, members of an organization which called itself the Ilion Typewriter Employees Protective Association.

At the proper moment the plant gates opened, and the I.T.E.P.A. marched into the Remington Rand factory. No one was hurt. The strikers, behind the ropes and the phalanx of police and the nervous lads with the clubs, had done all they could. The strike was the only weapon they had, and they were still fighting; but it had been this way at Oriskany too, when Old Honikol's baggage train had fled in the face of an enemy which knew all the tricks of ambush and secret attack. No one was hurt in Ilion, for only the police and the deputies had the guns.

"Scabs! Look at them scabs!" I.T.E.P.A. had taken the citadel.

Inside the factory yard the wonderful Formula quieted fear and doubt and any lingering sense of cowardice. Reginald Boote, Rand workman and leader of the I.T.E.P.A., spoke to his followers. There would be no relaxing of police protection, now that the plants had been saved for Ilion by this fine demonstration of worker loyalty. Speeches were made by a Remington Rand home office official, by Ross, the local manager, and by others, all full of thanksgiving that the strike was over, that Ilion's $12,000 daily payroll had been saved, and that the future was to be so bright for all those who wished to work on Mr. Rand's terms. Then the giant "For Sale" sign came down and the American flag was run up on the factory flagstaff. James H. Rand, Jr., with a fine sense of timing, now appeared before his loyal employees and congratulated them on their victory over the dark powers that had almost driven his company out of the Mohawk Valley.

That night a state of siege was declared in Ilion. Rumors had been spread that five hundred strikers were marching on the community, coming in from Syracuse to stop the I.T.E.P.A.'s back-to-work movement. Barney Allen, the Ilion storekeeper who had enlisted local business men in a stirring crusade to keep Remington Rand in the town at any cost, tried to get New York's acting governor, Bray, to send in a force of state police. The local hysteria sounded shrill and unconvincing in Albany, and Allen's request was refused.

The village Board of Trustees then met and passed a resolution authorizing Mayor Whitney "to declare a state of emergency in the Village of Ilion and that all roads and entrances be blocked and nobody allowed to enter the village unless they have lawful business in the village."

From then on, things moved fast.

Mayor Whitney declared the emergency would be effective beginning at midnight. Ilion, according to the report of the National Labor Relations Board, now "became an armed camp, separated from the outside world." The report continued, "the number of deputies was increased to three hundred, many businessmen serving in that capacity. The main road leading into the village was barricaded with a large chain. Squads of special deputies and the local police armed with shotguns—consisting of four to six deputies and one policeman in a squad—stood guard at the entrances to the village and patrolled the streets. Only persons with passes of the association (the I.T.E.P.A.), those working for the Remington Arms plant, and others satisfactory to the guards were per-

mitted to enter the village. Arms had been secured that night
at the Remington Arms plant and were carried by many of
the special deputies and police. Others carried clubs. Private
cars were used to serve as police cars. The headquarters of
the Ilion unions, where the pickets gathered, and which were
across the street from the plant, were padlocked by the village board on the basis of one complaint from an adjoining
landowner. The chief of police, in answer to protests from
union leaders, stated that 'Lieutenant Governor Bray declared
martial law on the request of Mayor Whitney of Ilion' . . .
which was denied by Bray and was obviously false. When an
investigator attached to the New York Department of Labor,
who had been sent to Ilion to investigate the situation on the
complaint of the unions, questioned the necessity of such
measures, he was informed by the spokesman for the Joint
Valley Board [the local authorities of Ilion, Frankfort, Mohawk, and Herkimer] that 'as Mr. Rand had threatened to
move the plant from Ilion, and it would be the ruination of
all four villages . . . it was absolutely necessary that the
strikers were shown that they were in the wrong and have
them return to work.' "

The next day, Ilion was a fortress town. One of the local
union leaders got into it only by sneaking through the woods.
A number of Rand's foremen spent the day going around to
the homes of those strikers who had not yet capitulated. The
NLRB report put it all succinctly enough: "They stated that
the deadline for jobs was that evening. All they wanted them
to do was to enter the plant . . . they were not required to
work in the plant. For that they would receive $5 in cash and
$10 later. There was an exception . . . those who had been
too 'active' in the unions would not be permitted to return at
that time."

"These measures," the report continued, "could have but

one effect. The union ranks were broken and the employees began to enter the plant in large numbers. On June 12 about 1200 employees entered the plant. The barricades were withdrawn and deputies decreased, but the emergency declaration remained in force. The union headquarters were still padlocked, the authorities stating in answer to the contention that these actions were unlawful, 'Legal or not, we done it.' "

"Legal or not, we done it" would seem to belong with the classic understatement of John Erskine's Helen of Troy, who was said to have remarked, when she saw the Trojan horse parked before the temple steps of ancient Ilion, "Isn't it cute!"

It was at the big plant-reopening celebration held by the Citizens' Committee and the local civic dignitaries that the Mohawk Valley Formula was officially christened, and presented to America as a tested technique. "They were honored," said the Labor Board's report, "with a speech by Mr. Rand. He was effusive in his praise: Ilion was to be congratulated for the type of people it had and what they had done. 'Two million business men have been looking for a formula like this and business has hoped for, dreamed of and prayed for such an example as you have set,' . . . an example 'that would go down into history as the Mohawk Valley Formula.' "

Barney Allen of the Ilion Citizens' Committee wrote an article which appeared in the National Association of Manufacturers' *Labor Relations Bulletin,* telling how the local businessmen had fitted into the operations of the Formula. The *Bulletin* concluded Allen's account with the observation that "the N.A.M. appreciates the opportunity to bring to the attention of industrial America the constructive manner in which this controversy was handled by these villages. Regardless of the final settlement of this dispute, here or at other

Remington Rand plants, Ilion has made a real contribution to civic dignity."

Pearl Bergoff, "expert in the technique of strikebreaking" and the head of a large strikebreaking agency employed by Remington Rand, told the NLRB how civic dignity had been upheld by his refusal to send his boys into strikers' homes, along with the forty or fifty "loyal" Rand employees who were attempting to get the strikers to join the back-to-work movement. He also told the board how his boys "were simply mixing with the help, just hanging around, making themselves useful . . ." which, when interpreted by him for the board, meant "starting rumors," "whispering," what he called "a missionary job."

Captain Shaw, "the radical investigator," when asked if Mr. Rand "was following some plan he had worked out," told the board, "The first idea was to go to their homes, talk to their wives and families. The second was to have a lot of people go en masse into the plant and to come out en masse, and there were so many numerous propositions, I just don't remember off hand."

"In the light of such testimony," the report continued, "Allen, Mayor Whitney and their fellow citizens appear as mere puppets dangled on an economic lifeline held by the respondent." The report pointed out that Ilion's economic existence depended on Remington Rand, that since the beginning of 1936 the whole town had been on edge because of the rumors that Rand was going to move Madam X and his plant to Elmira, a state of nerves considerably heightened by Rand's refusal to affirm or deny the rumors. Then, when the strike appeared to be inevitable, Rand invited Barney Allen, a local businessman, and the local bankers to a "conference" in New York.

"Three things were accomplished at this conference," according to the board's report: "the business men were threatened with the removal of the plant because of alleged interferences of the unions; they were made to realize the strike would be a long and costly affair because of the impossibility of settlement, inasmuch as Rand was determined not to meet with the unions; they were introduced to Boote and his group (the ITEPA) purporting to represent a majority of the employees and informed by Boote that the employees did not desire a strike . . . as a result, when the strike actually came, Allen and the Citizens Committee joined with Boote in an attempt to end the strike through collective bargaining conferences."

The next objective, according to the report, was "a show of force to intimidate the striking employees and compel their return to work." Various dodges were tried. There were the threats to remove the plant. No one could miss the "For Sale" sign that hung like a backdrop from Rand's factory during the unraveling of the whole tragedy. There were mysterious shipments of machinery. The panicked mayors and the Citizens' Committee were told "that the pressure could be lifted if ample 'police protection' were provided for a back-to-work movement." Boote's I.T.E.P.A. and Pearl Bergoff's "missionaries" were then scheduled for active parts in breaking down the strikers' morale.

The local mayors were thoroughly intimidated. Ilion's Mayor Whitney according to the NLRB Report, told several union leaders that "he was being compelled to do things he didn't want to do . . . he could easily be a ruined man and have nothing left but his hat, coat, and pants if these people were to clamp down on him." The Citizens' Committee, displeased with the authorities' failure to assemble the kind of police protection the committee desired, challenged the mayor to act or resign. The mayor acted, although he refused to ring the village fire bell to summon Ilion's volunteer fire fighters for swearing-in as deputies.

"With the intimidating show of force now provided by the village itself," the report stated, "Rand was ready for the next move. A trial mass-meeting, accompanied by speeches, dramatic scenes, and Bergoff's 'Ballyhoo' showed that the back-to-work propoganda had been effective and the plant was ready for reopening." All these moves had their effect on the undisciplined strikers. Then came the rumors about the invasion from Syracuse, and, the report says, "a wave of mass hysteria swept the village and Ilion became an armed town ruled by citizens turned vigilantes and raised to a frenzied pitch by the delusions evoked by armed force and the swift seizure of power. The union ranks, subjected to that hysteria and being at the same time undermined by the respondent's threats of replacement and bonus offers . . . eight hundred $5 bills were distributed on June 10 . . . could not hold together and the strike was broken.

"There remained only the final touch . . . Rand's christening this technique the 'Mohawk Valley Formula' and proudly offering it to his fellow members in the National Association of Manufacturers as an example of modern strike-breaking."

The Rand unions lost the first round to those who rode a Trojan horse into their ranks. They won finally, however, when the National Labor Relations Board took the strike off the streets of Ilion, out of the valley itself, and gave it its proper proportions as a major clash in the running, never-ending battle to preserve and to extend the American way of life.

Such a strike could never really be lost. The federal courts upheld the major findings of the NLRB, and the workers, whose jobs are as real as farms and cattle, were reassured that their right to bargain collectively with their employers was a right which could not be abrogated.

The A.F.L. Joint Protective Board was vindicated in its demand that the Remington Rand Company talk with it as one talks with an equal, frankly and without reservations. The men and women who went on strike to defend so basic a democratic principle were told by the court that their jobs must be returned to them. The Mohawk Valley Formula had lost its power to intimidate or coerce. Perhaps it had become a dated weapon.

24

House of Magic

"Pioneering," said the professor, "began again along the Mohawk in 1886."

The old man closed his *Aristotle,* picked up his sheaf of notes, and walked to the door that led from his crowded classroom into the hall. He stopped there as usual, waiting for the hands of the clock above his desk to clasp themselves in their noon embrace.

"Someday the paths trod by Aristotle and his fellow philosophers," he went on, "great researchers in the realm of human values, must cross the paths traveled here by Steinmetz and the electrical pioneers."

It was probably the sound-wake of the General Electric Company's jet plane rolling through the valley that had made the professor swing back twenty-five hundred years along the time curve. His "Class dismissed" was hardly heard as the noon whistles roared above the "Big Shop" at ALCO, and a great amen swelled up from the "GE" on the river road.

It was Harry Livor who opened the Mohawk Valley's new pioneering age. If he had turned his head in some other direction as his train went past the empty McQueen Locomotive lofts huddled between the Mohawk River and the Erie Canal, on one side, and the railroad on the other, Schenectady might still be the brush-and-broom capital of America. The hypothetical "if," however, is anathema in this City-that-Lights-the-World. Harry Livor, being a man of action, hurried back to New York with the news for which Thomas A. Edison had been waiting. Schenectady was the place, all right for the Edison Machine Works. The location was perfect: every kind of transportation facility at the door, and plenty of room to expand into the broom-corn fields that spread across the big flats by the river.

How much? Thomas Edison thought $45,000 was too high for the unfinished pair of factory buildings. He would pay $37,500 for them, but that was the limit. Conference, and soul searching, and a dim vision of what might happen along the River Road prompted a group of Schenectady merchants to go into their tills for the $7,500 needed to bring the famous Edison to the quiet, small city by the Mohawk, where life for most of the nineteenth century had revolved around Union College, the "Big Shop" of the American Locomotive Company, and the broom-corn factories.

Sixty years are not much in the life of a river. A sand bank may crumble and yellow the waters for an hour. Spring floods may carry away the topsoil of a hundred farms or straighten an ancient curve in the river's trough. Sixty years aren't enough to change the river shapes much. Sixty years, however, are enough for determined and adventurous men to push back a frontier beyond any measurable barrier, against any opposition: virgin forests, the Iroquois, a dead feudal system, collapse before the pioneers and around them, and because of them, a new world emerges.

The Edison men followed Harry Livor into the Mohawk Valley and began again the timeless work of pioneers. Two years after they had settled down on the edge of the Groote Vlachte, south of the old dorp a visitor, awe-struck by what he termed the "noble machine shop," wrote in the *Electrical World:* "We are looking at one of the greatest exemplifications of the power of American inventive genius and at an establishment where, from the beginning to end, a new art is illustrated by new processes."

Clinton's Ditch and then the iron progeny spawned by the old Mohawk and Hudson Railroad Company merged life along the Mohawk River with the life in every valley in America. Now Edison's "new art" and his "new processes" which he housed in the McQueen buildings began to flow past national boundaries and carry the achievements of valley men wherever switches were thrown.

The professor, of course, had been wrong when he said that it was the General Electric Company that had brought the golden year to Schenectady. It was not until 1892 that America's two great electrical apparatus and lampmaking companies, the Edison General Electric and the Thomson-Houston Company of Lynn, Massachusetts, saw the handwriting on the wall: patent suits and court battles over "rights" to the incandescent lamp, which was lighting the way into the new wonderland of electricity, were slowing up the work of trail blazing. In order to ease the fear of investors and to make it possible to stake out more of the domain beyond the frontiers across which they were both moving, the two companies joined forces to become the "GE." The new company's headquarters remained in Schenectady, where frontiersmen had been gathering since the days of the Long House.

The year before the great consolidation, *Edisonia*, the parent company's paper, reported that the Schenectady works "grow with the rapidity of a western town . . . these huge cathedral shops, swarming, every one, with hundreds of busy

artisans . . . are filled to overflowing with machines and tools
and labor saving appliances . . . where huge cauldrons simmer
and huge piles of black iron pipe rise to the roof . . . an electric drill pounding away in a ferocious manner at the heart
of a block of granite, 'elbow to elbow' with demure young
ladies splitting mica."

"A new art . . . and new processes." Pioneers in a new
land make their own rules and adjust the laws of settled com-
munities to their own needs. The new frontiers now lay just
beyond the end of a power line, on the edge of those shadows
Edison's lamp had not yet dispelled.

Into Schenectady, at the turn of the century, moved a
strange troupe, the kind of pioneers the old town had never
seen before. Dr. Willis R. Whitney, one of these pioneers
himself, said that among these GE men were "highly individ-
ualistic engineers, strong-minded egoists, weak-minded al-
truists, sanguine inventors, phlegmatic pluggers, systematic
workers, optimistic spenders and pure researchers."

"GE engineers" now pioneered among the forests of
wire-carrying poles they and their rivals planted across America; they made iron hearts of dynamos and turbines to pump
life into their wires. The "phlegmatic pluggers" filled the expanding offices and shops, turned ledger pages and sent out
bills. Those who came to the Company's headquarters built
their homes in what Schenectady calls the "GE Plot." The
"optimistic spenders" were among the giants in the new
wilderness. They were the men who perfected the utilities
holding companies, those money pools on which they floated
the hundreds of buildings and the million-dollar payrolls that
were to mark their progress into the power world.

All these, however, were as a motley army which followed
the trail blaze of the researchers. They were the lead men.
Dr. Whitney was probably the first of industry's new breed,

the frontiersmen who worked apart among test tubes and instruments which in time were to become sensitive enough to measure thought.

Today GE's publicity department delights in talking about the House of Magic, the big laboratories between the Mohawk River and the road that runs through acres of company buildings, where hundreds of scientists are working their calculated miracles. The name is a godsend to the ad writers, although it probably torments many of the researchers. Their House of Magic, however, when Dr. Whitney came to Schenectady in 1900, was a barn behind a boardinghouse, hardly a home for Merlin.

There was a kind of Merlin in Schenectady already, waiting to welcome Dr. Whitney to the Mohawk Valley. Schenectadians were familiar with him, a gnomelike, hunchbacked little man, with a head that belonged to a giant; a generous-hearted genius whose high-pitched voice and shuffle and cigar stubs were to become the joy of the legendmakers. Charles Proteus Steinmetz and the Berg brothers lived in that boardinghouse behind which stood the memorable barn.

Steinmetz was the poet of the new wilderness. His language was mathematical formulae, a private language to most men, but to Willis Whitney and those who came to join him in the House of Magic it was music and imagery. It was this sadly twisted great mathematical engineer, who with the company's patent attorney, had dreamed of this research adventure and had persuaded GE to undertake it.

Steinmetz was a very simple man. The two rooms he loved best in the big house in Schenectady that he built in later years were those in which he housed his experimental equipment, and the glass room where he kept his alligators and Gila monsters which occasionally joined his guests by crawling through the always open door into the hallway. He

loved poker. He worried about his young students at Union College who, during his part-time service as head of the college's Electrical Engineering Department, often watched the flight of his chalk across the board with hopeless incomprehension. He was a socialist who hoped men could be led to accept something of the fruitful discipline he poured into his own work as a scientist.

This Merlin's barn, the first House of Magic, burned down three weeks after Willis Whitney moved into it. So these research pioneers moved down to the "Works" on the River Road, into "Building 10," their first company home. "New art . . . and new processes," with the spring floods of the Mohawk River moving into the cellar and tossing the apparatus around, were inclined to suffer, so Whitney and his growing staff of glass blowers, metallurgists, and shop workers, soon moved again, into a drier laboratory.

The older Mohawk Valley pioneers had been satisfied to stake out a royal land grant for themselves, to make a campfire deal for an Iroquois's bale of beaver skin, to cut farms out of the wilderness of trees and lay out villages next to the millsites. Canals and railroads, forges and looms, these visible things had been the earlier fruits of pioneering. Settlers and travelers could see them, gossip about them, watch them develop. In Building 19, however, the laboratory built on land high enough to escape the waters of the Mohawk, the fruits of a new pioneering first became visible as the solution of a mathematical equation, as a residue at the bottom of a test tube, or in the glow of a loop of wire. The excitement of pioneering in the new unknown belonged now to the Whitneys, to men like Steinmetz, and their colleagues—hardly a term for pioneers—who slept at home in their beds at night.

Out of Building 19 came the first fruits of GE's newest industrial adventure.

In 1905 America began to screw the GEM lamp into its lighting sockets. With it Willis Whitney gave what was tantamount to hundreds of millions of dollars to his fellow citizens. The excitement, however, that had greeted Edison's first electric light had long since cooled, and now the GEM was accepted as casually as small change, although Whitney's bulb was almost five times as efficient as Edison's, and far brighter. Whether or not Americans were aware of what GE's researchers were doing, the company was. The engineers, the "phlegmatic pluggers," the "optimistic spenders" knew now that their laboratories were gateways to a new West where there was wealth beyond imagining.

"Come, and bring your experiment along," Willis Whitney said in this same year to young William Coolidge, teaching and doing original work in chemistry at the Massachusetts Institute of Technology. Within three years of his arrival in Schenectady the new research man had become assistant director of the laboratory and was busy charting his own course into the power world.

If you had said "tungsten" to the average Schenectadian in those early research years he probably would have thought you were announcing your name. In the House of Magic, however, it meant an intractable metal, and to Dr. Coolidge it meant that, and six grueling years of work to change its very structure. Tungsten had already been used as the filament of an incandescent lamp, but a rough blow on the bulb destroyed it. When Dr. Coolidge suggested that perhaps tungsten could be made ductile, pliable as a copper wire, he was told that such a search would be hopeless.

"Let's try!" If he had disappeared up the beach of a new continent he could not have had fewer guides to take him where he was going. Explorers sometimes come back from a pioneering adventure scarred by their hardships. Dr. Coolidge still carries the marks of his day-and-night search for ductile tungsten in the deep seams of his face.

He found, finally, what he had set out to find: a tungsten wire that would absorb even the jouncing an automobile bulb must take. In order to use it the GE had to scrap a half million dollars' worth of machinery that had been used in making the old carbon filament; but the "Coolidge wire" performed a lighting miracle and would have justified the rebuilding of the whole industry. In 1914, three years after the new lamp had become a laboratory success, it saved Americans a fifth of a billion dollars in illumination bills.

"Good morning; having good fun today?" Bending over a microscope or jotting down the record of a chemical experiment, a researcher would look up for a moment as Dr. Whitney made his rounds of the laboratories. "Fun" meant any number of things: "Are you clearing new ground?" "Any new light on the problem?" or, "Can I help?" The man who had begun GE's adventure in industrial research in a barn behind a Schenectady boardinghouse, by the beginning of World War I had a new building along the Mohawk's banks devoted solely to the work "of moving out into an unknown land." The company equipped it as completely as it could for the work of pioneering, and then set the occupants free in its labyrinth "in the hope," said Owen D. Young, until recently chairman of General Electric's Board of Directors, "that they would bring back among their discovered treasures a few at least that would be of practicable advantage to the electrical industry."

". . . discovered treasures"? . . . Ophir and Samarkand, California gold and the gold acres of the Comstock Lode have meant less to mankind than the things Willis Whitney's team of researchers evolved out of the intricate mazes of their own minds. Good will and a belief in the soundness of their work echoed their director's casual "Good morning; having good fun?"

"Coolidge wire," hair fine, proved to be a path along which tides of power could be made to flow as Whitney's men willed. Irving Langmuir, one of the Building 19 pioneers, worked the last of the great lighting miracles with it when he banished the light-killing deposits that still formed on the inside of the incandescent bulb.

Whitney's pioneers signaled each other from the remote regions where they sought "a knowledge of causes, and the true motions of things." Langmuir's work touched off fires in whose light Coolidge soon read directions for the opening of new territory. X rays had once burned him terribly. These mysterious emanations which would filter through steel or flesh onto a photographic plate and write there a record of metal fractures, or of hidden disease, he knew could be some thousand times more useful if they could be made as tractable as he had already made the reluctant tungsten.

When he finished his work, and the "Coolidge tube" was a reality, doctors had an X-ray instrument as precise as a fine gauge, and industry a giant eye of one million volts that could look through inches of steel as though it were window glass. This eye will see far more tomorrow, for GE is making a 100,000,000-volt Coolidge tube which will see into a darkness men have never penetrated.

The new pioneers along the Mohawk River were something like the men of Solomon's House, that laboratory imagined by Francis Bacon, Elizabethan politician, author, and scientist. Like the men of Solomon's House, the Whitney men too, increasing in number each year, worked singly and in groups, verifying, classifying, traveling down any path that promised knowledge, to the end, as Bacon wrote of his imaginary researchers, that there should be ". . . the enlargement of the bounds of human empire to the effecting of all things possible."

The House of Magic has dramatic achievements to boast and the names of real pioneers to write on its walls. Steinmetz, who had a profound understanding of the basic principles of the "new art" and its "new processes," was one of the greatest. Willis Whitney, freed by the General Electric Company to explore any realm he chose to invade, gave us the first great improvement in the light with which Thomas Edison had created a new industry. Whitney's device for inducing artificial fever has given our doctors a new weapon against pain. Perhaps Whitney's greatest achievement, however, was his pioneering work as the director of industry's first program of pure research; it was he who laid out the plans here by the Mohawk River for one of the great invasions of new frontiers.

William Coolidge's victory over the intractable tungsten and Irving Langmuir's success in evolving high-vacuum, high-voltage tubes have given us modern lighting and the mixed blessing of radio broadcasting. Alexanderson built a generator here which, with Langmuir's high-vacuum tubes, gave radio a voice loud enough to be heard around the world.

In the House of Magic radio's first tin trumpeting became the articulate full-throated voice it is today, when GE's research men developed the electromagnetic speaker, and gave us sound which had fidelity as well as volume.

Research paths break into strange clearings, cross trails which lead to promontories from which one can see new rivers running down nameless valleys. Whitney's men have been moving down those paths for almost half a century now, bringing back what they could, reporting in the journals of the great scientific associations on what they saw.

Instead of Coolidge wire, they are now studying the mysteries of gas turbines, and jet engines, developing temperatures greater than those at the sun's surface, and producing pressures born of atom smashing. These new pioneers are searching for the atom's heart where the Long House had its eastern door, the "Schonowe" of the Iroquois and their league of the Tree of the Great Long Leaves. Here, on the doorstep of the Long House, there is a new vocabulary: "cyclotron," "betatron," "fission pile," and "linear accelerator," names for new gear with which men must equip themselves to break down the new frontiers.

Walk down the old Indian trail, a dirt road today, that parallels the north edge of the Mohawk River palisades, east of the abandoned Erie Canal aqueduct at Rexford. If you look across the river to the south shore you will see the walls of the new House of Magic. There on a beautiful plateau called "the Knolls," high above the palisaded river, eight hundred men will soon carry on the work Willis Whitney began in the barn behind Charles Steinmetz's boardinghouse. The rules of procedure will still be the same, those which were to govern the men of Solomon's House: to seek "a knowledge of causes, and the secret motion of things. . . ."

Next to the General Electric Company's Knolls Research Laboratory the United States government is building the Knolls Atomic Power Laboratory which will be operated by the men of the House of Magic. There on the Mohawk palisades the cyclotrons and the betatrons, the fission piles and the linear accelerators will explore the heart of creation, and the researchers will try to give meaning to Hiroshima and Nagasaki.

"New frontiers," the professor had said, "opened up again along the Mohawk in 1886." The old man had gone on to say that the paths first cleared by the prophets and the philosophers, pioneers in the study of human values, must one day cross the paths of these pioneers of science.

"It makes no difference," he said later, "in what valley, or by what river, they meet. If they do not meet soon, however, those ancient potholes along the Mohawk River, below the Knolls and running down to the falls may someday be crowded with the broken skeletons of a race which was no more able to meet the challenge of new times than was the Cohoes mastodon and his breed. For them, you remember, the melting of the glaciers meant death in the drying marshes of a warming world."

The professor, of course, was an alarmist.

Acknowledgments

Dixon Ryan Fox, the late president of Union College, loved this Mohawk River, and its valley, as one must who knows what its trails and highways and harvest lands have meant to America. He saw the valley and its people as part of a huge, shifting design. He was no antiquarian, collecting only shards and kitchen middens and cracker barrel stories. He read history, and taught it, with an artist's appreciation. I owe him far more than a student's debt.

I know "C.N.W." so well that I find it hard to separate the historian in him from the friend. What I've said of the late Dr. Fox, however, is true too of "Charley" Waldron . . . Charles Newman Waldron, professor emeritus of American history at Union College and, until recently, secretary of the college's Alumni Association. Charley and "Heidi," his Seeing Eye dog, have visited up and down the valley for years, Charley talking history and "Union" to a legion of friends. His firm "No" to dead-end themes and quaint characterizations have saved me from many digressions. His "Yes," which I now have, is reward enough for writing *The Mohawk*.

To write of the past is to make a part of one's own paragraphs the facts others have worked hard to unearth. If an author were to thank all those who have thus helped him prepare his book he would have as many lines of footnotes as he has of text. Occasionally, however, the debt is so great that it must be acknowledged. I owe much of the Dekana-wida-Hiawatha legend to Mr. A. C. Parker's *The Constitution of the Five Nations,* whose author is New York State's eminent authority on Iroquois history, and who is himself a chief of the Seneca Nation. I owe special thanks to Noble Whitford, whose records of the history of the Erie Canal have given me the basis for my canal chapters, and to Howard Swiggett, whose story of Walter Butler in *War Out of Niagara* helped me to understand that maligned Mohawk Valley Tory. I want also to thank Mr. Nelson Greene of Fort Plain, New York, for granting me permission to borrow as I wished from his *Mohawk Valley,* a rich compendium of Mohawk history and pictures.

Mr. Helmar Webb, Union College's librarian, and Mr. Harold O'Neal, his assistant, indeed, the whole library staff, have been patient guides through a wilderness of Mohawk River material, supplying not only hard-to-get books and pamphlets, but many other research services. Professor E. S. C. Smith, head of the college's Geology Department, has approved the chapter that deals with the birth of the valley. Miss Travis, of the administrative staff, found new Erie Canal material for me. Professor Philip Stanley, and my cousin, F. W. Frost, did a much-needed job of excising what they called the "nonsemantic" passages, those words and ideas which they thought had meaning for me alone.

Schenectady friends always seemed to have time when I came to them for assistance. Mrs. Van Vranken, of the Schenectady Historical Society, was able to put her hands unerringly on what I wanted from the Society's library. Mr. John

Vrooman helped me particularly with the Sir William Johnson chapters, and Mr. Giles Van Der Bogaert, who knows the valley's architecture so well, has approved the things said in the chapter I've called "Union Street." I also want to thank Mr. Jonathan Pearson for letting me use passages from his great-grandfather's manuscript diary of a trip on the Erie Canal, a little volume hard to read because, as the diarist notes on the last page, it fell overboard on one occasion.

I hope Mr. Guy Bartlett and others at GE in Schenectady forgive me for taking quite a different tack in the General Electric chapter than the one I had expected to take. They and Mr. Roland Thomson gave me enough material to write a definitive history of the electrical industry. Mrs. Herbert MacMaster, of Schenectady, and Mr. Charles Thompson, of Herkimer, helped me often by asking those casual questions which usually catch up with an author after the presses begin to roll.

Very special thanks go to Professor Frederick L. Bronner, of the Union College History Department, for reading the manuscript with a sharp, professional eye; to Mrs. Phyllis McKnight, of Schenectady, and to Mrs. George Hanson for taking infinite pains in typing the author's script—"odd" was their kind word for some pretty crabbed handwriting. My wife's reward for her part in the project will be a summer's foot trip along the Iroquois Trail.

Bibliography

THIS *Mohawk River* bibliography makes no pretense of completeness, though here the reader can pick up the old trails leading to the doorways of once-great houses, and through "canawl" towns, and the palisaded villages of the warrior Mohawks, and on backward through time until he stands on the shores of the ancient Iromohawk. The inquiring reader will find dozens of titles, caches of manuscript material, and helpful guides in the valley's fine historical societies, in the libraries of the larger towns, at Hamilton and Union colleges, and among the historical collections of the State Library, at Albany, New York.

BOOKS

ALBANY COUNTY, N.Y., *Committee of Correspondence*, 1775-1778 (2 vols.). Albany: University of the State of New York, 1923-1925.

ALBANY, COURT OF ALBANY, Colony of Rensselaerswyck and Schaenhectede. *Minutes of the Court of Albany, Rensselaerswyck and Schenectady*, 1668-1685 (3 vols.). Albany: University of the State of New York, 1926-1932.

ALVORD, CLARENCE WALWORTH, *The Mississippi Valley in British Politics* (2 vols.). Cleveland: The Arthur N. Clark Co., 1917.

BAGG, MOSES MEARS, *The Pioneers of Utica*. Utica: Curtis and Childs, 1877.

BARNES, RUTH A., *I Hear America Singing; an anthology of folk poetry*. Philadelphia: John C. Winston Co., 1937.

BARTH, LAURA F. AND LEFFERTS, *The Mohawk River and Its Valley-New York's great pathway*. Philadelphia: F. A. Davis Co., 1941.

BEAUCHAMP, WILLIAM MARTIN, *A History of the New York Iroquois, now commonly called the Six Nations*. Albany: New York State Education Department, Bulletin No. 329, 1905.

—— *Civil, religious and Mourning Councils and ceremonies of Adoption of the New York Indians*. New York State Education Department. Albany: New York State Museum Bulletin No. 113, 1907.

—— *The Iroquois trail; or, Foot-prints of the Six Nations in Customs, traditions, and history . . . in which are included David Cusick's sketches of ancient history of the Six Nations*. Fayetteville: H. C. Beauchamp, 1892.

BENNETT, CLARENCE E., *Many Mohawk Moons*. Schenectady: The Gazette Press, 1938.

BENTON, NATHANIEL SOLEY, *A History of Herkimer County, including the Upper Mohawk Valley*. Albany: J. Munsell, 1856.

BEST, MRS. ALLENA CHAMPLIN, *Lock Her Through*. New York: Oxford University Press, 1940.

BIGELOW, TIMOTHY, *Journal of a Tour to Niagara Falls in the year 1805*. Boston: J. Wilson and Son, 1876.

BOBBÉ, MRS. DOROTHIE DE BEAR, *De Witt Clinton*. New York: Minton, Balch and Co., 1933.

BRODERICK, JOHN THOMAS, *Forty Years With General Electric*. Albany: Fort Orange Press, 1929.

—— *Pulling Together*. Schenectady: Robson and Adee, 1922.

—— *Willis Rodney Whitney, pioneer of industrial research*. Albany: Fort Orange Press, 1945.

BROWN, JOHN MATHIAS, *A brief sketch of the First Settlement of the County of Scoharie*. Scoharie: L. Cuthbert, 1823.

CAMP, PHINEAS, *Poems of the Mohawk Valley, and on scenes in Palestine*. Utica: Curtis and White, 1859.

CAMPBELL, WILLIAM W., *Annals of Tryon County; or, the Border Warfare of New York during the Revolution*. New York: J. and J. Harper, 1831.

CANFIELD, WILLIAM WALKER, *The Legends of the Iroquois, told by "the Cornplanter."* New York: A. Wessels Co., 1902.

CARMER, CARL LAMSON, *Listen for a Lonesome Drum.* New York: Farrar and Rinehart, 1936.

CHALMERS, HARVEY, *West to the Setting Sun.* Toronto: The Macmillan Company of Canada, Ltd., 1943.

CLARK, JOSHUA, V. H., *Onondaga; . . . with notes on the several towns in the county, and Oswego.* Syracuse: Stoddard and Babcock, 1849.

CLARKE, THOMAS WOOD, *The Bloody Mohawk.* New York: The Macmillan Co., 1940.

CLINTON, DE WITT, *The Life and Writings of De Witt Clinton,* by William W. Campbell. New York: Baker and Scribner, 1849.

COLDEN, CADWALLADER, *The History of the Five Nations of Canada* (2 vols.). New York: A. S. Barnes and Co., 1904.

CONVERSE, MRS. HARRIET MAXWELL, *Myths and Legends of the New York State Iroquois.* Edited and annotated by Arthur Caswell Parker. Albany: New York State Bulletin No. 125, 1908.

COOKINHAM, HENRY J., *History of Oneida County, N.Y.* Chicago: S. J. Clarke Pub. Co., 1912.

COOPER, WILLIAM, *A Guide in the Wilderness; or, The History of the First Settlement in the western counties of New York, with useful instructions to future settlers.* Cooperstown, N.Y., 1936.

CORNPLANTER, JESSE J., *Legends of the Longhouse.* Philadelphia: J. B. Lippincott Co., 1938.

CROWNFIELD, GERTRUDE, *Alison Blair.* New York: E. P. Dutton and Co., 1927.

CRUIKSHANK, ERNEST ALEXANDER, *The Story of Butler's Rangers and the settlement of Niagara.* Ontario: Tribune Printing House, 1893.

DAILEY, WILLIAM NELSON POTTER, *History of the Old Fort Herkimer Church, German Flatts Reformed Church, 1723.* St. Johnsville: St. Johnsville Enterprise and News, 1929.

DALES, FREDERICK, *Story of Schenectady and the Mohawk Valley.* Schenectady: The Maqua Co., 1926.

DIEFENDORF, MARY RIGGS, *The Historic Mohawk.* New York and London: G. P. Putnam's Sons, 1910.

Documentary history of the State of New York; arranged . . . by E. B. O'Callaghan (4 vols.). Albany: Weed, Parsons and Co., 1849-1851.

Documents relating to the colonial history of the State of New York (15 vols.). Albany: Weed, Parsons and Co., 1853-1887.

DURANT, SAMUEL W., *History of Oneida County, New York.* Philadelphia: Everts and Fariss, 1878.

DWIGHT, TIMOTHY, *Travels in New England and New York* (4 vols.). New Haven: T. Dwight, 1821-1822.

EATON, M., *Five Years on the Erie Canal.* Utica: Bennett, Backus and Hawley, 1845.

EDMONDS, WALTER DUMAUX, *Rome Haul.* Boston: Little, Brown and Co., 1929.

—— *Erie Water.* Boston: Little, Brown and Co., 1934.

—— *Mostly Canallers.* Boston: Little, Brown and Co., 1934.

—— *Drums Along the Mohawk.* Boston: Little, Brown and Co., 1936.

—— *The Wedding Journey.* Boston: Little, Brown and Co., 1947.

FISKE, JOHN, *The Dutch and Quaker Colonies in America* (2 vols.). Boston and New York: Houghton Mifflin Co., 1899.

FLICK, ALEXANDER CLARENCE, *Loyalism in New York during the American Revolution.* New York: Columbia University Press, 1901.

FREDERIC, HAROLD, *In the Valley.* New York: Charles Scribner's Sons, 1890.

FROTHINGHAM, WASHINGTON, *History of Fulton County.* Syracuse: D. Mason and Co., 1892.

—— *History of Montgomery County.* Syracuse: D. Mason and Co., 1892.

GRANT, MRS. ANNE MACVICAR, *Memoirs of An American Lady.* Philadelphia: D. Appleton and Co., 1846.

GREGG, ARTHUR B., *Old Hellebergh; Historical sketches of the West Manor of Rennsselaerswyck.* Altamont: The Altamont Enterprise, 1936.

GREENE, NELSON, *The old Mohawk turnpike book.* Fort Plain: N. Greene, 1924.

HALE, HORATIO EMMONS, *The Iroquois Book of Rites.* Philadelphia: D. G. Brinton, 1883.

HALSEY, FRANCIS WHITING, *The Old New York Frontier.* New York: Charles Scribner's Sons, 1901.

HAMMOND, JOHN WINTHROP, *Men and Volts;* The Story of General Electric. Philadelphia: J. B. Lippincott Co., 1941.

HANSON, WILLIS TRACEY, JR., *History of Schenectady During the Revolution.* Brattleboro: E. L. Hildreth and Co., 1916.

HARDIN, GEORGE ANSON, *History of Herkimer County.* Syracuse: D. Mason and Co., 1893.

HARLOW, ALVIN FAY, *Old Towpaths; the story of the American canal era.* New York and London: D. Appleton and Co., 1926.

HEDRICK, ULYSSES PRENTISS, *A History of Agriculture in the State of New York.* Albany: 1933. Printed for the Society.

HEWITT, JOHN NAPOLEON BRINTON, *Iroquoian Cosmology.* Washington, D.C.: U.S. Bureau of American Ethnology, Part 1, 21st annual report 1899-1900; Part 2, 43rd annual report 1925-1926.

HIGGINS, RUTH LOVING, *Expansion in New York, with especial reference to the eighteenth century.* Columbus: Ohio State University, 1931.

History of Herkimer County, N.Y. New York: F. W. Beers & Co., 1879.

History of Montgomery and Fulton Counties, N.Y. New York: F. W. Beers & Co., 1878.

History of the County of Schenectady. Schenectady: Burhyte & Birch, 1887.

History of the Mohawk Valley, gateway to the west, 1614-1925; covering the six counties of Schenectady, Schoharie, Montgomery, Fulton, Herkimer and Oneida (4 vols.). Edited by Nelson Greene. Chicago: S. J. Clarke Pub. Co., 1925.

HOFFMAN, CHARLES FENNO, *Greyslaer: a romance of the Mohawk* (2 vols.). New York: Harper Bros., 1840.

HOSACK, DAVID, *Memoir of De Witt Clinton.* New York: J. Seymour, 1829.

HOUGH, FRANKLIN BENJAMIN, *The Northern Invasion of October, 1780 . . . relating to the expeditions from Canada under Sir John Johnson.* Bradford Club Series, No. 6. New York, 1866.

HOWELL, GEORGE ROGERS AND TENNEY, JONATHAN, *Bi-centennial history of Albany and History of the County of Albany, N.Y., from 1609 to 1886.* New York: W. W. Munsell Co., 1886.

HOWELL, GEORGE ROGERS, AND JOHN MUNSELL, *History of the County of Schenectady, N.Y., from 1662-1886.* New York: W. W. Munsell and Co., 1886.

HUDLESTON, FRANCIS JOSIAH, *Gentleman Johnny Burgoyne; Misadventures of an English general in the revolution.* Indianapolis: Bobbs-Merrill Co., 1927.

HULBERT, ARCHER BUTLER, *The Great American Canals.* (Vol. 2 deals with the Erie Canal.) Cleveland: 1904.

—— *Historic Highways of America.* Cleveland: A. H. Clarke Co., 1904.

HUNGERFORD, EDWARD, *Men and Iron; the history of New York Central.* New York: Thomas Y. Crowell Co., 1938.

HUNT, GEORGE T., *The Wars of the Iroquois; a study in intertribal trade relations.* Madison: University of Wisconsin Press, 1940.

JACOBSON, HAROLD S., *For the Freedom of the Mohawk.* New York: E. P. Dutton and Co., 1931.

JAMISON, JOHN FRANKLIN (ed.), *Narratives of the New Netherland, 1609-1664.* New York: Charles Scribner's Sons, 1909.

Jesuit Relations and Allied Documents; 1610-1791, The (73 vols.). Edited by Reuben Gold Thwaites. Cleveland: Burrows Brothers Co., 1896-1901.

Jogues Papers, The, Translated and arranged, with a memoir, by John Gilmary Shea. New York: 1856. (In New York historical society. *Collections,* 2d series. N.Y. 1857, vol. III.)

JOHNSON, MRS. SUSAN GRIFFITH (COLPOYS), *Adventures of a lady in the war of independence in America.* Workington (Eng): P. D. Lambe, 1874.

JOHNSON, SIR JOHN, BART., *Orderly Book of Sir John Johnson during the Oriskany campaign, 1776-1777.* Albany: J. Munsell's Sons, 1882.

Papers of Sir William Johnson, The. Albany: University of the State of New York, 1921.

JONES, POMROY, *Annals and Recollections of Oneida County.* Rome: The Author, 1851.

KALM, PETER, *The America of 1750; Peter Kalm's Travels in North America . . .* Edited by Adolph B. Benson. New York: Wilson, Erickson, Inc., 1937.

KIMBALL, FRANCIS P., *New York, the Canal State.* Albany: Argus Press, 1937.

KNITTLE, WALTER ALLEN, *The Early eighteenth century Palatine Emigration.* Philadelphia: Dorrance and Co., 1937.

LAING, MARY ELIZABETH, *The Hero of the Long House.* Yonkers: World Book Co., 1920.

LANGDALE, MRS. HAZEL LOUISE (RAYBOLD), *Mark of Seneca Basin.* New York: E. P. Dutton Co., 1942.

LINCOLN, CHARLES ZEBINA, *Constitutional history of New York* (5 vols.). Rochester: Lawyers Cooperative Pub. Co., 1906.

LYDEKKER, JOHN WOLFE, *The Faithful Mohawks.* Cambridge (Eng.): The University Press, 1938.

MACDONALD, ZILLAH K., *Two on a Tow.* Boston: Houghton Mifflin Co., 1942.

MacLeod, William Christie, *The American Indian Frontier.* New York: A. A. Knopf, 1928.

MacWethy, Lou D., *The book of Names, especially relating to the early Palatines and the first settlers in the Mohawk Valley.* St. Johnsville: The Enterprise and News, 1933.

Martin, Felix, *The Life of Father Isaac Joques.* New York: Benziger Bros., 1885.

Masten, Arthur H., *History of Cohoes, New York.* Albany: J. Munsell, 1877.

Meadowcroft, Mrs. Enid La Monte, *Along the Erie Towpath.* New York: Thomas Y. Crowell Co., 1940.

Monroe, Joel Henry, *Schenectady, ancient and modern.* Geneva: W. F. Humphrey, 1914.

Morgan, Lewis Henry, *Ancient Society.* New York: H. Holt and and Co., 1877.

—— *League of the Ho-de-no-saw-nee or Iroquois* (2 vols.). New York: Dodd, Mead and Co., 1901.

Munsell, Joel, *The Annals of Albany* (10 vols.). Albany: J. J. Munsell, 1850-1859.

Murdock, George Peter, *Our Primitive Contemporaries.* New York: The Macmillan Co., 1934.

New York State Department of Commerce, *A Graphic Survey of the Mohawk River Basin.* New York State Bulletin No. 42, June, 1939.

New York State Department of Commerce, *New York State Means Business in the Mohawk Valley Area.* Albany, 1944.

New York State. Secretary of State, *Journals of the military expedition of Major General John Sullivan against the Six Nations of Indians in 1779.* Auburn: Knapp, Peck and Thomson, 1887.

New York State Historical Association, *History of the state of New York* (10 vols.). Edited by A. C. Flick. New York: Columbia University Press, 1933-1937.

Nissenson, Samuel George, *The Patroon's Domain.* New York: Columbia University Press, 1937.

Orton, Helen Fuller, *The Brave Frontier; a story of old Scoharie.* New York: F. A. Stokes Co., 1940.

Parker, Arthur Caswell, *The Archeological History of New York* (2 vols.). Albany: University of the State of New York, 1922.

—— *The Constitution of the Five Nations.* Albany: University of the State of New York, 1916.

PARKMAN, FRANCIS, *Count Frontenac and New France under Louis XIV*. Boston: Little, Brown and Co., 1877.

—— *Half-century of Conflict* (2 vols.). Boston: Little, Brown and Co., 1939.

PARTRIDGE, BELLAMY, *Country Lawyer*. New York: Whittlesey House, 1939.

PEARSON, JONATHAN, *A history of the Schenectady patent in the Dutch and English times*. Albany: J. Munsell's Sons, 1883.

POUND, ARTHUR AND RICHARD E. DAY, *Johnson of the Mohawks*. New York: The Macmillan Co., 1930.

RADIN, PAUL, *The Story of the American Indian*. New York: Liveright Pub. Corp., 1927.

RAYMOND, ANDREW VAN VRANKEN, *Union University* (3 vols.). New York: Lewis Pub. Co., 1907.

REID, WILLIAM MAXWELL, *The Mohawk Valley, its legends and its history*. New York: G. P. Putnam's Sons, 1904.

—— *The story of Old Fort Johnson*. New York: G. P. Putnam's Sons, 1906.

REYNOLDS, CUYLER (ed.), *Hudson-Mohawk Genealogical and Family Memoirs* (4 vols.). New York: Lewis Pub. Co., 1911.

ROBERTS, GEORGE SIMON, *Old Schenectady*. Schenectady: Robson and Adee, 1904.

ROOT, EDWARD WALES, *Philip Hooker*. New York: Charles Scribner's Sons, 1929.

ROSCOE, WILLIAM E., *History of Schoharie County, New York, 1713*. Syracuse: D. Mason Co., 1882.

RYERSON, ADOLPHUS EGETON, *The Loyalists of America and their Times* (2 vols.). Toronto: W. Briggs, 1880.

SABINE, LORENZO, *Biographical sketches of loyalists of the American revolution, with an historical essay* (2 vols.). Boston: Little, Brown and Co., 1864.

SANDERS, JOHN, *Centennial address relating to the early history of Schenectady, and its first settlers*. Delivered 1876. Albany: Van Benthuyson, 1879.

SCOTT, JOHN ALBERT, *Fort Stanwix (Fort Schuyler) and Oriskany*. Rome: Rome Sentinal Co., 1927.

SEVERANCE, FRANK HAYWARD, *Old Trails on the Niagara Frontier*. Buffalo: Mathews-Northrup, 1899.

SEYMOUR, FLORA WARREN (SMITH), *Lords of the Valley, Sir William Johnson and his Mohawk brothers*. London and New York: Longmans, Green and Co., 1930.

SHAFER, DONALD CAMERON, *Smokefires in Schoharie*. New York: Longmans, Green and Co., 1938.

SINGMASTER, ELSIE, *The Long Journey*. Boston: Houghton Mifflin Co., 1917.

SIMMS, JEPTHA ROOT, *History of Schoharie County*. Albany: Munsell and Tanner, 1845.

—— *Trappers of New York; a biography of Nicholas Stoner and Nathaniel Foster*. Albany: J. Munsell, 1850.

SINGLETON, ESTHER, *Dutch New York*. New York: Dodd, Mead and Co., 1909.

SMITH, MRS. ERMINNIE ADELE (PLATT), *Myths of the Iroquois*. (In 2nd Annual Report, U.S. Bureau of American Ethnology, 1880-1881.)

SMITH, RICHARD, *A Tour of Four Great Rivers: Hudson, Mohawk, Susquehanna and Delaware in 1769*. New York: Charles Scribner's Sons, 1906.

STEVENS, FRANK WALKER, *The Beginnings of the New York Central Railroad; a history*. New York: G. P. Putnam's Sons, 1926.

STOLLER, JAMES HOUGH, *Geological excursions; a guide to localities in the region of Schenectady and the Mohawk Valley and the vicinity of Saratoga Springs*. Schenectady: Union Book Co., 1932.

STONE, WILLIAM LEETE, JR., *The Life and Times of Sir William Johnson, bart.* (2 vols.). Albany: J. Munsell, 1865.

STONE, WILLIAM LEETE, SR., *Life of Joseph Brant* (2 vols.). New York: G. Dearborn and Co., 1838.

STREET, ALFRED BILLINGS, *Burning of Schenectady, and other poems*. Albany: W. C. Little, 1842.

SWIFT, HILDEGARDE HOYT, *Little Blacknose; the story of a pioneer*. New York: Harcourt, Brace and Co., 1929.

SWIGGETT, HOWARD, *War out of Niagara; Walter Butler and the Tory Rangers*. New York: Columbia University Press, 1933.

THOMPSON, HAROLD WILLIAM, *Body, Boots & Britches*. Philadelphia: J. B. Lippincott Co., 1940.

TRYON COUNTY, NEW YORK, *The Minute Book of the Committee of Safety of Tryon County; with an introduction by J. Howard Hanson, and notes by Samuel Ludlow Frey*. New York: Dodd, Mead and Co., 1905.

TURNER, CHIPMAN P., *The Pioneer Period of Western New York*. Buffalo: Bigelow Bros., 1888.

U.S. NATIONAL LABOR RELATIONS BOARD, *Decisions and orders of the national labor relations board* (Vol. 2). Washington: Government Printing Office, 1936.

VANDEWATER, ROBERT J., *The Tourist, or Pocket Manual for*

travellers on the Hudson River, the western canal, and stage road to Niagara Falls . . . New York: Harper and Bros., 1834.

VAN EPPS, PERCY MEYERS, *Stories and Legends of Our Indian Paths.* Glenville: The Town Board, 1940.

VAN TYNE, CLAUDE HALSTEAD, *The Loyalists in the American Revolution.* New York: The Macmillan Co., 1902.

VAN WAGNER, EDITH, *Agricultural Manual of New York State.* Albany: Division of Agriculture, Bulletin No. 133, 1922.

VROOMAN, JOHN J., *Forts and Firesides of the Mohawk Country.* Compiled and published by Elijah Ellsworth Brownell. Philadelphia: published, 1943.

WAGER, DANIEL ELBRIDGE (Ed.), *Our City and Its People; A Descriptive Work on the City of Rome, New York.* Boston: The Boston History Co., 1896.

—— *Our county and its people; a descriptive work on Oneida County, New York.* Boston: The Boston History Co., 1896.

WALLACE, PAUL A. W., *Conrad Weiser, 1696-1760, friend of colonist and Mohawk.* Philadelphia: University of Pennsylvania Press, 1945.

WALTON, JOSEPH SOLOMON, *Conrad Weiser and the Indian policy of colonial Pennsylvania.* Philadelphia: G. W. Jacobs and Co., 1900.

WATSON, ELKANAH, *History . . . of the Western Canals in the State of New-York, from September 1788-to . . . 1819.* Albany: D. Steele, 1820.

WELLER, W. EARL, *Tales of Old Dorp.* Schenectady: Robson and Adee, 1907.

WESTOVER, MYRON F. (Ed.), *Schenectady, Past and Present.* Strasburg, Va.: Shenandoah Pub. House, 1931.

WHITFORD, N. E., *History of the Canal System of the State of New York.* Albany: State of New York, 1905, 2 vols.

WILLETT, WILLIAM MARINUS, *A narrative of the military actions of Colonel Marinus Willett, taken chiefly from his own manuscript.* New York: G. and C. and H. Carrill, 1831.

WISSLER, CLARK, *Indians of the United States; Four centuries of their History and Culture.* Garden City: Doubleday, Doran and Co., 1941.

WRITERS' PROGRAM, *New York, A guide to the Empire State.* American Guide Series. New York: Oxford University Press, 1940.

YATES, AUSTIN ANDREW, *Schenectady County New York; its history to the close of the nineteenth century.* New York: 1902.

PERIODICALS AND BULLETINS

ALVORD, C. W., "The British Ministry and the Treaty of Fort Stanwix," Wisconsin Historical Society. *Proceedings*, 1908.

BEAUCHAMP, W. M., "Aboriginal Place Names in New York," Bulletin No. 108, New York State Museum, Albany, N.Y., 1907.

—— "The Iroquois and the Colony of New York," Oneida County Historical Society, *Transactions* No. 2, 1889-1891.

BOSHAR, HELEN, "The First Push Westward of the Albany Fur Traders," Massachusetts Valley *Historical Review*, No. VII.

BRIGHAM, A. P., "The Mohawk Valley—The Eastern Gateway of the United States," *Geographical Journal* (London), Vol. 13.

BROWNE, DOUGLAS G., "Butlers of Butlersbury," *Cornhill Magazine* (London), November 19, 1921.

BUFFINGTON, ARTHUR, "The Policy of Albany and English Expansion Westward," Mississippi Valley *Historical Review*, March, 1922.

EARL, ROBERT, "The Mohawk Valley in History," Herkimer County Historical Society *Papers*, 1896.

ELLSWORTH, W. W., "The Palatines in the Mohawk Valley," New York State Historical Association, *Proceedings*, Vol. XIV, 1915.

FARRAND, MAX, "The Indian Boundary Line," *American Historical Review*, Vol. X, No. 4.

FREY, S. L., "Relic Hunting on the Mohawk," *American Naturalist*, Vol. 12.

GRIFFIS, W. E., "Arendt Van Curler, First Superintendent of Rensselaerswick, Founder of Schenectady, and the Dutch Policy of Peace with the Iroquois," The Albany Institute, *Transactions*, Vol. XI, 1887.

HALL, JAMES, "Notes and Observations on the Cohoes Mastodon," Twenty-First *Annual Report*, Regents of the University of New York, April 20, 1868.

JOHNSON, GEORGE L., "Pioneer Times in the Royal Grant," Herkimer County Historical Society *Papers*, Vol. II.

LARRABEE, HAROLD ATKINS, "How Ramée Came to Schenectady," Union College *Alumni Monthly*, February, 1937.

MAYER, W. G., "The History of Transportation in the Mohawk Valley," New York Historical Association, *Proceedings*, Vol. XIV.

MORGAN, L. H., "Government and Institutions of the Iroquois" (edited by A. C. Parker), New York State Archeological Association, Vol. VII, Rochester, 1928.

NILES, C. M., "Mohawk River—Making Friends of the Floods," *Technical World,* Vol. 21, May, 1914.

ROORBACK, B. J., "Geographic Influences in the Development of the Manufacturing Industry of the Mohawk Valley," *Journal of Geography,* Vol. X, November, 1910.

RUTTENBER, E. N., "Indian Geographic Names," New York Historical Society, *Proceedings,* Vol. VI, 1906.

SHAFER, D. C., "Schenectady, Treasure House of Colonial Days," *American Homes,* Vol. II, April, 1914.

VOSBURGH, FREDERICK, "Drums to Dynamos on the Mohawk," *National Geographic Magazine,* July, 1947.

WAGNER, D. F., "Forts Stanwix and Bull and other Forts at Rome," Oneida County Historical Society, *Transactions,* 1885.

WARREN, M. S., "The First Settlers of the Mohawk Valley," Herkimer County Historical Society, *Papers,* 1896.

WHITFORD, NOBLE E., "Effects of the Erie Canal on New York History," New York Historical Association, Vol. XXIV, 1926.

Index

351